W9-BMC-663

A
Wollstonecraft
Anthology

Mary Wollstonecraft by John Opie.

A 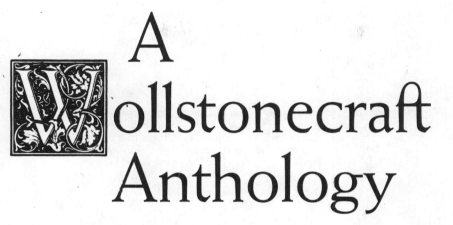ollstonecraft Anthology

EDITED
WITH AN INTRODUCTION BY
Janet M. Todd

Indiana University Press • Bloomington • London

Part title illustrations for "Works of Controversy" and "Works of
Commentary" sections reprinted by permission of the Service
photographique, Bibliothèque Nationale, Paris. Part title
illustration for "Letters" section reprinted by permission of Rare
Book Division, The New York Public Library, Astor, Lenox
and Tilden Foundations.

Published in Canada by Fitzhenry & Whiteside Limited, Don Mills, Ontario

Manufactured in the United States of America

Library of Congress Cataloging in Publication Data

Wollstonecraft, Mary, 1759–1797.
A Wollstonecraft anthology.

Bibliography: p.
I. Todd, Janet M., 1942–   II. Title.
PR5841.W8A6   1977   828'.6'09   77–72192
ISBN 0–253–36605–4   1 2 3 4 5 81 80 79 78 77

Contents

ILLUSTRATIONS

PREFACE

Selecting from any writer is justified by the hope that readers will go from passages to works. If no writer actually benefits from selection, it may yet be maintained that some appear more easily accessible and appealing in that form. I believe that Mary Wollstonecraft is one of them. She is a repetitive writer, whose works are embedded in the literary and political world of the late eighteenth century. Unless one recreates this world to understand her context and respond to her need of repetition, it is possible to come from much of her writing with a sense of frustration. With these selections I have tried to prune Wollstonecraft in such a way that the reader will, when finished, wish to come to terms with the full growth of her work.

The selections have been chosen to suggest Wollstonecraft's literary powers, her use of a wide range of styles, and her philosophical progress, especially in her understanding of women and of emotion. I have tried to include examples of the simplicity of statement, most attractive to twentieth-century readers, and of rhetorical inflation, perhaps less so. Where the work exists in print only in a facsimile edition, I have taken large continuous extracts; where the work is easily available, I have chosen short passages.

The categories are arbitrary. Although I have entitled one "Courtesy Books" or works of education, and another "Works of Controversy," it can certainly be argued that most books Wollstonecraft wrote were both educational and controversial. Some categories were necessary, however, and I have chosen those which suggest the main genres in which Wollstonecraft worked. The first category includes a pedagogical treatise and a collection of children's stories, both early books. The second concerns polemical works that formed part of political debates in the 1790s; these works belong to the middle years of Wollstonecraft's literary life. The third category has books and essays designed to inform and comment; these were written primarily during her wanderings in France and Scandinavia. The fourth section includes novels and is the least chronological since it extracts from her early work, *Mary, A Fiction* and from her late one, *The Wrongs of Woman*. The final section is devoted to the two series of letters Wollstonecraft wrote in her final years, the letters to Gilbert Imlay and William Godwin. Whatever the genre, Wollstonecraft constantly alludes to and recreates her life; the introduction is therefore primarily biographical.

THE TEXT

The excerpts follow closely the original editions brought out by Wollstonecraft in her lifetime and by Godwin after her death. Extracts from *A*

Vindication of the Rights of Woman are taken from the second edition of 1792. The letters to Imlay follow the text in *Posthumous Works* (1798) and the numbers refer to this text. The Godwin letters are numbered according to the edition of Ralph Wardle, entitled *Godwin and Mary: Letters of William Godwin and Mary Wollstonecraft*, from which the text is also taken. As far as possible I have followed what Wollstonecraft wrote and have changed irregularities in spelling and punctuation only where noted. Throughout, however, the apostrophe in the possessive pronoun has been eliminated.

Footnotes from the Wollstonecraft and Godwin texts are followed by the names to distinguish them from other editorial notes. Wollstonecraft's writing is a tissue of quotations, some accurately and some inaccurately reproduced. Most of them are passing allusions to Shakespeare or Milton, or phrases from the poets of sensibility, much in vogue when she wrote, especially Edward Young and William Cowper. In an anthology for the general reader, it would be pedantic to footnote all these quoted fragments even if it were possible, and unnecessary to indicate how they frequently diverge from the originals. I have, however, given some bibliographical information on quotations that seem important for Wollstonecraft's argument or effect, for example the quotations from Edmund Burke in *A Vindication of the Rights of Men*.

I would like to thank the many people who encouraged me in this project and contributed to it with advice and comments. I am especially grateful to Catherine Dammeyer, Godelieve Mercken-Spaas, and Aaron R. Todd for reading parts of the book and to Anna Zalarick for many hours of typing and copying. Professor Ralph M. Wardle aided indirectly with his excellent biography of Wollstonecraft and directly with his trenchant comments and criticism.

A
Wollstonecraft
Anthology

Introduction

In the last book published before her death in 1797, Mary Wollstonecraft wrote:

> All the world is a stage, thought I; and few are there in it who do not
> play the part they have learnt by rote; and those who do not, seem
> marks set up to be pelted at by fortune; or rather as sign-posts, which
> point out the road to others, whilst forced to stand still themselves
> amidst the mud and dust.[1]

In her time and later, Wollstonecraft was certainly "amid the mud and
dust" of calumny and abuse. After her death in childbirth she was
branded an "unsex'd female" and "whore," whose vices and follies had
brought about her providential end; in the twentieth century, she has
been portrayed as the mentally sick originator of the disease of femi-
nism.[2] She was right too in seeing her life and works as "sign-posts."
Her story tells how difficult and dangerous it was for a woman to flout
social convention, and how courageous, tough, and sometimes hard
such an unconventional woman had to be. Wollstonecraft's works and
letters, taken together, suggest why she was publicly vilified; at the
same time they show how strenuously and successfully she struggled to
develop in intellect and emotion.

Wollstonecraft was born in April 1759 in London, the second of
seven children. Her grandfather was a prosperous weaver, whose financial success formed the basis of his son's rise into the middle class as a
gentleman farmer. It was an unfortunate rise, for the son had neither
the ability nor the resources to maintain the position, and Wollstonecraft's life was early marred by her father's failed aspirations. As his
fortunes declined, he took to a peripatetic life, and, dragging his family
across England and Wales, he became increasingly more drunken, feck-
less, and domineering, especially over his subservient wife. Wollstonecraft's early view of the relations of man and woman was not therefore
a happy one and it is reflected in her later extreme attitudes to marriage,
ranging from fearful detestation to intense idealization.

As their own hopes failed, the Wollstonecraft parents invested them anew in their eldest son, Edward. The custom of primogeniture and the privilege accorded to his sex gave Edward a favored position, but the situation was made worse for Wollstonecraft by their mother's preference for her first child. In her autobiographical novel, entitled with some irony *Mary, A Fiction*, the eldest son is made to die; in real life, his presence ensured that by the end of her childhood Wollstonecraft would instinctively distrust privilege and authority of all kinds.

Fortunately Wollstonecraft was not always confined to home and her father's wanderings were punctuated with occasional lengthy stops. One entrenchment occurred in Beverley in Yorkshire, where she spent the formative years from nine to fifteen. Here she ran wild in the hills and dales, picked up some education at the local school, and established her pattern of friendship. She liked other girls and with them felt and expressed the emotions she had curbed with her family, but the family clearly lent its pattern to her relationships. Her early letters to her Yorkshire friend Jane Arden show Wollstonecraft viewing friendship as a matter of domination and submission, rather as she must have understood marriage: "I am a little singular in my thoughts of love and friendship," she wrote, "I must have the first place or none."[3] She justified such selfishness by asserting that her feelings were uniquely strong and compelling.

When she was sixteen, Wollstonecraft met her next friend in Hoxton near London. The friend was Fanny Blood, whose impoverished family was a sadder version of Wollstonecraft's, but whose character seemed an ideal version of her own. Fanny Blood appeared immediately to write, paint, and think on a higher plane than her untutored friend; later in their relationship Wollstonecraft would come to see how much she excelled with her own vigorous mind and independent spirit.

The friendship with Fanny Blood was deep and close. Years later, after the death of her friend, Wollstonecraft named her child Fanny and in her last completed book, *Letters Written . . . in Sweden*, she was clearly writing of Fanny when she described a dear friend who in spite of death was always present to her.

Soon of course the Wollstonecraft family had to move from Hoxton. By this time she had vowed to spend her days with Fanny Blood and to put a period to her dreary home life. At the age of nineteen she left her family for her first job, sustained by her hope of one day joining her friend and by her desire of freeing herself from a family that had failed to love her.

As if preparing for the writing of her major work, *A Vindication of the Rights of Woman*, in the next few years Wollstonecraft tried almost all the positions open to respectable but impoverished middle-class women. Her first one was as a companion to a wealthy widow in Bath. This was not an easy situation for she was already headstrong and assertive. She struggled to maintain both the necessary subservience and her own self-respect, and the letters she wrote at this time record this struggle; in them she pities herself profusely while asserting her own emotional superiority—compensation perhaps for her social inferiority. Incessantly she describes her mental and physical sufferings: "My health is ruined, my spirits broken, and I have a constant pain in my side. . . . My head aches with holding it down."[4]

Yet, with all her debility, Wollstonecraft managed to satisfy her difficult employer and to keep an observant eye on the doings of the fashionable world of Bath. It was her first contact with this world and she found it distasteful; in this attitude she was no doubt influenced by her situation as an upper servant: "You cannot imagine how amazingly they dress here;—It is the important business that takes up great part of the time of both old and young.—I believe I am thought a very poor creature. . . ."[5]

From Bath in 1781 Wollstonecraft was suddenly recalled home, now in Enfield, to tend her dying mother. She had been embittered by her family's lack of concern for her and she was much moved by the summons. In Godwin's version of the last illness and death, she became at the end indispensable to the mother who had earlier scorned her.

After her mother died, Wollstonecraft felt responsible for "the welfare of every member of her family" and she energetically set about organizing the lives of her younger siblings.[6] Shortly after, she moved in with Fanny Blood and soon came to dominate and care for the Blood family as well as for her own. Yet, throughout her days, she was haunted by her mother's dying words "A little patience, and all will be over!" which suggested a suffering passivity also attractive to her.[7] Repeatedly in times of crisis and depression and in her autobiographical writings, she would echo these words.

From the Bloods, Wollstonecraft was once more summoned home to a family crisis. Her younger sister Eliza had married and borne a child. Suffering a postpartum depression bordering on madness, Eliza came to detest her husband. Wollstonecraft understood this situation in terms of her own experience of male tyranny and she resolved it by dramatically abducting Eliza from her husband and baby. It was impulsively done, perhaps wrongheadedly, but it reveals much about Wollstonecraft's longing for vigorous action at this stage and her tendency toward simple judgment. At least she was aware of her appearance before the world: "I knew I should be . . . the *shameful incendiary*," she wrote, "in this shocking affair of a woman's leaving her bed-fellow."[8]

Established in secret lodgings, the Wollstonecraft sisters pondered the limited options open to women situated like themselves. They chose the most accessible option and, together with Fanny Blood, in 1784 the young women opened a school in Newington Green, a town just north of London. They were joined there later by Everina, the youngest of the Wollstonecraft sisters.

The choice of Newington Green was fortunate. A community of intellectual Dissenters had lived there for some years, among whom Dr. Richard Price was perhaps the most notable. At sixty he was a veteran of many political battles and he would soon enter the fight again as a supporter of the principles of the French Revolution. In Newington Green, Wollstonecraft quickly came to know Price and the liberal men and women acquainted with him. Their conversation and literary works stimulated her to consider the social basis of the tyranny she had endured at home and in Bath and they provided her with a framework of ideas into which her own experiences could fit. She came to see her personal struggle for independence as part of a larger political struggle and, through Price, to understand that a person required freedom to cultivate reason and so achieve true humanity.

In its early days Wollstonecraft's school prospered in spite of the personal problems of its teachers. Eliza grieved for her baby, and Fanny Blood, growing consumptive, longed for a young man named Hugh Skeys to whom she had long before given her heart but who seemed reluctant to commit himself to Fanny with her train of shiftless relatives. Wollstonecraft frequently saw herself shut out from the life of domestic and intellectual joys for which she had so much zest and her letters of the time show her again retreating into herself, taking comfort in the kind of resignation exemplified earlier by her mother on her deathbed. "I have lost all relish for life," she wrote at this time, "and my almost broken heart is only cheared by the prospect of death. I may be years a-dying tho', and so I ought to be patient."[9]

Wollstonecraft's school eventually disintegrated because of the characters of its teachers. Fanny Blood finally left for Portugal to marry Skeys, who was working there; her friends hoped she would regain her failing health in the drier, warmer climate. The following year, in late 1785, Wollstonecraft heard of Fanny's approaching confinement and, aware of her consumptive state, took the dramatic step of abandoning the school and traveling to Portugal. She arrived in time to see her friend die. The death was a crushing blow to Wollstonecraft. Her own words later about her loneliness and friendlessness, like the words of her dying mother, echo and reecho through her letters and novels.

As on other occasions of emotional upheaval, Wollstonecraft's misery did not prevent her from observing her surroundings. Her brief, melancholy stay in Portugal impressed her deeply with the sad condition of humanity and with the evils of poverty. She saw superstition and cruelty at every turn, and the sight strengthened her belief, derived in part from Price, that reason and civilization were essential to virtue. It was a belief that was shaken only when she came to contemplate the barbarous actions of the civilized French during their Revolution.

Back in England in 1786, heavily in debt, Wollstonecraft found her school foundering, and without Fanny Blood she was not inclined to rescue it. Needing money for herself and her numerous assumed dependents, she decided to turn her experience to use and write a book on the subject about which she knew much: how girls should and should not be educated. The book, *Thoughts on the Education of Daughters*, was published in 1787 by Joseph Johnson. An interesting first work, it makes plain that Wollstonecraft was already dissatisfied with the status of women but that she still accepted their primary roles of mother and wife. Of daughters she wrote: "I wish them to be taught to think," while at the same time she stressed that they must learn restraint and submission.[10] The book earned her ten guineas, which, in spite of her own need, she used to pay the Bloods' fare to Dublin where they had more hope of earning a living.

The publication of her work provided Wollstonecraft with a new definition of herself, that of author, but it did not change her sorry financial condition. Extricating herself from her school as best she could, she accepted a position as a governess; in so doing she tried the third of the main employment options open to the respectable woman. In 1786 she traveled to Ireland to assume charge of the three eldest daughters of Lord and Lady Kingsborough.

Wollstonecraft entered on her new life with no illusions: in *Thoughts on the Education of Daughters* she had written, "A governess to young ladies is . . . disagreeable. It is ten to one if they meet with a reasonable mother. . . . The children treat them with disrespect, and often with insolence. In the mean time life glides away, and the spirits with it"; in a letter of the time she showed herself acutely aware of the problems of living surrounded only by "unequals."[11] Given such awareness, it was largely inevitable that she should dislike Lady Kingsborough, who although often kind to her governess—whom she treated as "a gentlewoman"—yet combined aristocratic privilege with feminine passivity and triviality in a way Wollstonecraft had to deplore.[12] Forced again into a position of inappropriate dependence, she responded to it by scorning her employer and pitying herself. Frequently in her writ-

ings, in her letters and novels, and later in her polemical works, she
portrayed Lady Kingsborough in the vapid yet pernicious aristocratic
ladies she created; herself she pictured at this time as a poor, solitary
soul doomed to mental and physical anguish which could only end in
death. "My mind preys on my body," she complained, momentarily
aware of the mental source of much of her suffering in Ireland.[13]

During her time with the Kingsboroughs, Wollstonecraft turned
her misery to account in her first novel. Growing out of her partly
morbid, partly just contemplation of her early life and present situation,
Mary, A Fiction provided an idealized and simplified account of her
childhood. At the same time it betrayed her longing to be loved and to
find an object worthy of love. Fanny Blood clearly appears as Ann,
the friend much regarded but ultimately found wanting. At this stage
in Wollstonecraft's life there seems to have been no counterpart to the
hero, a man combining intellect with warmth of sentiment. The end
of the work reflects its author's desolate and lonely state and suggests
her early habit of consoling herself with images of a compensatory
afterlife:

> [Mary's] delicate state of health did not promise long life. In moments
> of solitary sadness, a gleam of joy would dart across her mind—She
> thought she was hastening to that world *where there is neither marry-
> ing*, nor giving in marriage.[14]

The writing of *Mary, A Fiction* seems to have purged Wollstonecraft for a time of her melancholia and self-pity. In addition it re-
asserted her right to the active title of author. When Lady Kingsborough finally dismissed her insubordinate governess, it was as an
author that she resolved to earn her living.

In 1787 Wollstonecraft moved alone to London to work for Joseph
Johnson, first as translator and reader and later as reviewer and editorial
assistant on the *Analytical Review*, the new journal Johnson and his
friends were starting at the time. Over the next years Johnson acted
as father and friend to the headstrong woman whom he had encouraged
into letters. His belief in her enabled her to move from dependent to
independent life in London; through his social circle—which included
Tom Paine, supporter and apologist of the American Revolution;
Henry Fuseli, the German-Swiss painter and commentator on Rousseau; William Blake, the poet and radical thinker; William Godwin,
the political and social theorist; and Thomas Holcroft, the novelist—
Johnson provided her with the kind of intellectual stimulation she had
missed since leaving Newington Green and with the kind of friends
she found most congenial. In the pride of her new role, she wrote

excitedly to her sister: "I am then going to be the first of a new genus.
. . . You know I am not born to tread in the beaten track, the peculiar
bent of my nature pushes me on. . . ."[15]

Wollstonecraft was of course not the "first of a new genus," but one
of the first. Several women in the late seventeenth and early eighteenth
centuries, from Aphra Behn to Eliza Haywood and Delariviere Manley,
had been professional writers. In her own age women authors abounded
too. The majority were novelists writing for polite amusement to lighten
the boredom of middle-class female life; others certainly wrote to earn
a living, such as Charlotte Smith and Elizabeth Inchbald, who made
no attempt to hide their financial motives. Still others, such as the
poet and chronicler Helen Maria Williams and the novelist and polemi-
cist Mary Hays, combined a commitment to the profession of letters
with a passionate concern for ideas, the hallmark of Wollstonecraft.
Many of these women came from Dissenting backgrounds and had
been stimulated by the same ideas as Wollstonecraft in Newington
Green. Some in the 1780s and 1790s were groping toward those views
which were to be so vehemently expressed for their generation in *A
Vindication of the Rights of Woman*.

In 1788, Wollstonecraft's third book, *Original Stories from Real
Life; with Conversations, Calculated to Regulate the Affections, and
Form the Mind to Truth and Goodness*, was published by Johnson. It
was written for children and presented her vision of the reasonable
mother, a rather cold, stern, but not altogether unsympathetic character named Mrs. Mason, who has in her charge, as Wollstonecraft had
with the Kingsboroughs, two girls of twelve and fourteen. Through cautionary tales and exemplary situations, the girls are taught the virtues,
especially those of benevolence and patience. The book reiterates Wollstonecraft's views that the years of childhood are all-important for the
creation of character and that more is learned from experience than
precept. The character of Mrs. Mason certainly had one admirer. Years
later Margaret, the eldest of the Kingsborough daughters, showed her
affection and respect for her former governess by adopting the name of
Mrs. Mason. She was known by this name when in Italy she befriended
Mary Shelley, Wollstonecraft's second daughter.

By the time the French Revolution broke out in 1789, Wollstonecraft was already established as a translator, reviewer, and minor author
and she was well aware of her position: "My die is cast!" she wrote
dramatically, "I could not now resign intellectual pursuits for domestic
comforts."[16]

During her early years with Johnson she worked incessantly. In
1788 she was translating Jacques Necker's *Of the Importance of Reli-*

gious Opinions and in 1790 Christian Gotthilf Salzmann's *Elements of Morality for the Use of Children*, both written in languages which she had to master as she went along. She reviewed works as diverse as Dr. Johnson's *Sermon on the Death of His Wife, La Vie Privée du Cardinal Dubois*, and Charlotte Smith's *Ethelinda*.[17] These reviews, and many others she wrote for Johnson's journal between 1788 and 1790, suggest her shifting opinions. At first unconcerned with politics or the political causes of the social malaise, she still accepted an afterlife as compensation for the evils of this world. By 1790, however, she had come to see doctrinal Christianity as a "fable," the work of priestcraft, and to connect social ills with political institutions and privilege. As the rationalist belief in the perfectibility of humanity superseded the Christian belief in human limitation, she came to accept that compensation could and must occur in this life.

Clearly authorship and the reading it required provided intellectual stimulus and comfort for Wollstonecraft, but it was never quite sufficient for all her needs. When she wrote of her enjoyment of intellectual pursuits, she added rather wistfully: "Yet I think I could form an idea of more *elegant* felicity—where mind chastened sensation, and rational converse gave a little dignity to fondness."[18] She still yearned for the human closeness unknown since Fanny Blood's death and in her yearning she again referred much to her solitariness and often echoed her mother's dying words.

The literary events of 1789 and 1790 gave Wollstonecraft the opportunity to combine brilliantly many facets of her complex personality, her tendency to emotional attachments and her enjoyment of intellectual struggle. She rose magnificently to the occasion. Her old friend and mentor, Dr. Price, had preached a sermon before the Society for Commemorating the Glorious Revolution of 1688, in which he welcomed the revolutionary events in France and called for reform in England. A few weeks later, answers to Price began and a year after the event Burke renewed the controversy with his reply, *Reflections on the Revolution in France*, a work that went far beyond Price's sermon in passion and length of argument.

With great eloquence Burke stated the conservative position on the Revolution, arguing forcefully against disregarding tradition and experience in pursuit of the chimerical and conflicting ideals of equality and liberty. Predicated on a pessimistic view of humanity as indelibly flawed and incipiently brutish, Burke's book assailed those beliefs in the perfectibility and reason of humanity that Wollstonecraft had come to hold so dear. By so doing, it was attacking not only Price, a man she revered, but herself, for if the rebuttal were true it suggested that she erred in her own principles and unconventional practice.

Equipped with reasoning arguments and inspired by affection for Price, Wollstonecraft made herself into a famous author by her speedy answer to Burke entitled *A Vindication of the Rights of Men*, the first of many replies, which included Paine's *Rights of Man*. In her book she reasoned against the irrationality and sentimentality of Burke; at the same time she gave reign to her emotions in outbursts of sympathy for Price, intended to demonstrate the nature of genuine feeling in contrast to the kind affected in the *Reflections*.

In *A Vindication of the Rights of Men* Wollstonecraft argued eloquently for the essential liberty of humanity and against the encroachment on it of "the demon of property," seen as a main cause of privilege and subordination.[19] She inveighed against primogeniture, supported by Burke as part of the foundation of the social order, and against the social order itself insofar as it derived from traditions of injustice and oppression. Her arguments are based on her own experience and the theories of liberal thinkers such as John Locke and Jean-Jacques Rousseau. Part of her tribute to Price is found in her use of his philosophy, especially in her emphasis on the dependence of morality on reason.

The Rights of Men is a digressive work, which yet has considerable power. It is given unity by its overall argument that the poison of privilege and subordination caused by property, rank, and privilege has eaten into all people and all classes: "The tremendous mountain of woe . . . defaces our globe," she wrote toward the end of her work.[20]

When Wollstonecraft regarded the subordinate class in early 1790, she saw primarily working men; she failed to perceive her own sex as a group distinctly oppressed. Yet *The Rights of Men* contains in embryo the ideas of its successor, *A Vindication of the Rights of Woman*; in both works Wollstonecraft argued against women's triviality and ignorance and for their moral and intellectual cultivation.

Clearly Wollstonecraft came to her ideas on women's sorry situation from her own experiences as a dependent and independent woman. She may also have found support and stimulus for such ideas among her friends within Johnson's circle; certainly she received both from a work she reviewed in November 1790: Catherine Macaulay's *Letters on Education*. Like Wollstonecraft later, Macaulay argued that women must be educated before they could develop morally, and she blamed their apparent triviality on the predominantly sexual character they had been forced to adopt in a male society. She scorned female accomplishments designed solely to make women sexually attractive and she criticized a harem mentality that allowed exclusive cultivation of the trivial. To Macaulay's ideas Wollstonecraft brought in 1791 her own experience, analytical power, and emphatic style. The resulting work, *A Vindication of the Rights of Woman*, was published in 1792 by Johnson.

Like its predecessor *The Rights of Men*, *A Vindication of the Rights of Woman* is rooted in controversy. The French National Assembly was concerned with education and was considering a plan by Talleyrand to provide it for boys but limit it for girls. Such a proposal emphasized that the rights envisioned by the Assembly in its *Declaration of the Rights of Men* were indeed just that, and, while Wollstonecraft was at work on her book, a Frenchwoman, Olympe de Gouges, was penning her ironic commentary on her government's attitude to women, *A Declaration of the Rights of Woman*. Wollstonecraft's work was dedicated to Talleyrand and was, rather optimistically, designed to influence French events in favor of women.

The book is, of course, more than an element in a controversy. Pedagogical like her early works, it goes far beyond them in expression and implication. Her previous aim had been to teach women to think. This was still her aim but it is expressed now in more striking terms, with full awareness of its revolutionary implications. "It is time," she states, "to effect a revolution in female manners—time to restore to them their lost dignity."[21] Clearly Wollstonecraft saw what her opponents also saw, that the assertion of the right of women to reason was a revolutionary act and that a change such as she advocated would have vast social and political consequences: "I love man as my fellow; but his sceptre, real, or usurped, extends not to me."[22]

Partly in response to her fame as the author of *The Rights of Men*, Wollstonecraft in 1791 consciously changed her appearance; putting off the guise of "philosophical sloven," she smartened herself up in more fashionable clothes than the coarse drab ones she had so far been known for and she moved into finer lodgings.[23] Her transformation was, however, not entirely due to fame of authorship. Long starved of love, Wollstonecraft felt that she had at last found in life the intellectual and sensitive hero she had imagined in her letters and novel. Henry Fuseli, the object of her affections, had indeed the intellectual power she sought but little of the sensitivity. In his writings he described women as childlike and feeble and in his art he often depicted them as insectlike victims. For Wollstonecraft at work on her polemic in support of independence and self-reliance for women, he was an ironic and unhappy choice.

Wollstonecraft's infatuation with Fuseli exemplified well the female tendency, which she had attacked in *The Rights of Woman*, to create and then be captured by an imaginary figure. She bombarded Fuseli with love and letters, to neither of which he responded. Finally, obsessed with the figure she had created, she went to his wife and proposed joining the family. The proposal was summarily rejected and the earlier idea of a joint trip to France of Johnson, the Fuselis, and herself was abandoned. In December of 1792, Wollstonecraft set off for France alone. Her sister, the sufferer from much of her well-intentioned but sometimes ill-advised help, commented more truthfully than she knew: "So the author of The Rights of Women is going to France . . . in spite of Reason, when Mrs W reaches the Continent she will be but a woman."[24]

Wollstonecraft arrived in Paris at a critical point in the Revolution. A few months earlier, with the rising of the Paris Commune, the September Massacres of political prisoners, and the imprisonment of Louis XVI, the Revolution had been moving from its reformist to its revolutionary phase. One of the first public sights she witnessed was the passing of the King to his trial, a dramatic event which aroused her sympathy and unsettled some of her favorable preconceptions about the Revolution.

A few weeks later, Wollstonecraft wrote her "Letter on the Present Character of the French Nation," by which time the King had been beheaded and war with England had broken out. The "Letter" revealed the impact of such events; it renounced belief both in humanity's perfectibility and in revolution—sudden political and social change—and it cast doubts on the ability of the French to better their condition at all, characterized as they were by vanity and triviality. Sadly Wollstonecraft wrote of her disillusion; she saw vices, follies, and prejudice where she had expected virtue and the "fair form of Liberty."[25] It seemed that the hated aristocracy of birth had merely given way to an aristocracy of riches, even more pernicious to freedom and dignity. Vice and evil, not virtue, had become "the grand mobile of action."[26]

Wollstonecraft's response was extreme and emotional. When she came later to write her history of the genesis of the Revolution, *An Historical and Moral View of the Origin and Progress of the French Revolution,* she warned readers against judging with emotions instead of reason, for she knew from experience the danger. In this work she partially reaffirmed her old rationalist beliefs in humanity.

Wollstonecraft's history of the French Revolution concerned only the events of the early months, in 1789, but since the book was written in 1793 and 1794, it is informed with her knowledge of the later violent events of the Jacobin period under Robespierre. Opposing tyranny of any kind, Wollstonecraft responded to the sufferings of the dispossessed and politically disfavored as surely as to the miseries of the poor. Yet by the time she started to write her book she had come to terms with the violence and initial chaos of change and had accepted that the

Revolution, in spite of its barbarous aspect, was the natural outcome of intellectual development in Europe and a sign of genuine social improvement. Such a view represents a considerable struggle on Wollstonecraft's part, one undertaken by few of the idealistic English visitors to revolutionary France. She had intellectual company, however, in her friend and fellow historian, Helen Maria Williams, who, in her *Letters from France*, managed to achieve a similar view in spite of her personal suffering under the Jacobin repression.

In Britain the favorable view of the Revolution put forward by Wollstonecraft and Williams was certainly not the common one. Wollstonecraft's warning against judging events with the emotions alone went unheeded and the British responded harshly to the French situation. They repudiated all liberal theory as "Jacobin," tainted with French crimes, and in Wales, early in 1793, Eliza Wollstonecraft described the people's burning of Paine's effigy; she added that there was a chance of their "immortalizing Miss Wollstonecraft in the like manner."[27]

In France Wollstonecraft was, however, far from being associated with the Jacobin policies that caused much of the English reaction. Through her friends at Johnson's she had become immediately aligned with the opposing moderate faction of the Revolution, the Girondists, and their group of expatriate friends and sympathizers, which included Paine, the American Joel Barlow, and Helen Maria Williams. In October and November of 1793 Jacobin hostility to this group caused the death of many of Wollstonecraft's French associates, such as Madame Roland, and the imprisonment of many of their expatriate friends. The ideas in *The French Revolution* are clearly influenced by the progressive and evolutionary views of the Girondists, while Wollstonecraft's horror of mob violence and manipulation undoubtedly comes in part from her knowledge of the Jacobin campaign against her friends.

In the group of Girondists and Anglo-Americans, Wollstonecraft met Gilbert Imlay, a rather murky American speculator, bent like so many on using the Revolution for financial gain. She did not immediately see his speculating and mercenary side, which later struck her forcefully, but instead perceived in him the new man, untouched by the conventions and vices of the Old World. Soon he became a successor to Fuseli in her affections.

The ensuing months of late 1793 and early 1794 were joyful but lonely ones for Wollstonecraft, and her isolation may explain something of her obsessive relationship with Imlay. Her friends and associates had been guillotined or imprisoned and her faith in the anti-authoritarian basis of the Revolution was sorely tried. Since her feminist faith

was a part of a wider rationalist belief in the freedom and equality of
all humanity, her concept of women must have suffered some shock
too. In a small village near Paris where she had gone into hiding Wollstonecraft saw no one but Imlay, who visited her at intervals. In such a
situation, she seems to have forsaken her desire, so forcefully expressed
in *The Rights of Woman*, to become an independent and active woman;
instead she was happy to place her entire confidence in another person.
In a letter to Imlay, she imaged herself as a clinging female vine to the
male tree: "Let me indulge the thought that I have thrown out some
tendrils to cling to the elm by which I wish to be supported."[28] It was a
dangerous indulgence, as the author of *The Rights of Woman* well
knew.

By the time Imlay left Paris for Le Havre, Wollstonecraft was pregnant. She followed him in letters, some gaily asserting their cozy love
and happiness, others begging for proofs of a relationship that she felt
was already fading. The old picture of herself as a lone and suffering
female reappears in her letters, as, in Godwin's words, she gave "a loose
to all the sensibilities of her nature."[29] She spoke often of her tears and
agony, and of her need for patience.

After some months, Wollstonecraft followed Imlay to Le Havre,
where in May 1794 her daughter Fanny Imlay was born. The birth
proved easy and she found immediate and growing pleasure in motherhood. But such pleasure was insufficient to compensate for her other
pains: the relationship with Imlay was now clearly disintegrating. Wollstonecraft's pleading, cajoling, and reviling letters over the next few
months chart the course of disintegration. She came to see that the
deep feeling with which she had credited Imlay was, like Burke's, affected and she blamed him for a lack of the kind of emotion with which
she was only too well endowed. In her final novel, *The Wrongs of
Woman*, the faithless hero would be marked by Imlay's affectation of
feeling. Like Jane Austen later, Wollstonecraft came to distrust overtly
emotional men and to understand that men could be affected and trivial
as often as subordinate women.

Throughout the long agony of the Imlay affair, Wollstonecraft was
not without self-knowledge, although she seemed frequently to repress
it. Often she asserted her own part in the creation of the man she loved,
although at other times she blinded herself with the idea that Imlay was
other than the indifferent and mercenary person she experienced. Early
in 1795, worn out with the struggle, she returned with her daughter to
England, where Imlay was then living. There she learned of his infidelity. Her reaction was immediate and extreme: she attempted to poison
herself.

At this stage, a curious solution to the situation was proposed by Imlay and accepted by Wollstonecraft. With baby and nursemaid, she was dispatched to Scandinavia as his business representative. In this way Imlay intended to rid himself of a troublesome burden and Wollstonecraft perhaps hoped to gain some emotional strength. She went, however, expecting little success: "I shall make every effort to calm my mind," she wrote, "yet a strong conviction seems to whirl round in the very centre of my brain, which, like the fiat of fate, emphatically assures me that grief has a firm hold of my heart."[30] And, more briefly, "I never forget . . . the misery."[31]

Wollstonecraft's journey through Sweden, Norway, and Denmark is well described in semi-public letters to Imlay, published in 1796 as *Letters Written During a Short Residence in Sweden, Norway, and Denmark*, as well as in her private ones to him. Together they record her wanderings through the wild northern countryside of Scandinavia, revealing her response to the people and scenery she encountered there. Much of the book continues the argument of her work on the French Revolution, that progress is inevitable but gradual. In Scandinavia, the Revolution itself appeared more progressive than it had earlier, and the boorishness of the Scandinavians made the vices and frivolity of the civilized French less heinous.

The most immediately striking element of the *Letters Written . . . in Sweden* is Wollstonecraft's depiction of herself; among the cascades and lonely rocks of Scandinavia, she became a figure from a literary romance, a solitary wanderer whose bleeding heart is displayed on every page. Yet the work is not self-centered, for it shows a wider sympathy for the unfortunate than any of her previous works and it reaffirms her concern—little in evidence in *The French Revolution*—for the indignities and sufferings of women. In addition, although it talks much of her despair and yearning for death, its final effect is not depressing, perhaps because, in the middle of her grief, Wollstonecraft was penning one of her finest works. With it she was affirming herself as active and caring woman and author, and the moving dramatization of herself as inactive and sometimes self-centered female is belied by the effective literary creation and by the wide sympathy it reveals in its author.

Wollstonecraft's voyage to Scandinavia is bounded by suicide attempts; on her return to England in late 1795, she learned again that Imlay had been unfaithful. She responded by throwing herself in the Thames, having soaked her clothes to ensure her sinking. She was rescued from the water unconscious.

Still she was not cured of her obsession, and she made a last desperate effort to gain Imlay's attention with a proposal, painfully reminiscent of the Fuseli one years before, that she move in with him and his new mistress. The refusal she met with must have had a conviction lacking in Imlay's earlier refusals of her. In the spring of 1796 she wrote her last letter to him, ending "I part with you in peace."[32]

Perhaps Wollstonecraft never completely parted with Imlay, but she did make a valiant effort to take up again the strands of her old life. She began well by working her letters into a travel narrative of Scandinavia and producing a book that was better received by her contemporaries than any of her other works. In his memoirs of Wollstonecraft, Godwin wrote of the effect of this work on him: "If ever there was a book calculated to make a man in love with its author, this appears to me to be the book."[33]

In addition to reasserting herself as an author, Wollstonecraft reestablished herself as an independent and social woman. She took up with other professional writers such as Mary Hays, and it was at Hays's house that she met William Godwin again.

Now the successful author of *Political Justice* and *Caleb Williams*, Godwin when he met Wollstonecraft was also becoming less solitary and more sociable, and he was ready for a serious relationship with a woman. A firm believer in the power of reason, like many of his fellow rationalists he was by no means feminist in his views. He did, however, respect individual women and the relationship he formed with Wollstonecraft seems to have been based on his side on esteem and respect, as well as love. Later he wrote, "There was . . . no period of throes and resolute explanation attendant on the tale. It was friendship melting into love."[34] No doubt he idealized the past; yet the elements of love and friendship seem to have been present in the relationship at all times, if the obsessive passion of the Imlay affair was lacking.

With Godwin, Wollstonecraft gained a freedom, hitherto unknown in her relationships, to express the many aspects of her personality. Melancholy at times and distrustful of Godwin, she allowed her old views of herself, of solitary wanderer and suffering female, to come to the fore; at other times, however, she accepted her life, enjoyed her reasonable happiness and saw her troubled period as the necessary experience of an independent woman in a prejudiced society. With Godwin's encouragement she continued to write. "I think I may venture to say," wrote Godwin of their relationship, "that no two persons ever found in each other's society, a satisfaction more pure and refined."[35]

When Wollstonecraft found herself pregnant again, she and Godwin were privately married. News of their marriage provoked some ridicule, since both had condemned the institution, and some indignation, since by her act Wollstonecraft was admitting that she had not married

Imlay whose name she had borne since returning to England. A few friends responded kindly, among them Thomas Holcroft, Godwin's old friend and Wollstonecraft's associate from the early London days: "From my very heart and soul I give you joy. I think you the most extraordinary married pair in existence."[36]

During their few months of marriage, Wollstonecraft and Godwin tried to live both independent and close lives. They worked together, quarrelled and reaffirmed their love. Wollstonecraft was writing her novel, *The Wrongs of Woman,* which presents the many evils that women of the middle and lower classes suffer. The heroine is called Maria and her lover, who proves false, in many respects resembles Imlay. Her failure at love is the result both of the inordinate pressures of male society and of her own failure to know herself and follow reason. In fiction Wollstonecraft was taking stock of her past and assessing her own strengths and weaknesses.

The character of Maria is similar in many ways to the character of Mary in Wollstonecraft's first novel and to several other fictional heroines of deep feeling, found in the female novel of the late eighteenth century. The second heroine is, however, unique in women's fiction of the time. Jemima is a servant, thief, and whore; yet she is treated by her creator with a sympathy which suggests that in her final years Wollstonecraft had come to see her kinship with all women, however degraded.

On August 30, 1797, Wollstonecraft gave birth to a daughter, Mary, but the placenta did not follow and although most of it was removed—an agonizing process—some remained to infect her system. On the morning of September 10 she died. Godwin broke off his journal with a series of dashes after the note "20 minutes before 8."

Perhaps for Wollstonecraft's reputation in the nineteenth century it would have been better if Godwin had persisted in expressing his sorrow wordlessly. Soon, however, he felt the need of sharing with the public his view of Wollstonecraft as a courageous and tender woman. In 1798 he published her *Posthumous Works,* including the private letters to Imlay, which Godwin claimed "may possibly be found to contain the finest examples of the language of sentiment and passion ever presented to the world."[37] In addition he wrote *Memoirs of the Author of A Vindication of the Rights of Woman,* a courageous work, expressing his own love and esteem for his dead wife and depicting Wollstonecraft as she had depicted herself to him and as he had apprehended her. The work shirks nothing, mentioning the friendship with Fuseli and the painful liaison with Imlay. Such truthfulness from a grieving husband was too much for the age and a spate of vituperative attacks appeared, ridiculing both Godwin and the woman he had tried to honor.

Richard Polwhele's poem of 1798, *The Unsex'd Females,* is an early example. It attacks Wollstonecraft more for her personal unconventionality than for her works, although it does object to her desire to unsex women in her embracing of female reason. In her life she is said to have sunk from the height of reason into a "love-sick maid" through her passion for Fuseli.[38] With glee Polwhele describes her career of dissipation, licentiousness, and voluptuousness, checked only by the impious despair of the suicide attempts.

An even more powerful and shocking picture was created in 1801 in the anonymous poem, "The Vision of Liberty," published in the *Anti-Jacobin Review,* a periodical founded to express conservative political and social views and to taunt radicals into silence:

> Then saw I mounted on a braying ass,
> William and Mary, sooth, a couple jolly:
> Who married, note ye how it came to pass,
> Although each held that marriage was but folly?—
> And she of curses would discharge a volley
> If the ass stumbled, leaping pales or ditches:
> Her husband, sans-culottes, was melancholy,
> For Mary verily would wear the breeches—
> God help poor silly men from such usurping b——s.
>
> Whilom this dame the Rights of Women writ,
> This is the title to her book she places,
> Exhorting bashful womankind to quit
> All foolish modesty, and coy grimaces;
> And name their backsides as it were their faces;
> Such license loose-tongued liberty adores,
> Which adds to female speech exceeding graces;
> Lucky the maid that on her volume pores,
> A scripture, archly fram'd, for propagating w——s.
>
> William hath penn'd a waggon-load of stuff,
> And Mary's life at last he needs must write,
> Thinking her whoredoms were not known enough,
> Till fairly printed off in black and white.—
> With wondrous glee and pride, this simple wight
> Her brothel feats of wantonness sets down,
> Being her spouse, he tells, with huge delight,
> How oft she cuckolded the silly clown
> And lent, O lovely piece! herself to half the town.[39]

Novels were published presenting this licentious image and cautionary tales provided early deaths for numerous abandoned women.

George Walker in *The Vagabond* describes "Mary," who, mouthing Wollstonecraft's sentiments, prostituted herself to several men, and Charles Lucas in *The Infernal Quixote*, portraying another corrupted heroine, calls Godwin's *Memoirs* the history of his own wife's intrigues.

In America the attack was no less vicious: in *The Letters of Shahcoolen*, published in 1802, Wollstonecraft becomes a lewd woman and a lunatic, and in a satire on her in the *Mercury and New-England Palladium* (March 1802) she is referred to as a strumpet. The latter work anticipates twentieth-century attacks when it asserts that Wollstonecraft lived and wrote as she did because she was despised, unloved, and unmarried: in 1947 in *Modern Woman, The Lost Sex* Ferdinand Lundberg and Marynia Farnham found Wollstonecraft a neurotic character, afflicted from childhood deprivation by a severe case of penis envy; in a 1974 review of a Wollstonecraft biography, Marghanita Laski considered her life as primarily a search for respectability and marriage.[40]

If Wollstonecraft inspired the image of jealous and castrating woman, she was also accepted by many as an exemplary human being, a rare combination of reason and emotion. Immediately after her death, her friend Mary Hays wrote affectionately about her in the *Monthly Magazine*, stressing her great talents and understanding, as well as her qualities of heart. Hays presents an active, fighting Wollstonecraft, whose life is sorrowful and hard because of those very prejudices she had wished to remove through her work.[41] In lines prefixed to his poem "The Triumph of Woman," Robert Southey also praised Wollstonecraft for personal warmth and intellectual power.[42]

As the conservative reaction to all things radical or unconventional deepened during the early years of the nineteenth century, tributes to Wollstonecraft became rarer and less enthusiastic, although she remained a felt presence in the lives of many of the feminist thinkers. Several of her works fell out of print and she became for most merely a name, frequently misspelled, for wantonness and unfemininity. In 1855 George Eliot wrote in an essay on Wollstonecraft and Margaret Fuller that she was amazed to find *The Rights of Woman* a severely moral and serious work, markedly at odds with the wild image of its author.[43]

In the late nineteenth century with the agitation for women's rights, there grew a desire to reclaim Wollstonecraft from her licentious reputation and allow her a position as one of the first feminists. Perhaps learning from Wollstonecraft, this later movement sought to avoid the association of women's freedom and promiscuity, the legacy of the 1790s. Partially in fulfillment of this desire, C. Kegan Paul produced a whitewashed image with all embarrassing details omitted. The relationship with Fuseli was strenuously denied, despite Godwin's admission of it, and at about this time the Wollstonecraft letters to Fuseli seem to have been destroyed. The liaison with Imlay became a marriage without ceremony, this having been neglected owing to the difficult French situation.[44] As G. R. Stirling Taylor commented wryly in his biography of Wollstonecraft written early in the twentieth century, "There are some theories which are much weakened by the unfortunate presence of facts."[45]

Since the 1960s the image of Wollstonecraft has been rounded out to include her irregularities of conduct. Yet even now her personal struggle is often found embarrassing rather than enlightening. Modern biographers have sometimes considered the discrepancies between the arguments for independence of *The Rights of Woman* and the actions of the life too severe for acceptance and have suggested that, ignorant when she wrote the book, she later learned disillusion and sense through experience of male love.[46] Such a view is certainly understandable and indeed Wollstonecraft often showed herself the victim of the female social conditioning and education she proposed to change. In spite of this deficient education, however, she managed to keep herself economically independent in her adult years and frequently to support a whole host of relatives and friends; she achieved this independence through excelling in intellectual pursuits usually reserved for men.

Wollstonecraft never completely abandoned the ideals of *The Rights of Woman*, and her writings, taken together, reveal a woman striving from the beginning to the end against deeply ingrained images of feminine passivity and dependence to attain a complete humanity. Her life certainly had much sorrow and failure; it also had many positive achievements, the greatest of which was its transmutation into literary works.

NOTES

1. *Letters Written during a Short Residence in Sweden, Norway, and Denmark* (1796; Lincoln: University of Nebraska Press, 1976), pp. 180–181.

2. See Richard Polwhele's *Unsex'd Females* (1798), the anonymous "Vision of Liberty" (1801), and *Modern Woman: The Lost Sex* (1947) by Ferdinand Lundberg and Marynia F. Farnham.

3. *Shelley and His Circle 1773–1822* (Cambridge: Harvard University Press, 1961), II, 955.

4. *Shelley and His Circle*, II, 965.

5. *Shelley and His Circle*, II, 978.

6. William Godwin, *Memoirs of the Author of A Vindication of the Rights of Woman* (London: Joseph Johnson, 1798), p. 29.

7. *Memoirs*, p. 28.

8. See Emily Sunstein's *A Different Face: The Life of Mary Wollstonecraft* (New York: Harper & Row, 1975), p. 88.

9. See Ralph Wardle's *Mary Wollstonecraft: A Critical Biography* (1951; Lincoln: University of Nebraska Press, 1967), pp. 40–41.

10. *Thoughts on the Education of Daughters* (1787; Clifton: A. M. Kelley, 1972), p. 22.

11. *Thoughts on the Education of Daughters*, pp. 71–72; quoted in Sunstein, p. 117.

12. Wardle, p. 62.

13. *Letters to Joseph Johnson* in *Posthumous Works of the Author of A Vindication of the Rights of Woman* (Clifton: Augustus Kelley, 1972), II, 61.

14. *Mary, A Fiction* (1788; New York: Garland Publishing Inc., 1974), p. 187.

15. See C. Kegan Paul's *William Godwin: His Friends and Contemporaries* (London: Henry S. King, 1876), I, 191–192.

16. Wardle, p. 109.

17. The reviews appeared anonymously in the *Analytical Review* but they may be assigned to Wollstonecraft on the basis of the initial and the style.

18. Wardle, p. 109.

19. *A Vindication of the Rights of Men* (1790; Gainesville: Scholars' Facsimiles & Reprints, 1960), p. 8.

20. *The Rights of Men*, pp. 151–152.

21. *A Vindication of the Rights of Woman* (1792; New York: Norton, 1975), p. 45.

22. *The Rights of Woman*, p. 37.

23. John Knowles, *The Life and Writings of Henry Fuseli* (London: Henry Colburn and Richard Bentley, 1831), I, 164.

24. Wardle, p. 172.

25. *Posthumous Works*, II, 43.

26. *Posthumous Works*, II, 45.

27. Wardle, pp. 181–182.

28. *Letters to Imlay* (London: C. Kegan Paul, 1879), pp. 40–41.

29. *Memoirs*, p. 114.

30. *Letters to Imlay*, p. 115.

31. *Letters to Imlay*, p. 139.

32. *Letters to Imlay*, p. 207.

33. *Memoirs*, p. 129.

34. *Memoirs*, p. 153.

35. *Memoirs*, p. 165.

36. Wardle, p. 288.

37. *Posthumous Works*, Preface, II.

38. *The Unsex'd Females* (London, 1798).

39. *Anti-Jacobin Review and Magazine*, IX, (1801).

40. *Modern Woman: The Lost Sex* (New York: Harper & Brothers, 1947); "Mary Quite Contrary," *Observer* (September 8, 1974), 27.

41. *Monthly Magazine*, IV (September 1797), 232–233.

42. *Poetical Works of Robert Southey* (London: Longman, Brown, Green, and Longmans, 1845).

43. "Margaret Fuller and Mary Wollstonecraft," *Essays of George Eliot* (New York: Columbia University Press, 1963).

44. *William Godwin: His Friends and Contemporaries* (1876); *Letters to Imlay* (1879).

45. *Mary Wollstonecraft: A Study in Economics and Romance* (London: Martin Secker, 1911).

46. The view is held most notably by Claire Tomalin in *The Life and Death of Mary Wollstonecraft* (London: Weidenfeld and Nicolson, 1974).

Part I

Courtesy Books

Thoughts on the Education of Daughters

Original Stories from Real Life

"Letters on the Management of Infants"

During the eighteenth century courtesy books*—educational manuals and moral tales—became increasingly popular in England as the desire for improvement spread through the middle class. In the early part of the century most of these were male productions, but toward the end women wrote an increasingly large proportion and frequently they devoted their instructions to their own sex. Authors such as Catherine Macaulay, Maria Edgeworth, and Hannah More all wrote for and about children; although they differed widely in philosophies, they and the many other educating women of their time united in a strong desire to improve the moral and occasionally intellectual tone of young girls. They were alike too in viewing education as a rigorous process and in requiring for children a strong female figure of authority.

Wollstonecraft was first and last a writer on education. Her earliest book, written and published in 1786, was *Thoughts on the Education of Daughters* and at her death in 1797 she left unfinished "Letters on the Management of Infants." Her major work, *A Vindication of the Rights of Woman*, is in large part devoted to education and its neglect, while much of her reviewing for the *Analytical Review* treats pedagogical treatises and children's books.

Wollstonecraft's deep concern for education came in part from her rationalist philosophy which regarded character as determined by environment and upbringing; the vices of humanity and the resulting evils could therefore be prevented by proper treatment of children. The concern is also in part due to her own experience; as a young adult she was a schoolteacher and a governess, while in her last years she had the care of her daughter Fanny, whose upbringing interested her intensely.

The development in Wollstonecraft's thinking through the decade of her literary works is recorded in her pedagogical writings. The early books, *Thoughts on the Education of Daughters* and *Original Stories*, show her mingling of rationalism and piety, her understanding of social as well as physical misery, and her firm belief in its divine purpose. By the end of her life—as "Letters on the Management of Infants" suggests —she felt misery should be avoided rather than suffered. Other marks of development are equally striking. In her early books Wollstonecraft is dismissive of certain classes, even hostile, especially to servants, whom

* The term is discussed by Ellen Moers in *Literary Women: The Great Writers* (New York: Doubleday and Company, 1976).

she regarded as inherently immoral or ineducable. Later she came to
realize that the classes were interdependent in morality and that there
existed potential for good even in the lowest.

The development should not, however, be overstressed. Throughout her writing life Wollstonecraft stuck fast to certain opinions: from
beginning to end she despised affectation and all assumption of power
—from kings over subjects to boys over insects—and she always valued
kindness, self-respect, and intellectual independence, the best fruits of
education.

Thoughts on the Education of Daughters

This book of 160 pages was written in six weeks during 1786. It aimed to show the sad results of the faulty education usually afforded to females and to outline a more rational and suitable one. Much of the argument is based on the theories of John Locke who, nearly a century before, had started the trend toward dealing with children as individuals and adapting instruction to fit their capacities. Some of the illustration—notably that concerning the horrors of dependent females—clearly derives from Wollstonecraft's own experience as a companion and teacher.

PREFACE

IN THE FOLLOWING pages I have endeavoured to point out some important things with respect to female education. It is true, many treatises have been already written; yet it occurred to me, that much still remained to be said. I shall not swell these sheets by writing apologies for my attempt. I am afraid, indeed, the reflections will, by some, be thought too grave; but I could not make them less so without writing affectedly; yet, though they may be insipid to the gay, others may not think them so; and if they should prove useful to one fellow-creature, and beguile any hours, which sorrow has made heavy, I shall think I have not been employed in vain.

from
THE NURSERY

As I conceive it to be the duty of every rational creature to attend to its offspring, I am sorry to observe, that reason and duty together have not so powerful an influence over human conduct, as instinct has in the brute creation. Indolence, and a thoughtless disregard of every thing, except the present indulgence, make many mothers, who may have momentary starts of tenderness, neglect their children. They follow a pleasing impulse, and never reflect that reason should cultivate and govern those instincts which are implanted in us to render the path of duty pleasant—for if they are not governed they will run wild; and strengthen the passions which are ever endeavouring to obtain dominion—I mean vanity and self-love.

The first thing to be attended to, is laying the foundation of a good constitution. The mother (if there are not very weighty reasons to prevent her) ought to suckle her children.* Her milk is their proper nutriment, and for some time is quite sufficient. Were a regular mode of suckling adopted, it would be far from being a laborious task. Children, who are left to the care of ignorant nurses, have their stomachs overloaded with improper food, which turns acid, and renders them very uncomfortable. We should be particularly careful to guard them in their infant state from bodily pain; as their minds can then afford them no amusement to alleviate it. . . .

The suckling of a child also excites the warmest glow of tenderness—Its dependant, helpless state produces an affection, which may properly be termed maternal. I have even felt it, when I have seen a mother perform that office; and am of opinion, that maternal tenderness arises quite as much from habit as instinct. It is possible, I am convinced, to acquire the affection of a parent for an adopted child; it is necessary, therefore, for a mother to perform the office of one, in order to produce in herself a rational affection for her offspring.

from
MORAL DISCIPLINE

The marriage state is too often a state of discord; it does not always happen that both parents are rational, and the weakest have it in their power to do most mischief.

How then are the tender minds of children to be cultivated?— Mamma is only anxious that they should love her best, and perhaps takes pains to sow those seeds, which have produced such luxuriant weeds in her own mind. Or, what still more frequently occurs, the children are at first made play-things of, and when their tempers have been spoiled by indiscreet indulgence, they become troublesome, and are

* It was the custom in the eighteenth century for middle and upper class women to employ wet nurses for their babies.—Editor.

mostly left with servants; the first notions they imbibe, therefore, are mean and vulgar. They are taught cunning, the wisdom of that class of people, and a love of truth, the foundation of virtue, is soon obliterated from their minds. It is, in my opinion, a well-proved fact, that principles of truth are innate. Without reasoning we assent to many truths; we feel their force, and artful sophistry can only blunt those feelings which nature has implanted in us as instinctive guards to virtue. Dissimulation and cunning will soon drive all other good qualities before them, and deprive the mind of that beautiful simplicity, which can never be too much cherished. . . .

The riot . . . of the kitchen, or any other place where children are left only with servants, makes the decent restraint of the parlour irksome. A girl, who has vivacity, soon grows a romp; and if there are male servants, they go out a walking with them, and will frequently take little freedoms with Miss, the bearing with which gives a forwardness to her air, and makes her pert. The becoming modesty, which being accustomed to converse with superiors, will give a girl, is entirely done away. I must own, I am quite charmed when I see a sweet young creature, shrinking as it were from observation, and listening rather than talking. It is possible a girl may have this manner without having a very good understanding. If it should be so, this diffidence prevents her from being troublesome. . . .

The first things . . . that children ought to be encouraged to observe, are a strict adherence to truth; a proper submission to superiors; and condescension to inferiors. These are the main articles; but there are many others, which compared to them are trivial, and yet are of importance. It is not pleasing to see a child full of bows and grimaces; yet they need not be suffered to be rude. They should be employed, and such fables and tales may be culled out for them as would excite their curiosity. A taste for the beauties of nature should be very early cultivated: many things, with respect to the vegetable and animal world, may be explained in an amusing way; and this is an innocent source of pleasure within every one's reach.

Above all, try to teach them to combine their ideas. It is of more use than can be conceived, for a child to learn to compare things that are similar in some respects, and different in others. I wish them to be taught to think—thinking, indeed, is a severe exercise, and exercise of either mind or body will not at first be entered on, but with a view to pleasure. Not that I would have them make long reflections; for when they do not arise from experience, they are mostly absurd.

from
ARTIFICIAL MANNERS

The emotions of the mind often appear conspicuous in the countenance and manner. These emotions, when they arise from sensibility and virtue, are inexpressibly pleasing. But it is easier to copy the cast of countenance, than to cultivate the virtues which animate and improve it.

How many people are like whitened sepulchres, and careful only about appearances! yet if we are too anxious to gain the approbation of the world, we must often forfeit our own.

How bewitching is that humble softness of manners which humility gives birth to, and how faint are the imitations of affectation! That gentleness of behaviour, which makes us courteous to all, and that benevolence, which makes us loth to offend any, and studious to please every creature, is sometimes copied by the polite; but how aukward is the copy! The warmest professions of regard are prostituted on all occasions. No distinctions are made, and the esteem which is only due to merit, appears to be lavished on all—Nay, affection is affected; at least, the language is borrowed, when there is no glow of it in the heart. Civility is due to all, but regard or admiration should never be expressed when it is not felt.

As humility gives the most pleasing cast to the countenance, so from sincerity arises that artlessness of manners which is so engaging. She who suffers herself to be seen as she really is, can never be thought affected. She is not solicitous to act a part; her endeavour is not to hide; but correct her failings, and her face has of course that beauty, which an attention to the mind only gives. I never knew a person really ugly, who was not foolish or vicious; and I have seen the most beautiful features deformed by passion and vice. It is true, regular features strike at first; but it is a well ordered mind which occasions those turns of expression in the countenance, which make a lasting impression.

Feeling is ridiculous when affected, and even when felt, ought not to be displayed. It will appear if genuine, but when pushed forward to notice, it is obvious vanity has rivalled sorrow, and that the prettiness of the thing is thought of. Let the manners arise from the mind, and let there be no disguise for the genuine emotions of the heart.

Things merely ornamental are soon disregarded, and disregard can scarcely be borne when there is no internal support.

In "An Establishment for Young Ladies" Edward F. Burney carica-
tures the education in fashion and female graces which Wollstonecraft
was attacking.

from
DRESS

In the article of dress may be included the whole tribe of beauty-washes, cosmetics, Olympian dew, oriental herbs, liquid bloom, and the paint which enlivened Ninon's face, and bid defiance to time.* These numerous and essential articles are advertised in so ridiculous a style, that the rapid sale of them is a very severe reflection on the understanding of those females who encourage it. The dew and herbs, I imagine, are very harmless, but I do not know whether the same may be said of the paint. White† is certainly very prejudicial to the health, and never can be made to resemble nature. The red,‡ too, takes off from the expression of the countenance, and the beautiful glow which modesty, affection, or any other emotion of the mind, gives, can never be seen. It is not "a mind-illumined face." "The body does not charm, because the mind is seen," but just the contrary; and if caught by it a man marries a woman thus disguised, he may chance not to be satisfied with her real person. A made-up face may strike visitors, but will certainly disgust domestic friends. And one obvious inference is drawn, truth is not expected to govern the inhabitant of so artificial a form. The false life with which rouge animates the eyes, is not of the most delicate kind; nor does a woman's dressing herself in a way to attract languishing glances, give us the most advantageous opinion of the purity of her mind.

UNFORTUNATE SITUATION OF FEMALES, FASHIONABLY EDUCATED, AND LEFT WITHOUT A FORTUNE

I have hitherto only spoken of those females, who will have a provision made for them by their parents. But many who have been well, or at least fashionably educated, are left without a fortune, and if they

---

* Beauty washes were intended to improve the complexion; they were made from a variety of ingredients ranging from bean water to minced pigeon. Olympian dew was probably a cleansing agent, while liquid bloom was a vegetable extract designed to give an instant and lasting rosy hue to the cheeks. Ninon may be Ninon de Lenclos (1620–1705), a woman famous in youth and old age for her salon and liaisons.—Editor.

† Lead and bismuth were used to give whiteness and polish to the face; they were absorbed by the skin and eventually poisoned the system.—Editor.

‡ Red paint was a preparation of cochineal in nitrous acid or, more cheaply, of vermilion, a product of mercury.—Editor.

are not entirely devoid of delicacy, they must frequently remain single.

Few are the modes of earning a subsistence, and those very humiliating. Perhaps to be an humble companion to some rich old cousin, or what is still worse, to live with strangers, who are so intolerably tyrannical, that none of their own relations can bear to live with them, though they should even expect a fortune in reversion. It is impossible to enumerate the many hours of anguish such a person must spend. Above the servants, yet considered by them as a spy, and ever reminded of her inferiority when in conversation with the superiors. If she cannot condescend to mean flattery, she has not a chance of being a favorite; and should any of the visitors take notice of her, and she for a moment forget her subordinate state, she is sure to be reminded of it.

Painfully sensible of unkindness, she is alive to every thing, and many sarcasms reach her, which were perhaps directed another way. She is alone, shut out from equality and confidence, and the concealed anxiety impairs her constitution; for she must wear a cheerful face, or be dismissed. The being dependant on the caprice of a fellow-creature, though certainly very necessary in this state of discipline, is yet a very bitter corrective, which we would fain shrink from.

A teacher at a school is only a kind of upper servant, who has more work than the menial ones.

A governess to young ladies is equally disagreeable. It is ten to one if they meet with a reasonable mother; and if she is not so, she will be continually finding fault to prove she is not ignorant, and be displeased if her pupils do not improve, but angry if the proper methods are taken to make them do so. The children treat them with disrespect, and often with insolence. In the mean time life glides away, and the spirits with it; "and when youth and genial years are flown," they have nothing to subsist on; or, perhaps, on some extraordinary occasion, some small allowance may be made for them, which is thought a great charity.

The few trades which are left, are now gradually falling into the hands of the men, and certainly they are not very respectable.

It is hard for a person who has a relish for polished society, to herd with the vulgar, or to condescend to mix with her former equals when she is considered in a different light. What unwelcome heart-breaking knowledge is then poured in on her! I mean a view of the selfishness and depravity of the world; for every other acquirement is a source of pleasure, though they may occasion temporary inconveniences. How cutting is the contempt she meets with!—A young mind looks round for love and friendship; but love and friendship fly from poverty: expect them not if you are poor! The mind must then sink into meanness, and accommodate itself to its new state, or dare to be unhappy. Yet I think no reflecting person would give up the experience and improvement they have gained, to have avoided the misfortunes; on the contrary, they are thankfully ranked amongst the choicest blessings of life, when we are not under their immediate pressure.

How earnestly does a mind full of sensibility look for disinterested friendship, and long to meet with good unalloyed. When fortune smiles they hug the dear delusion; but dream not that it is one. The painted cloud disappears suddenly, the scene is changed, and what an aching void is left in the heart! a void which only religion can fill up—and how few seek this internal comfort!

A woman, who has beauty without sentiment, is in great danger of being seduced; and if she has any, cannot guard herself from painful mortifications. It is very disagreeable to keep up a continual reserve with men she has been formerly familiar with; yet if she places confidence, it is ten to one but she is deceived. Few men seriously think of marrying an inferior; and if they have honor enough not to take advantage of the artless tenderness of a woman who loves, and thinks not of the difference of rank, they do not undeceive her until she has anticipated happiness, which, contrasted with her dependant situation, appears delightful. The disappointment is severe; and the heart receives a wound which does not easily admit of a compleat cure, as the good that is missed is not valued according to its real worth: for fancy drew the picture, and grief delights to create food to feed on.

If what I have written should be read by parents, who are now going on in thoughtless extravagance, and anxious only that their daughters may be *genteelly educated*, let them consider to what sorrows they expose them; for I have not over-coloured the picture.

Though I warn parents to guard against leaving their daughters to encounter so much misery; yet if a young woman falls into it, she ought not to be discontented. Good must ultimately arise from every thing, to those who look beyond this infancy of their being; and here the comfort of a good conscience is our only stable support. The main business of our lives is to learn to be virtuous; and He who is training us up for immortal bliss, knows best what trials will contribute to make us so; and our resignation and improvement will render us respectable to ourselves, and to that Being, whose approbation is of more value than life itself. It is true, tribulation produces anguish, and we would fain avoid the bitter cup, though convinced its effects would be the most salutary. The Almighty is then the kind parent, who chastens and educates, and indulges us not when it would tend to our hurt. He is compassion itself, and never wounds but to heal, when the ends of correction are answered.

from
LOVE

There are quite as many male coquets as female, and they are far more pernicious pests to society, as their sphere of action is larger, and they are less exposed to the censure of the world. A smothered sigh, downcast look, and the many other little arts which are played off, may give extreme pain to a sincere, artless woman, though she cannot resent, or complain of, the injury. This kind of trifling, I think, much more inexcusable than inconstancy. . . .

People of sense and reflection are most apt to have violent and constant passions, and to be preyed on by them. Neither can they, for the sake of present pleasure, bear to act in such a manner, as that the retrospect should fill them with confusion and regret. Perhaps a delicate mind is not susceptible of a greater degree of misery, putting guilt out of the question, than what must arise from the consciousness of loving a person whom their reason does not approve. This, I am persuaded, has often been the case; and the passion must either be rooted out, or the continual allowances and excuses that are made will hurt the mind, and lessen the respect for virtue. Love, unsupported by esteem, must soon expire, or lead to depravity; as, on the contrary, when a worthy person is the object, it is the greatest incentive to improvement, and has the best effect on the manners and temper. We should always try to fix in our minds the rational grounds we have for loving a person, that we may be able to recollect them when we feel disgust or resentment; we should then habitually practise forbearance, and the many petty disputes which interrupt domestic peace would be avoided. A woman cannot reasonably be unhappy, if she is attached to a man of sense and goodness, though he may not be all she could wish.

from
MATRIMONY

Early marriages are, in my opinion, a stop to improvement. If we were born only "to draw nutrition, propagate and rot," the sooner the end of creation was answered the better; but as women are here allowed to have souls, the soul ought to be attended to. In youth a woman endeavours to please the other sex, in order, generally speaking, to get married, and this endeavour calls forth all her powers. If she has had a tolerable education, the foundation only is laid, for the mind does not soon arrive at maturity, and should not be engrossed by domestic cares before any habits are fixed. The passions also have too much influence over the judgment to suffer it to direct her in this most important affair; and many women, I am persuaded, marry a man before they are twenty, whom they would have rejected some years after. Very frequently, when the education has been neglected, the mind improves itself, if it has leisure for reflection, and experience to reflect on; but how can this happen when they are forced to act before they have had time to think, or find that they are unhappily married? Nay, should they be so fortunate as to get a good husband, they will not set a proper value on him; he will be found much inferior to the lovers described in novels, and their want of knowledge makes them frequently disgusted with the man, when the fault is in human nature. . . .

. . . Women are often before marriage prudish, and afterwards they think they may innocently give way to fondness, and overwhelm the poor man with it. They think they have a legal right to his affections, and grow remiss in their endeavours to please. There are a thousand nameless decencies which good sense gives rise to, and artless proofs of regard which flow from the heart, and will reach it, if it is not depraved. It has ever occurred to me, that it* was sufficient for a woman to receive caresses, and not bestow them. She ought to distinguish between fondness and tenderness. The latter is the sweetest cordial of life; but, like all other cordials, should be reserved for particular occasions; to exhilarate the spirits, when depressed by sickness, or lost in sorrow. Sensibility will best instruct. Some delicacies can never be pointed out or described, though they sink deep into the heart, and render the hours of distress supportable. . . .

Women are said to be the weaker vessel, and many are the miseries which this weakness brings on them. Men have in some respects very much the advantage. If they have a tolerable understanding, it has a chance to be cultivated. They are forced to see human nature as it is, and are not left to dwell on the pictures of their own imaginations. Nothing, I am sure, calls forth the faculties so much as the being obliged to struggle with the world; and this is not a woman's province in a married state. Her sphere of action is not large, and if she is not taught to look into her own heart, how trivial are her occupations and pursuits! What little arts engross and narrow her mind! "Cunning fills

* "is" in original.—Editor.

up the mighty void of sense;" and cares, which do not improve the heart or understanding, take up her attention. Of course, she falls a prey to childish anger, and silly capricious humors, which render her rather insignificant than vicious.

In a comfortable situation, a cultivated mind is necessary to render a woman contented; and in a miserable one, it is her only consolation. A sensible, delicate woman, who by some strange accident, or mistake, is joined to a fool or a brute, must be wretched beyond all names of wretchedness, if her views are confined to the present scene. Of what importance, then, is intellectual improvement, when our comfort here, and happiness hereafter, depends upon it.

from
THE BENEFITS WHICH ARISE FROM DISAPPOINTMENTS

Most women, and men too, have no character at all.* Just opinions and virtuous passions appear by starts, and while we are giving way to the love and admiration which those qualities raise, they are quite different creatures. It is reflection which forms habits, and fixes principles indelibly on the heart; without it, the mind is like a wreck drifted about by every squall. The passion that we think most of will soon rival all the rest; it is then in our power, this way, to strengthen our good dispositions, and in some measure to establish a character, which will not depend on every accidental impulse. To be convinced of truths, and yet not to feel or act up to them, is a common thing. Present pleasure drives all before it, and adversity is mercifully sent to force us to think.

In the school of adversity we learn knowledge as well as virtue; yet we lament our hard fate, dwell on our disappointments, and never consider that our own wayward minds, and inconsistent hearts, require these needful correctives. Medicines are not sent to persons in health. . . .

I have very often heard it made a subject of ridicule, that when a person is disappointed in this world, they turn to the next. Nothing can be more natural than the transition; and it seems to me the scheme of Providence, that our finding things unsatisfactory here, should force us to think of the better country to which we are going.

---

* Pope wrote "Most women have no characters at all," *Moral Essays* II.—Editor.

from
BENEVOLENCE

Women too often confine their love and charity to their own families. They fix not in their minds the precedency of moral obligations, or make their feelings give way to duty. Goodwill to all the human race should dwell in our bosoms, nor should love to individuals induce us to violate this first of duties, or make us sacrifice the interest of any fellow-creature, to promote that of another, whom we happen to be more partial to. A parent, under distressed circumstances, should be supported, even though it should prevent our saving a fortune for a child; nay more, should they be both in distress at the same time, the prior obligation should be first discharged.

· *from*
THE THEATRE

Until very lately I never had the courage even to look at a person dying on the stage. The hour of death is not the time for the display of passions; nor do I think it natural it should: the mind is then dreadfully disturbed, and the trifling sorrows of this world not thought of. The deaths on the stage, in spite of the boasted sensibility of the age, seem to have much the same effect on a polite audience, as the execution of malefactors has on the mob that follow them to Tyburn*. . . .

Young persons, who are happily situated, do well to enter into fictitious distress; and if they have any judicious person to direct their judgment, it may be improved while their hearts are melted. Yet I would not have them confine their compassion to the distresses occasioned by love; and perhaps their feelings might more profitably be roused, if they were to see sometimes the complicated misery of sickness and poverty, and weep for the beggar instead of the king.

from
PUBLIC PLACES

There seems at present such a rage for pleasure, that when adversity does not call home the thoughts, the whole day is mostly spent in

* The principal place of public execution in London until the late eighteenth century.—Editor.

preparations and plans, or in actual dissipation. Solitude appears insupportable, and domestic comfort stupid. And though the amusements may not always be relished, the mind is so enervated it cannot exert itself to find out any other substitute. An immoderate fondness for dress is acquired, and many fashionable females spend half the night in going from one place to another to display their finery, repeat commonplace compliments, and raise envy in their acquaintance whom they endeavour to outshine. Women, who are engaged in those scenes, must spend more time in dress than they ought to do, and it will occupy their thoughts when they should be better employed.

In the fine Lady how few traits do we observe of those affections which dignify human nature! If she has any maternal tenderness, it is of a childish kind. We cannot be too careful not to verge on this character; though she lives many years she is still a child in understanding, and of so little use to society, that her death would scarcely be observed.

Original Stories from Real Life

Wollstonecraft's second educational book was published in 1788. It follows the advice in *Thoughts on the Education of Daughters* that children be instructed through amusing tales. Based on principles of education similar to those put forward in her first book, *Original Stories* reflects Wollstonecraft's year as governess to the Kingsborough children, as well as her reading of Rousseau's *Émile* during this time. Both led her to stress the role of experience in education.

Original Stories teaches through a Mrs. Mason, who takes in hand the moral education of two girls, Mary and Caroline. Through a series of melancholy tales and situations, they are led to understand the pleasures of virtue and the miseries of vice.

from the
PREFACE

THESE CONVERSATIONS and tales are accommodated to the present state of society; which obliges the author to attempt to cure those faults by reason, which ought never to have taken root in the infant mind. Good habits, imperceptibly fixed, are far preferable to the precepts of reason; but, as this task requires more judgment than generally falls to the lot of parents, substitutes must be sought for, and medicines given, when regimen would have answered the purpose much better. I believe those who examine their own minds, will readily agree with me, that reason, with difficulty, conquers settled habits, even when it is arrived at some degree of maturity: why then do we suffer children to be bound with fetters, which their half-formed faculties cannot break. . . .

The way to render instruction most useful cannot always be adopted; knowledge should be gradually imparted, and flow more from example than teaching: example directly addresses the senses, the first inlets to the heart; and the improvement of those instruments of the understanding is the object education should have constantly in view, and over which we have most power. But to wish that parents would, themselves, mould the ductile passions, is a chimerical wish, for the present generation have their own passions to combat with, and fastidious pleasures to pursue, neglecting those pointed out by nature: we must therefore pour premature knowledge into the succeeding one; and, teaching virtue, explain the nature of vice. Cruel necessity!

from
THE TREATMENT OF ANIMALS: THEIR DIFFERENT NATURE

What we call virtue, may be thus explained:—we exercise every benevolent affection to enjoy comfort here, and to fit ourselves to be angels hereafter.* And when we have acquired human virtues, we shall have a nobler employment in our Father's kingdom. But between angels and men a much greater resemblance subsists, than between men and the brute creation; because the two former seem capable of improvement.

The birds you saw to-day do not improve—or their improvement only tends to self-preservation; the first nest they make and the last are exactly the same; though in their flights they must see many others more beautiful if not more convenient, and, had they reason, they would probably shew something like individual taste in the form of their dwellings; but this is not the case. You saw the hen tear the down from her breast to make a nest for her eggs; you saw her beat the grain with her bill, and not swallow a bit, till the young were satisfied; and afterwards she covered them with her wings, and seemed perfectly happy, while she watched over her charge; if any one approached, she was ready to defend them, at the hazard of her life: yet, a fortnight hence, you will see the same hen drive the fledged chickens from the corn, and forget the fondness that seemed to be stronger than the first impulse of nature.

Animals have not the affections which arise from reason, nor can they do good, or acquire virtue. Every affection, and impulse, which I have observed in them, are like our inferior emotions, which do not depend entirely on our will, but are involuntary; they seem to have been implanted to preserve the species, and make the individual grateful for

* Mrs. Mason is speaking.—Editor.

actual kindness. If you caress and feed them, they will love you, as children do, without knowing why; but we neither see imagination nor wisdom in them; and, what principally exalts man, friendship and devotion, they seem incapable of forming the least idea of. Friendship is founded on knowledge and virtue, and these are human acquirements; and devotion is a preparation for eternity; because when we pray to God, we offer an affront to him, if we do not strive to imitate the perfections He displays every where for our imitation, that we may grow better and happier.

The children eagerly enquired in what manner they were to behave, to prove that they were superior to animals? The answer was short,—be tenderhearted; and let your superior endowments ward off the evils which they cannot foresee. It is only to animals that children *can* do good, men are their superiors. When I was a child, added their tender friend, I always made it my study and delight, to feed all the dumb family that surrounded our house; and when I could be of use to any one of them I was happy. This employment humanized my heart, while, like wax, it took every impression; and Providence has since made me an instrument of good—I have been useful to my fellow-creatures. I, who never wantonly trod on an insect, or disregarded the plaint of the speechless beast, can now give bread to the hungry, physic to the sick, comfort to the afflicted, and, above all, am preparing you, who are to live for ever, to be fit for the society of angels, and good men made perfect. This world, I told you, was a road to a better—a preparation for it; if we suffer, we grow humbler and wiser: but animals have not this advantage, and man should not prevent their enjoying all the happiness of which they are capable.

A she-cat or dog have such strong parental affection, that if you take away their young, it almost kills them; some have actually died of grief when all have been taken away; though they do not seem to miss the greatest part.

A bitch had once all her litter stolen from her, and drowned in a neighbouring brook: she sought them out, and brought them one by one, laid them at the feet of her cruel master;—and looking wistfully at them for some time, in dumb anguish, turning her eyes on the destroyer, she expired!

I myself knew a man who had hardened his heart to such a degree, that he found pleasure in tormenting every creature whom he had any power over. I saw him let two guinea-pigs roll down sloping tiles, to see if the fall would kill them. And were they killed? cried Caroline. Certainly; and it is well they were, or he would have found some other mode of torment. When he became a father, he not only neglected to educate his children, and set them a good example, but he taught them to be cruel while he tormented them: the consequence was, that they neglected him when he was old and feeble; and he died in a ditch.

You may now go and feed your birds, and tie some of the straggling flowers round the garden sticks. After dinner, if the weather continues fine, we will walk to the wood, and I will shew you the hole in the lime-stone mountain (a mountain whose bowels, as we call them, are lime-stones) in which poor crazy Robin and his dog lived.

THE TREATMENT OF ANIMALS: CRAZY ROBIN

In the afternoon the children bounded over the short grass of the common, and walked under the shadow of the mountain till they came to a craggy part; where a stream broke out, and ran down the declivity, struggling with the huge stones which impeded its progress, and occasioned a noise that did not unpleasantly interrupt the solemn silence of the place. The brook was soon lost in a neighbouring wood, and the children turned their eyes to the broken side of the mountain, over which ivy grew in great profusion. Mrs. Mason pointed out a little cave, and desired them to sit down on some stumps of trees, whilst she related the promised story.

In yonder cave once lived a poor man, who generally went by the name of crazy Robin. In his youth he was very industrious, and married my father's dairy-maid; a girl deserving of such a good husband. For some time they continued to live very comfortably; their daily labour procured their daily bread; but Robin, finding it was likely he should have a large family, borrowed a trifle, to add to the small pittance which they had saved in service, and took a little farm in a neighbouring county. I was then a child.

Ten or twelve years after, I heard that a crazy man, who appeared very harmless, had piled by the side of the brook a great number of stones; he would wade into the river for them, followed by a cur dog, whom he would frequently call his Jacky, and even his Nancy; and then mumble to himself,—thou wilt not leave me—we will dwell with the owls in the ivy.—A number of owls had taken shelter in it. The stones which he waded for he carried to the mouth of the hole, and only just left room enough to creep in. Some of the neighbours at last recollected his face; and I sent to enquire what misfortune had reduced him to such a deplorable state.

The information I received from different persons, I will communicate to you in as few words as I can.

Several of his children died in their infancy; and, two years before he came to his native place, one misfortune had followed another till he had sunk under their accumulated weight. Through various accidents he was long in arrears to his landlord; who, seeing that he was an honest man, who endeavoured to bring up his family, did not distress him; but when his wife was lying-in of her last child, the landlord dying, his heir sent and seized the stock for the rent; and the person from whom he had borrowed some money, exasperated to see all gone, arresting him immediately, he was hurried to gaol, without being able to leave any money for his family. The poor woman could not see them starve, and trying to support her children before she had gained sufficient strength, she caught cold; and through neglect, and her want of proper nourishment, her illness turned to a putrid fever; which two of the children caught from her, and died with her. The two who were left, Jacky and Nancy, went to their father, and took with them a cur dog, that had long shared their frugal meals.

The children begged in the day, and at night slept with their wretched father. Poverty and dirt soon robbed their cheeks of the roses which the country air made bloom with a peculiar freshness; so that they soon caught a jail fever,—and died. The poor father, who was now bereft of all his children, hung over their bed in speechless anguish; not a groan or a tear escaped from him, whilst he stood, two or three hours, in the same attitude, looking at the dead bodies of his little darlings. The dog licked his hands, and strove to attract his attention; but for awhile he seemed not to observe his caresses; when he did, he said, mournfully, thou wilt not leave me—and then he began to laugh. The bodies were removed; and he remained in an unsettled state, often frantic; at length the phrenzy subsided, and he grew melancholy and harmless. He was not then so closely watched; and one day he contrived to make his escape, the dog followed him, and came directly to his native village.

After I had received this account, I determined he should live in the place he had chosen, undisturbed. I sent some conveniences, all of which he rejected, except a mat; on which he sometimes slept—the dog always did. I tried to induce him to eat, but he constantly gave the dog whatever I sent him, and lived on haws and blackberries, and every kind of trash. I used to call frequently on him; and he sometimes followed me to the house I now live in, and in winter he would come of his own accord, and take a crust of bread. He gathered water-cresses out of the pool, and would bring them to me, with nosegays of wild thyme, which he plucked from the sides of the mountain. I mentioned before, that the dog was a cur. It had, indeed, the bad trick of a cur, and would run barking after horses heels. One day, when his master was gathering water-

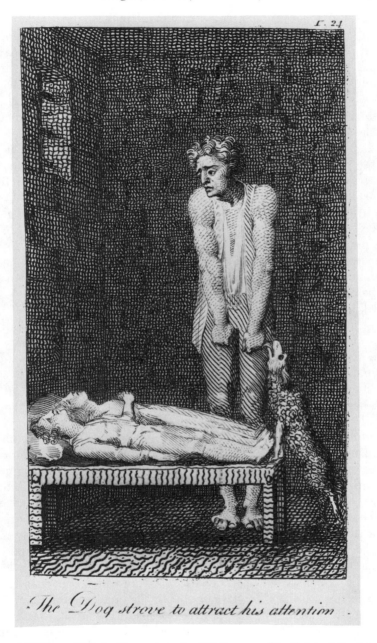

The Dog strove to attract his attention.

One of William Blake's illustrations for Wollstonecraft's *Original Stories.*

cresses, the dog running after a young gentleman's horse, made it start, and almost threw the rider; who grew so angry, that though he knew it was the poor madman's dog, he levelled his gun at his head—shot him, —and instantly rode off. Robin ran to his dog,—he looked at his wounds, and not sensible that he was dead, called to him to follow him; but when he found that he could not, he took him to the pool, and washed off the blood before it began to clot, and then brought him home, and laid him on the mat.

I observed that I had not seen him pacing up the hills as usual, and sent to enquire about him. He was found sitting by the dog, and no entreaties could prevail on him to quit the body, or receive any refreshment. I instantly set off for this place, hoping, as I had always been a favourite, that I should be able to persuade him to eat something. But when I came to him, I found the hand of death was upon him. He was still melancholy; yet there was not such a mixture of wildness in it as formerly. I pressed him to take some food; but, instead of answering me, or turning away, he burst into tears,—a thing I had never seen him do before, and, sobbing, he said, Will any one be kind to me!—you will kill me!—I saw not my wife die—No!—they dragged me from her—but I saw Jacky and Nancy die—and who pitied me?—but my dog! He turned his eyes to the body—I wept with him. He would then have taken some nourishment, but nature was exhausted—and he expired.—

Was that the cave? said Mary. They ran to it. Poor Robin! Did you ever hear of any thing so cruel? Yes, answered Mrs. Mason; and as we walk home I will relate an instance of still greater barbarity.

I told you, that Robin was confined in a jail. In France they have a dreadful one, called the Bastille. The poor wretches who are confined in it live entirely alone; have not the pleasure of seeing men or animals; nor are they allowed books.—They live in comfortless solitude. Some have amused themselves by making figures on the wall; and others have laid straws in rows. One miserable captive found a spider; he nourished it for two or three years; it grew tame, and partook of his lonely meal. The keeper observed it, and mentioned the circumstance to a superiour, who ordered him to crush it. In vain did the man beg to have his spider spared. You find, Mary, that the nasty creature which you despised was a comfort in solitude. The keeper obeyed the cruel command; and the unhappy wretch felt more pain when he heard the crush, than he had ever experienced during his long confinement. He looked round a dreary apartment, and the small portion of light which the grated bars admitted, only served to shew him, that he breathed where nothing else drew breath.

THE BENEFITS ARISING
FROM DEVOTION:
THE HISTORY OF MR. LOFTY

The next morning Mrs. Mason desired the children to get their work, and draw near the table whilst she related the promised history; and in the afternoon, if the weather be fine, they were to visit the village school-mistress.

Her father, the honourable Mr. Lofty, was the youngest son of a noble family; his education had been liberal, though his fortune was small. His relations, however, seemed determined to push him forward in life, before he disobliged them by marrying the daughter of a country clergyman, an accomplished, sensible woman.

Some time after the birth of his daughter Anna, his elder brother, the Earl of Caermarthen, was reconciled to him; but this reconciliation only led him into expences, which his limited fortune could not bear. Mr. Lofty had a high sense of honour, and rather a profuse turn; he was, beside, a very humane man, and gave away much more than he could afford to give, when his compassion was excited. He never did a mean action; but sometimes an ostentatious pride tarnished the lustre of very splendid ones, made them appear to judicious eyes, more like tinsel, than gold. I will account for it. His first impulse arose from sensibility, and the second from an immoderate desire of human applause: for he seemed not to be alive to devotional feelings, or to have that rock to rest on, which will support a frail being, and give true dignity to a character, though all nature combined to crush it.

Mrs. Lofty was not a shining character—but I will read you a part of a letter, which her daughter, the lady we are to visit, wrote to me.

'This being the anniversary of the day on which an ever loved, and much revered parent was released from the bondage of mortality, I ob-serve it with particular seriousness, and with gratitude; for her sorrows were great, her trials severe—but her conduct was blameless: yet the world admired her not; her silent, modest virtues, were not formed to attract the notice of the injudicious crowd, and her understanding was not brilliant enough to excite admiration. But she was regardless of the opinion of the world; she sought her reward in the source from whence her virtue was derived—and she found it.—He, who, for wise and merciful purposes, suffered her to be afflicted, supported her under her trials; thereby calling forth the exercise of those virtues with which He had adorned her gentle soul; and imparting to her a degree of heart-felt comfort, which no earthly blessing could afford.'

This amiable parent died when Anna was near eighteen, and left her to the care of her father, whose high spirit she had imbibed. However, the religious principles which her mother had instilled regulated her notions of honour, and so elevated her character, that her heart was regulated by her understanding.

Her father who had insensibly involved himself in debt, after her mother's death, tried many different schemes of life, all of which, at first wore a promising aspect; but wanting that suppleness of temper, that enables people to rise in the world, his struggles, instead of extricating, sunk him still deeper. Wanting also the support of religion, he became sour, easily irritated, and almost hated a world whose applause he had once eagerly courted. His affairs were at last in such a desperate state, that he was obliged, reluctantly, to accept of an invitation from his brother, who with his wife, a weak fine lady, intended to spend some time on the continent; his daughter was, of course, to be of the party.

The restraint of obligations did not suit his temper, and feeling himself dependent, he imagined every one meant to insult him.

Some sarcasms were thrown out one day by a gentleman, in a large company; they were not personal, yet he took fire. His sore mind was easily hurt, he resented them; and heated by wine, they both said more than their cool reason would have suggested. Mr. Lofty imagined his honour was wounded, and the next morning sent him a challenge— They met—and he killed his antagonist, who, dying, pardoned him, and declared that the sentiments which had given him so much offence, fell from him by accident, and were not levelled at any person.

The dying man lamented, that the thread of a thoughtless life had been so suddenly snapped—the name of his wife and children he could not articulate, when something like a prayer for them escaped his livid lips, and shook his exhausted frame—The blood flowed in a copious stream—vainly did Mr. Lofty endeavour to staunch it—the heart lost its vital nourishment—and the soul escaped as he pressed the hand of his destroyer.—Who, when he found him breathless, ran home, and rushed in a hurry into his own chamber. The dead man's image haunted his imagination—he started—imagined that he was at his elbow—and shook the hand that had received the dying grasp—yet still it was pressed, and the pressure entered into his very soul—On the table lay two pistols, he caught up one,—and shot himself.—The report alarmed the family—the servants and his daughter, for his brother was not at home, broke open the door,—and she saw the dreadful sight! As there was still some appearance of life, a trembling ray—she supported the body, and sent for assistance. But he soon died in her arms without speaking, before the servant returned with a surgeon.

Horror seized her, another pistol lay charged on the table, she caught it up, but religion held her hand—she knelt down by a dead father, and prayed to a superior one. Her mind grew calmer—yet still she passionately wished she had but heard him speak, or that she had conveyed comfort to his departing spirit—where, where would it find comfort? again she was obliged to have recourse to prayer.

After the death of her father, her aunt treated her as if she were a mere dependent on her bounty; and expected her to be an humble companion in every sense of the word. The visitors took the tone from her ladyship, and numberless were the mortifications she had to bear.

The entrance of a person about business interrupted the narration; but Mrs. Mason promised to resume it after dinner.

THE BENEFITS ARISING FROM DEVOTION: THE HISTORY OF THE VILLAGE SCHOOL-MISTRESS

As soon as the cloth was removed, Mrs. Mason concluded the narration; and the girls forgot their fruit whilst they were listening to the sequel.

Anna endured this treatment some years, and had an opportunity of acquiring a knowledge of the world and her own heart. She visited her mother's father, and would have remained with him; but she determined not to lessen the small pittance which he had anxiously saved out of a scanty income for two other grand-children. She thought continually of her situation, and found, on examining her understanding, that the fashionable circle in which she moved, could not at any rate have afforded her much satisfaction, or even amusement; though the neglect and contempt that she met with rendered her very uncomfortable. She had her father's spirit of independence, and determined to shake off the galling yoke which she had long struggled with, and try to earn her own subsistence. Her acquaintance expostulated with her, and represented the miseries of poverty, and the mortifications and difficulties that she would have to encounter. Let it be so, she replied, it is much preferable to swelling the train of the proud or vicious great, and despising myself for bearing their impertinence, for eating their bitter bread;—better, indeed, is a dinner of herbs with contentment. My wants are few. When I am my own mistress, the crust I earn will be sweet, and the water that moistens it will not be mingled with tears of sorrow or indignation.

To shorten my story; she came to me, after she had attempted several plans, and requested my advice. She would not accept of any considerable favour, and declared that the greatest would be, to put her in a

way of supporting herself, without forfeiting her highly valued independence. I knew not what to advise; but whilst I was debating the matter with myself, I happened to mention, that we were in want of a
school-mistress. She eagerly adopted the plan, and persevering in it these
last ten years, I find her a most valuable acquisition to our society.

She was formed to shine in the most brilliant circle—yet she relin-
quished it, and patiently labours to improve the children consigned to
her management, and tranquillize her own mind. She succeeds in both.

She lives indeed alone, and has all day only the society of children;
yet she enjoys many true pleasures; dependence on God is her support,
and devotion her comfort.. Her lively affections are therefore changed
into a love of virtue and truth: and these exalted speculations have given
an uncommon dignity to her manners; for she seems above the world,
and its trifling commotions. At her meals, gratitude to Heaven supplies
the place of society. She has a tender, social heart, and, as she cannot
sweeten her solitary draught, by expressing her good wishes to her
fellow-creatures, an ejaculation to Heaven for the welfare of her friends
is the substitute. This circumstance I heard her mention to her grandfather, who sometimes visits her.

I will now make some alteration in my dress, for when I visit those
who have been reduced from their original place in society by misfortunes, I always attend a little to ceremony; lest too much familiarity
should appear like disrespect.

THE BENEFIT OF BODILY PAIN: FORTITUDE THE BASIS OF VIRTUE

The children had been playing in the garden for some time, whilst
Mrs. Mason was reading alone. But she was suddenly alarmed by the
cries of Caroline, who ran into the room in great distress. Mary quickly
followed, and explaining the matter said, that her sister had accidently
disturbed some wasps, who were terrified, and of course stung her.
Remedies were applied to assuage the pain; yet all the time she uttered
the loudest and most silly complaints, regardless of the uneasiness she
gave those who were exerting themselves to relieve her.

In a short time the smart abated, and then her friend thus addressed
her, with more than usual gravity. I am sorry to see a girl of your age
weep on account of bodily pain; it is a proof of a weak mind—a proof
that you cannot employ yourself about things of consequence. How
often must I tell you that the Most High is educating us for eternity?

'The term virtue, comes from a word signifying strength. Fortitude
of mind is, therefore, the basis of every virtue, and virtue belongs to a

being, that is weak in its nature, and strong only in will and resolution.'

Children early feel bodily pain, to habituate them to bear the conflicts of the soul, when they become reasonable creatures. This, I say, is the first trial, and I like to see that proper pride which strives to conceal its sufferings. Those who, when young, weep if the least trifle annoys them, will never, I fear, have sufficient strength of mind, to encounter all the miseries that can afflict the body, rather than act meanly to avoid them. Indeed, this seems to be the essential difference between a great and a little mind: the former knows how to endure—whilst the latter suffers an immortal soul to be depressed, lost in its abode; suffers the inconveniences which attack the one to overwhelm the other. The soul would always support the body, if its superiority was felt, and invigorated by exercise. The Almighty, who never afflicts but to produce some good end, first sends diseases to children to teach them patience and fortitude; and when by degrees they have learned to bear them, they have acquired some virtue.

In the same manner, cold or hunger, when accidentally encountered, are not evils; they make *us feel what wretches feel,* and teach us to be tenderhearted. Many of your fellow-creatures daily bear what you cannot for a moment endure without complaint. Besides, another advantage arises from it, after you have felt hunger, you will not be very anxious to choose the particular kind of food that is to satisfy it. You will then be freed from a frivolous care.

When it is necessary to take a nauseous draught, swallow it at once, and do not make others sick whilst you are hesitating, though you know that you ought to take it. If a tooth is to be drawn, or any other disagreeable operation to be performed, determine resolutely that it shall be done immediately; and debate not, when you clearly see the step that you ought to take. If I see a child act in this way, I am ready to embrace it, my soul yearns for it—I perceive the dawning of a character that will be useful to society, as it prepares its soul for a nobler field of action.

Believe me, it is the patient endurance of pain, that will enable you to resist your passions; after you have borne bodily pain, you will have firmness enough to sustain the still more excruciating agonies of the mind. You will not, to banish momentary cares, plunge into dissipation, nor to escape a present inconvenience, forget that you should hold fast virtue as the only substantial good.

I should not value the affection of a person who would not bear pain and hunger to serve me; nor is that benevolence warm, which shrinks from encountering difficulties, when it is necessary, in order to be useful to any fellow-creature.

There is a just pride, a noble ambition in some minds, that I greatly admire. I have seen a little of it in Mary! for whilst she pities others, she imagines that she could bear their inconveniences herself; and she seems to feel more uneasiness, when she observes the sufferings of others, than I could ever trace on her countenance under the immediate pressure of pain.

Remember you are to bear patiently the infirmities of the weakest of your fellow-creatures; but to yourselves you are not to be equally indulgent.

JOURNEY TO LONDON

The girls were visibly improved; an air of intelligence began to animate Caroline's fine features; and benevolence gave her eyes the humid sparkle which is so beautiful and engaging. The interest that we take in the fate of others, attaches them to ourselves;—thus Caroline's goodness inspired more affection than her beauty.

Mary's judgment grew every day clearer; or, more properly speaking, she acquired experience; and her lively feelings fixed the conclusions of reason in her mind. Whilst Mrs. Mason was rejoicing in their apparent improvement, she received a letter from their father, requesting her to allow his daughters to spend the winter in town, as he wished to procure them the best masters, an advantage that the country did not afford. With reluctance she consented, determining to remain with them a short time; and preparations were quickly made for the journey.

The wished for morning arrived, and they set off in a tumult of spirits; sorry to leave the country, yet delighted with the prospect of visiting the metropolis. This hope soon dried the tears which had bedewed their cheeks; for the parting with Mrs. Mason was not anticipated. The autumnal views were new to them; they saw the hedges exhibit various colours, and the trees stripped of their leaves; but they were not disposed to moralize.

For some time after their arrival, every thing they saw excited wonder and admiration; and not till they were a little familiarized with the new objects, did they ask reasonable questions.

Several presents recruited their purses; and they requested Mrs. Mason to allow them to buy some trifles they were in want of. The request was modest and she complied.

CHARITY:
THE DISTRESSED STATIONER

As they walked in search of a shop, they both determined to purchase pocket-books; but their friend desired them not to spend all their money at once, as they would meet many objects of charity in the numerous streets of the metropolis. I do not wish you, she continued, to relieve every beggar that you casually meet; yet should any one attract your attention, obey the impulse of your heart, which will lead you to pay them for exercising your compassion, and do not suffer the whispers of selfishness, that they may be imposters, to deter you. However, I would have you give but a trifle when you are not certain the distress is real, and reckon it given for pleasure. I for my part would rather be deceived five hundred times, than doubt once without reason.

They stopped at a small shop, Mrs. Mason always sought out such; for, said she, I may help those who perhaps want assistance; bargains I never seek, for I wish every one to receive the just value for their goods.

In the shop which they chanced to enter, they did not find the kind of pocket-book that they had previously fixed on, and therefore wished precipitately to leave it; but were detained by their more considerate friend. While they had been turning over the trinkets, the countenance of the woman, who served them, caught her eye, and she observed her eager manner of recommending the books. You have given much unnecessary trouble, said she, to the mistress of the shop; the books are better, and more expensive than you intended to purchase, but I will make up the deficiency. A beam of pleasure enlivened the woman's swollen eyes; and Mrs. Mason, in the mild accents of compassion, said, if it is not an impertinent question, will you tell me from what cause your visible distress arises? perhaps I may have it in my power to relieve you. —The woman burst into tears.—Indeed, Madam, you have already relieved me; for the money you have laid out will enable me to procure some food for my poor little grandchildren, and to send a meal to their poor father, who is now confined for debt, though a more honest man never breathed. Ah! Madam, I little thought I should come to this— Yesterday his wife died, poor soul! I really believe things going so cross broke her heart. He has been in jail these five months; I could not manage the shop, or buy what was proper to keep up the credit of it, so business has been continually falling off; yet, if his debts were paid, he would now be here, and we should have money in our pockets. And what renders it more provoking, the people who owe us most are very rich. It is true, they live in such a very high style, and keep such a number of horses and servants, that they are often in want of money, and when they have it, they mostly have some freak in their heads, and do not think of paying poor trades-people. At first we were afraid to ask for payment lest we should lose their custom, and so it proved; when we did venture, forced by necessity, they sent to other shops, without discharging our demand.

And, my dear Madam, this is not all my grief; my son, before his misfortunes, was one of the most sober, industrious young men in London; but now he is not like the same man. He had nothing to do in the jail, and to drive away care he learned to drink; he said it was a comfort to forget himself, and he would add an oath—I never heard him swear till then. I took pains when he was a child to teach him his prayers, and he rewarded me by being a dutiful son. The case is quite altered now—he seems to have lost all natural affection—he heeds not his mother's tears.—Her sobs almost suffocated her, as she strove to go on—He will bring my grey hairs with sorrow to the grave—and yet I pity my poor boy, he is shut up with such a number of profligate wretches, who laugh at what is right. Every farthing I send him he spends in liquor, and used to make his poor wife pawn her clothes to buy him drink—she was happy to die, it was well for her not to live to hear the babe she gave suck to despise her!

A passion of tears relieved the sufferer, and she called her grandchildren; these innocent babes, said she, I shall not be able to keep them, they must go to the workhouse. If the quality did but know what they make us poor industrious people suffer—surely they would be more considerate.

Mrs. Mason gave her something to supply her present wants, and promised to call on her again before she left town.

They walked silently down two or three streets; I hope you have learned to think, my dear girls, said Mrs. Mason, and that your hearts have felt the emotions of compassion; need I make any comments on the situation of the poor woman we have just left. You perceive that those who neglect to pay their debts, do more harm than they imagine; perhaps, indeed, some of these very people do, what is called, a noble action, give away a large sum, and are termed generous; nay, very probably, weep at a tragedy, or when reading an affecting tale. They then boast of their sensibility—when, alas! neglecting the foundation of all virtue, *justice,* they have occasioned exquisite distress;—led a poor wretch into vice; heaped misery on helpless infancy, and drawn tears from the aged widow.

VISIT TO A POOR FAMILY IN LONDON

After the impression which the story, and the sight of the family had made, was a little worn off; Caroline begged leave to buy one toy, and then another, till her money was quite gone. When Mrs. Mason found it was all expended, she looked round for an object in distress; a poor woman soon presented herself, and her meagre countenance gave weight to her tale.—A babe, as meagre, hung at her breast, which did not seem to contain sufficient moisture to wet its parched lips.

On enquiry they found that she lodged in a neighbouring garret. Her husband had been out of employment a long time, and was now sick. The master who had formerly given him work, lost gradually great part of his business; for his best customers were grown so fond of foreign articles, that his goods grew old in the warehouse. Consequently a number of hands were dismissed, who not immediately finding employment elsewhere, were reduced to the most extreme distress. The truth of this account a reputable shopkeeper attested; and he added that many of the unhappy creatures, who die unpitied at the gallows, were first led into vice by accidental idleness.

They ascended the dark stairs, scarcely able to bear the bad smells that flew from every part of a small house, that contained in each room a family, occupied in such an anxious manner to obtain the necessaries of life, that its comforts never engaged their thoughts. The precarious meal was snatched, and the stomach did not turn, though the cloth, on which it was laid, was died in dirt. When to-morrow's bread is uncertain, who thinks of cleanliness? Thus does despair encrease the misery, and consequent disease aggravate the horrors of poverty!

They followed the woman into a low garret, that was never visited by the chearful rays of the sun.—A man, with a sallow complexion, and long beard, sat shivering over a few cinders in the bottom of a broken grate, and two more children were on the ground, half naked, near him, breathing the same noxious air. The gaiety natural to their age, did not animate their eyes, half sunk in their sockets; and, instead of smiles, premature wrinkles had found a place in their lengthened visages. Life was nipped in the bud; shut up just as it began to unfold itself. 'A frost, a killing frost,' had destroyed the parent's hopes; they seemed to come into the world only to crawl half formed,—to suffer, and to die.

Mrs. Mason desired the girls to relieve the family; Caroline hung down her head abashed—wishing the paltry ornaments which she had thoughtlessly bought, in the bottom of the sea. Mary, meanwhile, proud of the new privilege, emptied her purse; and Caroline, in a supplicating tone, entreated Mrs. Mason to allow her to give her neck-handkerchief to the little infant.

Mrs. Mason desired the woman to call on her the next day; and they left the family cheered by their bounty.

Caroline expected the reproof that soon proceeded from the mouth of her true friend. I am glad that this accident has occurred, to prove to you that prodigality and generosity are incompatible. Æconomy and self-denial are necessary in every station, to enable us to be generous, and to act conformably to the rules of justice.

Mary may this night enjoy peaceful slumbers; idle fancies, foolishly indulged, will not float in her brain; she may, before she closes her eyes, thank God, for allowing her to be His instrument of mercy. Will the trifles that you have purchased, afford you such heartfelt delight, Caroline?

Selfish people save to gratify their own caprices and appetites; the benevolent curb both, to give scope to the nobler feelings of the human heart. When we squander money idly, we defraud the poor, and deprive our own souls of their most exalted food. If you wish to be useful, govern your desires, and wait not till distress obtrudes itself—search it out. In the country it is not always attended with such shocking circumstances as at present; but in large cities, many garrets contain families, similar to those we have seen this afternoon. The money spent in indulging the vain wishes of idleness, and a childish fondness for pretty things not regulated by reason, would relieve the misery that my soul shrinks back from contemplating.

MRS. MASON'S FAREWELL ADVICE
TO HER YOUNG FRIENDS

The day before Mrs. Mason was to leave her pupils, she took a hand of each, and pressing them tenderly in her own, tears started into her eyes—I tremble for you, my dear girls, for you must now practise by yourselves some of the virtues which I have been endeavouring to inculcate; and I shall anxiously wait for the summer, to see what progress you have made by yourselves.

We have conversed on several very important subjects; pray do not forget the conclusions I have drawn.

I now, as my last present, give you a book, in which I have written the subjects that we have discussed. Recur frequently to it, for the stories illustrating the instruction it contains, you will not feel in such a great degree the want of my personal advice. Some of the reasoning you may not thoroughly comprehend, but, as your understandings ripen, you will feel its full force.

Avoid anger; exercise compassion; and love truth. Recollect, that from religion your chief comfort must spring, and never neglect the duty of prayer. Learn from experience the comfort that arises from making known your wants and sorrows to the wisest and best of Beings, in whose hands are the issues, not only of this life, but of that which is to come.

Your father will allow you a certain stipend; you have already *felt* the pleasure of doing good; ever recollect that the wild pursuits of fancy must be conquered, to enable you to gratify benevolent wishes, and that you must practise œconomy in trifles to have it in your power to be gen-

Œconomy & Self denial are necessary, in every station, to enable us to be generous.

One of William Blake's illustrations for Wollstonecraft's *Original Stories*.

erous on great occasions. And the good you intend to do, do quickly;—
for know that a trifling duty neglected, is a great fault, and the present
time only is at your command.

You are now candidates for my friendship, and on your advancement in virtue my regard will in future depend. Write often to me, I will
punctually answer your letters; but let me have the genuine sentiments
of your hearts. In expressions of affection and respect, do not deviate
from truth to gain what you wish for, or to turn a period prettily.

Adieu! when you think of your friend, observe her precepts; and let
the recollection of my affection, give additional weight to the truths
which I have endeavoured to instill; and, to reward my care, let me hear
that you love and practice virtue.

"Letters on the Management of Infants"

This fragment, consisting of a table of contents and part of an introductory letter, was first published in *Posthumous Works* in 1798. The series was presumably to have been based on Wollstonecraft's experience with her daughter, Fanny, whose birth had not been attended by the usual trappings of eighteenth-century midwifery and whose childhood illnesses had been successfully and simply treated.

CONTENTS

INTRODUCTORY LETTER

I OUGHT TO apologize for not having written to you on the subject you mentioned; but, to tell you the truth, it grew upon me: and, instead of an answer, I have begun a series of letters on the management of children in their infancy. Replying then to your question, I have the public in my thoughts, and shall endeavour to show what modes appear to me necessary, to render the infancy of children more healthy and happy.

I have long thought, that the cause which renders children as hard to rear as the most fragile plant, is our deviation from simplicity. I know that some able physicians have recommended the method I have pursued, and I mean to point out the good effects I have observed in practice. I am aware that many matrons will exclaim against me, and dwell on the number of children they have brought up, as their mothers did before them, without troubling themselves with new-fangled notions; yet, though, in my uncle Toby's words, they should attempt to silence me, by "wishing I had seen their large" families,* I must suppose, while a third part of the human species, according to the most accurate calculation, die during their infancy, just at the threshold of life, that there is some error in the modes adopted by mothers and nurses, which counteracts their own endeavours. I may be mistaken in some particulars; for general rules, founded on the soundest reason, demand individual modification; but, if I can persuade any of the rising generation to exercise their reason on this head, I am content. My advice will probably be found most useful to mothers in the middle class; and it is from them that the lower imperceptibly gains improvement. Custom, produced by reason in one, may safely be the effect of imitation in the other.

—　　—　　—

[End of fragment]

---

* A reference to Laurence Sterne's *Tristram Shandy*, Book II, where uncle Toby breaks into a discourse on obstetrical improvements by remarking "I wish . . . you had seen what prodigious armies we had in *Flanders*."—Editor.

Part II

Works of Controversy

A Vindication of the Rights of Men
A Vindication of the Rights of Woman
Review of Catherine Macaulay's *Letters on Education*

All Wollstonecraft's work is polemical, but the two books she wrote in 1790 and 1791—*A Vindication of the Rights of Men* and *A Vindication of the Rights of Woman*—add controversy to polemic. With them she entered the lists against two of the most influential thinkers of her day, Edmund Burke and Jean-Jacques Rousseau; in so doing she expressed the revolutionary hopes of a whole generation of men and women.

The Rights of Men has long been overshadowed by its more famous successor, *The Rights of Woman*; yet it is Wollstonecraft's first major work and a powerful document of radical philosophy. Written to refute Burke's *Reflections on the Revolution in France*, it impulsively rejects the status quo and its apologists while arguing rigorously for a society based on principles of freedom and equality.

Wollstonecraft wrote *The Rights of Men* on behalf of men or humanity. Increasingly, however, she came to see that the two were not synonymous and that women were frequently excluded by both British and French when they disputed over the rights of men; *The Rights of Woman* aimed to draw attention to this exclusion and show how essential it was for women to be active members of society if it was to progress. Like her first published book, *Thoughts on the Education of Daughters*, *The Rights of Woman* treats education but it far surpasses that work in its demand for a revolution in female education and manners and in the forceful tone of its demand.

Wollstonecraft reviewed Catherine Macaulay's *Letters on Education* in 1790 just before writing *The Rights of Woman*. In this book she pays tribute to Macaulay and acknowledges her debt to her famous predecessor. A section of the Macaulay review is included to suggest the nature of this debt.

A Vindication of the Rights of Men

Wollstonecraft's answer to Edmund Burke's *Reflections on the Revolution in France* was hastily written in 1790 and published immediately by Joseph Johnson. It is a topical work that constantly refers to the book it is designed to refute and to political quarrels now largely forgotten. In the course of its argument, however, it forcefully states the rationalist philosophy Wollstonecraft held during her early years with Johnson, and in its numerous digressions it touches on subjects—such as women's association with weakness and the universal fear of madness—which are relevant to any age.

Wollstonecraft saw Burke in two main roles, both of which angered her. First, he was the chief proponent of a conservative philosophy which held that hereditary honors and property were sacred, necessary to the order and well-being of the state; since Burke considered humanity weak, flawed, and only intermittently rational, he felt that custom and privilege, sanctioned by time, were the only safeguards against social chaos. Second, he was an example for Wollstonecraft of the sentimental writer, a person who spurned reason and indulged in feeling for its own sake; thus in his book he could waste on the undeserving great—especially the French Queen, Marie Antoinette—that sympathy which should reasonably have gone to the wretched and poor. To these roles of conservative philosopher and sentimental writer, Burke added a further one, equally obnoxious to Wollstonecraft: he was the author of *A Philosophical Enquiry into the Sublime and the Beautiful* (1757); in this work he ascribed women's beauty to their littleness and fragility, and "clearly proved that one half of the human species . . . have not souls."

In *The Rights of Men* Wollstonecraft opposed Burke's ideas with a mixture of bare assertion, reasoned argument, and personal abuse. She asserted vehemently and often that reason should be supreme in humanity and she argued movingly that the social situation in England prevented most people from cultivating this important faculty. In the course of her argument she drew attention to specific social abuses, such as the impressing of seamen; this practice forced poor men to leave the families of which they were often the sole support. The personal criticism of Burke runs throughout the book; it centers on his callousness, a result of his excessive sentimentality, and his ambition. The former allowed him to be indifferent to the sufferings of the poor, while the latter caused him—through concern for his party and so for his own career—to ignore the misery of the mad King, George III.

The Rights of Men was the first of Wollstonecraft's works to be widely reviewed and few journals could omit mention of the sex of its author. The *Analytical Review* of 1790 applauded the book and then anticipated Burke's annoyance at finding his antagonist to be a woman; the *Critical Review* of 1790 criticized it harshly and later apologized for having to treat a woman so bluntly. Most hostile of all was the *Gentleman's Magazine* of 1791, which found it ridiculous that the rights of men should be asserted by a woman.

THE BIRTHRIGHT of man, to give you, Sir, a short definition of this disputed right, is such a degree of liberty, civil and religious, as is compatible with the liberty of every other individual with whom he is united in a social compact, and the continued existence of that compact.

Liberty, in this simple, unsophisticated sense, I acknowledge, is a fair idea that has never yet received a form in the various governments that have been established on our beauteous globe; the demon of property has ever been at hand to encroach on the sacred rights of men, and to fence round with awful pomp laws that war with justice. But that it results from the eternal foundation of right—from immutable truth— who will presume to deny, that pretends to rationality—if reason has led them to build their morality and religion on an everlasting foundation —the attributes of God? . . .

I perceive, from the whole tenor of your Reflections, that you have a mortal antipathy to reason; but, if there is any thing like argument, or first principles, in your wild declamation, behold the result:—that we are to reverence the rust of antiquity, and term the unnatural customs, which ignorance and mistaken self-interest have consolidated, the sage fruit of experience: nay, that, if we do discover some errors, our *feelings* should lead us to excuse, with blind love, or unprincipled filial affection, the venerable vestiges of ancient days. These are gothic notions of beauty—the ivy is beautiful, but, when it insidiously destroys the trunk from which it receives support, who would not grub it up?

Further, that we ought cautiously to remain for ever in frozen inactivity, because a thaw, whilst it nourishes the soil, spreads a temporary

Edmund Burke in 1790 after J. Barry.

inundation; and the fear of risking any personal present convenience should prevent a struggle for the most estimable advantages. This is sound reasoning, I grant, in the mouth of the rich and short-sighted.

Yes, Sir, the strong gained riches, the few have sacrificed the many to their vices; and, to be able to pamper their appetites, and supinely exist without exercising mind or body, they have ceased to be men.— Lost to the relish of true pleasure, such beings would, indeed, deserve compassion, if injustice was not softened by the tyrant's plea—necessity; if prescription was not raised as an immortal boundary against innovation. Their minds, in fact, instead of being cultivated, have been so warped by education, that it may require some ages to bring them back to nature, and enable them to see their true interest, with that degree of conviction which is necessary to influence their conduct.

The civilization which has taken place in Europe has been very partial, and, like every custom that an arbitrary point of honour has established, refines the manners at the expence of morals, by making sentiments and opinions current in conversation that have no root in the heart, or weight in the cooler resolves of the mind.—And what has stopped its progress?—hereditary property—hereditary honours. The man has been changed into an artificial monster by the station in which he was born, and the consequent homage that benumbed his faculties like the torpedo's touch;—or a being, with a capacity of reasoning, would not have failed to discover, as his faculties unfolded, that true happiness arose from the friendship and intimacy which can only be enjoyed by equals; and that charity is not a condescending distribution of alms, but an intercourse of good offices and mutual benefits, founded on respect for justice and humanity. . . .

It is necessary emphatically to repeat, that there are rights which men inherit at their birth, as rational creatures, who were raised above the brute creation by their improvable faculties; and that, in receiving these, not from their forefathers but, from God, prescription can never undermine natural rights.

A father may dissipate his property without his child having any right to complain;—but should he attempt to sell him for a slave, or fetter him with laws contrary to reason; nature, in enabling him to discern good from evil, teaches him to break the ignoble chain, and not to believe that bread becomes flesh, and wine blood, because his parents swallowed the Eucharist with this blind persuasion.*

There is no end to this implicit submission to authority—some where it must stop, or we return to barbarism. . . .

* A reference to the Roman Catholic doctrine of Transubstantiation.—Editor.

Security of property! Behold, in a few words, the definition of English liberty. And to this selfish principle every nobler one is sacrificed. —The Briton takes place of the man, and the image of God is lost in the citizen! But it is not that enthusiastic flame which in Greece and Rome consumed every sordid passion: no, self is the focus; and the disparting* rays rise not above our foggy atmosphere. But softly—it is only the property of the rich that is secure; the man who lives by the sweat of his brow has no asylum from oppression; the strong man may enter—when was the castle of the poor sacred? and the base informer steal him from the family that depend on his industry for subsistence.

Fully sensible as you must be of the baneful consequences that inevitably follow this notorious infringement on the dearest rights of men, and that it is an infernal blot on the very face of our immaculate constitution, I cannot avoid expressing my surprise that when you recommended our form of government as a model, you did not caution the French against the arbitrary custom of pressing men for the sea service.† You should have hinted to them, that property in England is much more secure than liberty, and not have concealed that the liberty of an honest mechanic—his all—is often sacrificed to secure the property of the rich. For it is a farce to pretend that a man fights *for his country, his hearth, or his altars,* when he has neither liberty nor property.—His property is in his nervous arms—and they are compelled to pull a strange rope at the surly command of a tyrannic boy, who probably obtained his rank on account of his family connections, or the prostituted vote of his father, whose interest in a borough, or voice as a senator, was acceptable to the minister.

Our penal laws punish with death the thief who steals a few pounds;‡ but to take by violence, or trepan,§ a man, is no such heinous offence.—For who shall dare to complain of the venerable vestige of the law that rendered the life of a deer more sacred than that of a man? But it was the poor man with only his native dignity who was thus oppressed—and only metaphysical sophists and cold mathematicians can discern this insubstantial form; it is a work of abstraction— and a *gentleman* of lively imagination must borrow some drapery from fancy before he can love or pity a *man.*—Misery, to reach your heart, I perceive, must have its cap and bells; your tears are reserved, very *nat-*

* Separating and dissolving.—Editor.

† The forcing of able-bodied but unwilling men into the navy, a practice which continued into the second decade of the nineteenth century.—Editor.

‡ In the eighteenth century, there was a whole host of capital offences. As late as 1813 a person stealing less than five shillings could be punished by death.—Editor.

§ Entrap or decoy.—Editor.

urally considering your character, for the declamation of the theatre, or for the downfall of queens, whose rank alters the nature of folly, and throws a graceful veil over vices that degrade humanity; whilst the distress of many industrious mothers, whose *helpmates* have been torn from them, and the hungry cry of helpless babes, were vulgar sorrows that could not move your commiseration, though they might extort an alms. 'The tears that are shed for fictitious sorrow are admirably adapted,' says Rousseau, 'to make us proud of all the virtues which we do not possess.'* . . .

Man has been termed, with strict propriety, a microcosm, a little world in himself.—He is so;—yet must, however, be reckoned an ephemera, or, to adopt your figure of rhetoric, a summer's fly. The perpetuation of property in our families is one of the privileges you most warmly contend for; yet it would not be very difficult to prove that the mind must have a very limited range that thus confines its benevolence to such a narrow circle, which, with great propriety, may be included in the sordid calculations of blind self-love.

A brutal attachment to children has appeared most conspicuous in parents who have treated them like slaves, and demanded due homage for all the property they transferred to them, during their lives. It has led them to force their children to break the most sacred ties; to do violence to a natural impulse, and run into legal prostitution† to increase wealth or shun poverty; and, still worse, the dread of parental malediction has made many weak characters violate truth in the face of Heaven; and, to avoid a father's angry curse, the most sacred promises have been broken. It appears to be a natural suggestion of reason, that a man should be freed from implicit obedience to parents and private punishments, when he is of an age to be subject to the jurisdiction of the laws of his country; and that the barbarous cruelty of allowing parents to imprison their children, to prevent their contaminating their noble blood by following the dictates of nature when they chose to marry, or for any misdemeanor that does not come under the cognizance of public justice, is one of the most arbitrary violations of liberty.

Who can recount all the unnatural crimes which the *laudable, interesting* desire of perpetuating a name has produced? The younger children have been sacrificed to the eldest son; sent into exile, or confined in convents, that they might not encroach on what was called, with shameful falsehood, the *family* estate. Will Mr. Burke call this

* This sentiment is expressed in the letters of St. Preux to Julie in Part II of Rousseau's *La Nouvelle Heloïse.*—Editor.

† Wollstonecraft was the first writer to use this famous phrase.—Editor.

parental affection reasonable or virtuous?—No; it is the spurious offspring of over-weening, mistaken pride—and not that first source of
civilization, natural parental affection, that makes no difference between child and child, but what reason justifies by pointing out superior merit.

Another pernicious consequence which unavoidably arises from this
artificial affection is, the insuperable bar which it puts in the way of
early marriages. It would be difficult to determine whether the minds
or bodies of our youth are most injured by this impediment. Our young
men become selfish coxcombs, and gallantry with modest women, and
intrigues with those of another description, weaken both mind and
body, before either has arrived at maturity. The character of a master
of a family, a husband, and a father, forms the citizen imperceptibly,
by producing a sober manliness of thought, and orderly behaviour; but,
from the lax morals and depraved affections of the libertine, what results?—a finical* man of taste, who is only anxious to secure his own
private gratifications, and to maintain his rank in society.

The same system has an equally pernicious effect on female morals.
—Girls are sacrificed to family convenience, or else marry to settle themselves in a superior rank, and coquet, without restraint, with the fine
gentleman whom I have already described. And to such lengths has this
vanity, this desire of shining, carried them, that it is not now necessary
to guard girls against imprudent love matches; for if some widows did
not now and then *fall* in love, Love and Hymen† would seldom meet,
unless at a village church.

I do not intend to be sarcastically paradoxical when I say, that
women of fashion take husbands that they may have it in their power
to coquet, the grand business of genteel life, with a number of admirers,
and thus flutter the spring of life away, without laying up any store for
the winter of age, or being of any use to society. Affection in the marriage state can only be founded on respect—and are these weak beings
respectable? Children are neglected for lovers, and we express surprise
that adulteries are so common! A woman never forgets to adorn herself
to make an impression on the senses of the other sex, and to extort the
homage which it is gallant to pay, and yet we wonder that they have
such confined understandings!

Have ye not heard that we cannot serve two masters? an immoderate desire to please contracts the faculties, and immerges, to borrow

* Affectedly fastidious.—Editor.
† Marriage.—Editor.

the idea of a great philosopher, the soul in matter, till it becomes unable to mount on the wing of contemplation.*

It would be an arduous task to trace all the vice and misery that arise in society from the middle class of people apeing the manners of the great. All are aiming to procure respect on account of their property; and most places are considered as sinecures that enable men to start into notice. The grand concern of three parts out of four is to contrive to live above their equals, and to appear to be richer than they are. How much domestic comfort and private satisfaction is sacrificed to this irrational ambition! It is a destructive mildew that blights the fairest virtues; benevolence, friendship, generosity, and all those endearing charities which bind human hearts together, and the pursuits which raise the mind to higher contemplations, all that were not cankered in the bud by the false notions that 'grew with its growth and strengthened with its strength,' are crushed by the iron hand of property!

Property, I do not scruple to aver it, should be fluctuating, which would be the case, if it were more equally divided amongst all the children of a family; else it is an everlasting rampart, in consequence of a barbarous feudal institution, that enables the elder son to overpower talents and depress virtue.

Besides, an unmanly servility, most inimical to true dignity of character is, by this means, fostered in society. Men of some abilities play on the follies of the rich, and mounting to fortune as they degrade themselves, they stand in the way of men of superior talents, who cannot advance in such crooked paths, or wade through the filth which *parasites* never boggle at. Pursuing their way straight forward, their spirit is either bent or broken by the rich man's contumelies, or the difficulties they have to encounter.

The only security of property that nature authorizes and reason sanctions is, the right a man has to enjoy the acquisitions which his talents and industry have acquired; and to bequeath them to whom he chooses. Happy would it be for the world if there were no other road to wealth or honour; if pride, in the shape of parental affection, did not absorb the man, and prevent friendship from having the same weight as relationship. Luxury and effeminacy would not then introduce so much idiotism into the noble families which form one of the pillars of our state: the ground would not lie fallow, nor would undirected activity of mind spread the contagion of restless idleness, and its concomitant, vice, through the whole mass of society.

* Probably a reference to Plato's ideas in his *Phaedrus.*—Editor.

Instead of gaming they might nourish a virtuous ambition, and love might take place of the gallantry which you, with knightly fealty, venerate. Women would probably then act like mothers, and the fine lady, become a rational woman, might think it necessary to superintend her family and suckle her children, in order to fulfil her part of the social compact. But vain is the hope, whilst great masses of property are hedged round by hereditary honours; for numberless vices, forced in the hot-bed of wealth, assume a sightly form to dazzle the senses and cloud the understanding. The respect paid to rank and fortune damps every generous purpose of the soul, and stifles the natural affections on which human contentment ought to be built. Who will venturously ascend the steeps of virtue, or explore the great deep for knowledge, when *the one thing needful*, attained by less arduous exertions, if not inherited, procures the attention man naturally pants after, and vice 'loses half its evil by losing all its grossness.'*—What a sentiment to come from a moral pen! . . .

The sight of august ruins, of a depopulated country—what are they to a disordered soul!† when all the faculties are mixed in wild confusion. It is then indeed we tremble for humanity—and, if some wild fancy chance to cross the brain, we fearfully start, and pressing our hand against our brow, ask if we are yet men?—if our reason is undisturbed?—if judgment hold the helm? . . . poverty, shame, and even slavery, may be endured by the virtuous man—he has still a world to range in—but the loss of reason appears a monstrous flaw in the moral world, that eludes all investigation, and humbles without enlightening.

In this state was the King, when you, with unfeeling disrespect, and indecent haste, wished to strip him of all his hereditary honours.‡— You were so eager to taste the sweets of power, that you could not wait till time had determined, whether a dreadful delirium would settle into a confirmed madness; but, prying into the secrets of Omnipotence, you thundered out that God had *hurled him from his throne*, and that it was the most insulting mockery to recollect that he had been a king, or to treat him with any particular respect on account of his former dignity.§

* "It is gone—that sensibility of principle, that charity of honour . . . under which vice itself lost half its evil by losing all its grossness," *Reflections on the Revolution in France.*—Editor.

† Wollstonecraft is discussing the madness of George III.—Editor.

‡ A reference to Burke's arguments during the debate in the House of Commons on February 9, 1789, in support of investing the King's powers in the Prince Regent. —Editor.

§ ". . . did they recollect that they were talking of a sick king, of a monarch smitten

—And who was the monster whom Heaven had thus awfully deposed, and smitten with such an angry blow? Surely as harmless a character as Lewis XVIth; and the queen of Great Britain, though her heart may not be enlarged by generosity, who will presume to compare her character with that of the queen of France?

Where then was the infallibility of that extolled instinct which rises above reason?* was it warped by vanity, or *hurled* from its throne by self-interest? To your own heart answer these questions in the sober hours of reflection—and, after reviewing this gust of passion, learn to respect the sovereignty of reason.

I have, Sir, been reading, with a scrutinizing, comparative eye, several of your insensible and profane speeches during the King's illness. I disdain to take advantage of a man's weak side, or draw consequences from an unguarded transport—A lion preys not on carcasses! But on this occasion you acted systematically. It was not the passion of the moment, over which humanity draws a veil: no; what but the odious maxims of Machiavelian policy could have led you to have searched in the very dregs of misery for forcible arguments to support your party? Had not vanity or interest steeled your heart, you would have been shocked at the cold insensibility which could carry a man to those dreadful mansions, where human weakness appears in its most awful form to *calculate* the chances against the King's recovery. Impressed as *you are* with respect for royalty, I am astonished that you did not tremble at every step, lest Heaven should avenge on your guilty head the insult offered to its vicegerent. But the conscience that is under the direction of transient ebullitions of feeling, is not very tender or consistent, when the current runs another way. . . .

In what respect are we superior to the brute creation, if intellect is not allowed to be the guide of passion? Brutes hope and fear, love and hate; but, without a capacity to improve, a power of turning these passions to good or evil, they neither acquire virtue nor wisdom.—Why? Because the Creator has not given them reason.†

---

by the hand of Omnipotence, and that the Almighty had hurled him from his throne, and plunged him into a condition which drew upon him the pity of the meanest peasant in his kingdom," report of Burke's speech of February 9, 1789.—Editor.

   * Wollstonecraft constantly taunted Burke for placing sensibility or emotion above reason.—Editor.

   † I do not now mean to discuss the intricate subject of their mortality; reason may, perhaps, be given to them in the next stage of existence, if they are to mount in the scale of life, like men, by the medium of death.—Wollstonecraft.

But the cultivation of reason is an arduous task, and men of lively fancy, finding it easier to follow the impulse of passion, endeavour to persuade themselves and others that it is most *natural*. And happy is it for those, who indolently let that heaven-lighted spark rest like the ancient lamps in sepulchres, that some virtuous habits, with which the reason of others shackled them, supplies its place.—Affection for parents, reverence for superiors or antiquity, notions of honour, or that worldly self-interest that shrewdly shews them that honesty is the best policy: all proceed from the reason for which they serve as substitutes; —but it is reason at second-hand.

Children are born ignorant, consequently innocent; the passions, are neither good nor evil dispositions, till they receive a direction, and either bound over the feeble barrier raised by a faint glimmering of unexercised reason, called conscience, or strengthen her wavering dictates till sound principles are deeply rooted, and able to cope with the headstrong passions that often assume her awful form. What moral purpose can be answered by extolling good dispositions, as they are called, when these good dispositions are described as instincts: for instinct moves in a direct line to its ultimate end, and asks not for guide or support. But if virtue is to be acquired by experience, or taught by example, reason, perfected by reflection, must be the director of the whole host of passions, which produce a fructifying heat, but no light, that you would exalt into her place.—She must hold the rudder, or, let the wind blow which way it list, the vessel will never advance smoothly to its destined port; for the time lost in tacking about would dreadfully impede its progress. . . .

Who can deny, that has marked the slow progress of civilization, that men may become more virtuous and happy without any new discovery in morals? Who will venture to assert that virtue would not be promoted by the more extensive cultivation of reason? If nothing more is to be done, let us eat and drink, for to-morrow we die—and die for ever! Who will pretend to say, that there is as much happiness diffused on this globe as it is capable of affording? as many social virtues as reason would foster, if she could gain the strength she is able to acquire even in this imperfect state; if the voice of nature was allowed to speak audibly from the bottom of the heart, and the *native* unalienable rights of men were recognized in their full force; if factitious merit did not take place of genuine acquired virtue, and enable men to build their enjoyment on the misery of their fellow creatures; if men were more under the dominion of reason than opinion, and did not cherish their prejudices 'because they were prejudices?'* I am not, Sir, aware of your sneers, hailing a millennium, though a state of greater purity of morals may not be a mere poetic fiction; nor did my fancy ever create a heaven on earth, since reason threw off her swaddling clothes. I perceive, but too forcibly, that happiness, literally speaking, dwells not here;—and that we wander to and fro in a vale of darkness as well as tears. I perceive that my passions pursue objects that the imagination enlarges, till they become only a sublime idea that shrinks from the enquiry of sense, and mocks the experimental philosophers who would confine this spiritual phlogiston† in their material crucibles. I know that the human understanding is deluded with vain shadows, and that when we eagerly pursue any study, we only reach the boundary set to human enquires. —Thus far shalt thou go, and no further, says some stern difficulty; and the *cause* we were pursuing melts into utter darkness. But these are only the trials of contemplative minds, the foundation of virtue remains firm. —The power of exercising our understanding raises us above the brutes; and this exercise produces that 'primary morality,' which you term 'untaught feelings.'

If virtue be an instinct, I renounce all hope of immortality; and with it all the sublime reveries and dignified sentiments that have smoothed the rugged path of life: it is all a cheat, a lying vision; I have disquieted myself in vain; for in my eye all feelings are false and spurious, that do not rest on justice as their foundation, and are not concentred by universal love.

I reverence the rights of men.—Sacred rights! for which I acquire a more profound respect, the more I look into my own mind; and, professing these heterodox opinions, I still preserve my bowels; my heart is human, beats quick with human sympathies—and I FEAR God!

I bend with awful reverence when I enquire on what my fear is built.—I fear that sublime power, whose motive for creating me must have been wise and good; and I submit to the moral laws which my reason deduces from this view of my dependence on him.—It is not his power that I fear—it is not to an arbitrary will, but to unerring *reason* I submit.—Submit—yes; I disregard the charge of arrogance, to the law that regulates his just resolves; and the happiness I pant after must be the same in kind, and produced by the same exertions as his—though

* ". . . instead of casting away all our old prejudices, we cherish them to a very considerable degree, and . . . we cherish them because they are prejudices," *Reflections on the Revolution in France.*—Editor.

† A hypothetical substance regarded as the principle of fire; it was supposed to separate from matter through burning.—Editor.

unfeigned humility overwhelms every idea that would presume to compare the goodness which the most exalted created being could acquire, with the grand source of life and bliss.

This fear of God makes me reverence myself.—Yes, Sir, the regard I have for honest fame, and the friendship of the virtuous, falls far short of the respect which I have for myself. And this, enlightened self-love, if an epithet the meaning of which has been grossly perverted will convey my idea, forces me to see; and, if I may venture to borrow a prostituted term, to *feel*, that happiness is reflected, and that, in communicating good, my soul receives its noble aliment. . . .

. . . without fixed principles even goodness of heart is no security from inconsistency, and mild affectionate sensibility only renders a man more ingeniously cruel, when the pangs of hurt vanity are mistaken for virtuous indignation, and the gall of bitterness for the milk of Christian charity.

Where is the dignity, the infallibility of sensibility, in the fair ladies, whom, if the voice of rumour is to be credited, the captive negroes curse in all the agony of bodily pain, for the unheard of tortures they invent? It is probable that some of them, after the sight of a flagellation, compose their ruffled spirits and exercise their tender feelings by the perusal of the last imported novel.—How true these tears are to nature, I leave you to determine. But these ladies may have read your Enquiry concerning the origin of our ideas of the Sublime and Beautiful, and, convinced by your arguments, may have laboured to be pretty, by counterfeiting weakness.

You may have convinced them that *littleness* and *weakness* are the very essence of beauty;* and that the Supreme Being, in giving women beauty in the most supereminent degree, seemed to command them, by the powerful voice of Nature, not to cultivate the moral virtues that might chance to excite respect, and interfere with the pleasing sensations they were created to inspire. Thus confining truth, fortitude, and humanity, within the rigid pale of manly morals, they might justly argue, that to be loved, woman's high end and great distinction! they should 'learn to lisp, to totter in their walk, and nick-name God's creatures.' Never, they might repeat after you, was any man, much less a woman, rendered amiable by the force of those exalted qualities, fortitude, justice, wisdom, and truth; and thus forewarned of the sacrifice they must make to those austere, unnatural virtues, they would be au-

* "The beauty of women is considerably owing to their weakness or delicacy, and is even enhanced by their timidity, a quality of mind analogous to it," Edmund Burke's *Philosophical Enquiry into the Sublime and the Beautiful.*—Editor.

thorized to turn all their attention to their persons, systematically neglecting morals to secure beauty.—Some rational old woman indeed
might chance to stumble at this doctrine, and hint, that in avoiding
atheism you had not steered clear of the mussulman's creed;* but you
could readily exculpate yourself by turning the charge on Nature, who
made our idea of beauty independent of reason. Nor would it be necessary for you to recollect, that if virtue has any other foundation than
worldly utility, you have clearly proved that one half of the human
species, at least, have not souls; and that Nature, by making women
little, smooth, delicate, fair creatures, never designed that they should
exercise their reason to acquire the virtues that produce opposite, if not
contradictory, feelings. The affection they excite, to be uniform and
perfect, should not be tinctured with the respect which moral virtues
inspire, lest pain should be blended with pleasure, and admiration disturb the soft intimacy of love. This laxity of morals in the female world
is certainly more captivating to a libertine imagination than the cold
arguments of reason, that give no sex to virtue. If beautiful weakness
be interwoven in a woman's frame, if the chief business of her life be
(as you insinuate) to inspire love, and Nature has made an eternal distinction between the qualities that dignify a rational being and this
animal perfection, her duty and happiness in this life must clash with
any preparation for a more exalted state. So that Plato and Milton were
grossly mistaken in asserting that human love led to heavenly, and was
only an exaltation of the same affection; for the love of the Deity, which
is mixed with the most profound reverence, must be love of perfection,
and not compassion for weakness.

To say the truth, I not only tremble for the souls of women, but for
the good natured man, whom every one loves. The *amiable* weakness
of his mind is a strong argument against its immateriality, and seems to
prove that beauty relaxes the *solids* of the soul as well as the body.

It follows then immediately, from your own reasoning, that respect
and love are antagonist principles; and that, if we really wish to render
men more virtuous, we must endeavour to banish all enervating modifications of beauty from civil society. We must, to carry your argument a
little further, return to the Spartan regulations, and settle the virtues of
men on the stern foundation of mortification and self-denial; for any
attempt to civilize the heart, to make it humane by implanting reasonable principles, is a mere philosophic dream. If refinement inevitably

* The Koran makes general statements about women's equality and Mohammed
asserted that men and women could both achieve paradise. The status of women in
Moslem countries was, however, very low and no doubt contributed to the widespread
Christian belief that the Moslem religion denied that women had souls.—Editor.

lessens respect for virtue, by rendering beauty, the grand tempter, more seductive; if these relaxing feelings are incompatible with the nervous exertions of morality, the sun of Europe is not set; it begins to dawn, when cold metaphysicians try to make the head give laws to the heart.

But should experience prove that there is a beauty in virtue, a charm in order, which necessarily implies exertion, a depraved sensual taste may give way to a more manly one—and *melting* feelings to rational satisfactions. Both may be equally natural to man; the test is their moral difference, and that point reason alone can decide.

Such a glorious change can only be produced by liberty. . . .

Almost every vice that has degraded our nature might be justified by shewing that it had been productive of *some* benefit to society: for it would be as difficult to point out positive evil as unallayed good, in this imperfect state. What indeed would become of morals, if they had no other test than prescription? The manners of men may change without end; but, wherever reason receives the least cultivation—wherever men rise above brutes, morality must rest on the same base. And the more man discovers of the nature of his mind and body, the more clearly he is convinced, that to act according to the dictates of reason is to conform to the law of God.

The test of honour may be arbitrary and fallacious, and, retiring into subterfuge, elude close enquiry; but true morality shuns not the day, nor shrinks from the ordeal of investigation. Most of the happy revolutions that have taken place in the world have happened when weak princes held the reins they could not manage; but are they, on that account, to be canonized as saints or demi-gods, and pushed forward to notice on the throne of ignorance? Pleasure wants a zest, if experience cannot compare it with pain; but who courts pain to heighten his pleasures? A transient view of society will further illustrate arguments which appear so obvious that I am almost ashamed to produce illustrations. How many children have been taught œconomy, and many other virtues, by the extravagant thoughtlessness of their parents; yet a good education is allowed to be an inestimable blessing. The tenderest mothers are often the most unhappy wives; but can the good that accrues from the private distress that produces a sober dignity of mind justify the inflictor? Right or wrong may be estimated according to the point of sight, and other adventitious circumstances; but, to discover its real nature, the enquiry must go deeper than the surface, and beyond the local consequences that confound good and evil together. The rich and weak, a numerous train, will certainly applaud your system, and loudly celebrate your pious reverence for authority and establishments

—they find it pleasanter to enjoy than to think; to justify oppression than correct abuses.—*The rights of men* are grating sounds that set their teeth on edge; the impertinent enquiry of philosophic meddling innovation. If the poor are in distress, they will make some *benevolent* exertions to assist them; they will confer obligations, but not do justice. Benevolence is a very amiable specious quality; yet the aversion which men feel to accept a right as a favour, should rather be extolled as a vestige of native dignity, than stigmatized as the odious offspring of ingratitude. The poor consider the rich as their lawful prey; but we ought not too severely to animadvert on their ingratitude. When they receive an alms they are commonly grateful at the moment; but old habits quickly return, and cunning has ever been a substitute for force.

That both physical and moral evil were not only foreseen, but entered into the scheme of Providence, when this world was contemplated in the Divine mind, who can doubt, without robbing Omnipotence of a most exalted attribute? But the business of the life of a good man should be, to separate light from darkness; to diffuse happiness, whilst he submits to unavoidable misery. And a conviction that there is much unavoidable wretchedness, appointed by the grand Disposer of all events, should not slacken his exertions: the extent of what is possible can only be discerned by God. The justice of God may be vindicated by a belief in a future state; but, only by believing that evil is educing good for the individual, and not for an imaginary whole. The happiness of the whole must arise from the happiness of the constituent parts, or the essence of justice is sacrificed to a supposed grand arrangement. And that may be good for the whole of a creature's existence, that disturbs the comfort of a small portion. The evil which an individual suffers for the good of the community is partial, it must be allowed, if the account is settled by death.—But the partial evil which it suffers, during one stage of existence, to render another stage more perfect, is strictly just. The Father of all only can regulate the education of his children. To suppose that, during the whole or part of its existence, the happiness of any individual is sacrificed to promote the welfare of ten, or ten thousand, other beings—is impious. But to suppose that the happiness, or animal enjoyment, of one portion of existence is sacrificed to improve and ennoble the being itself, and render it capable of more perfect happiness, is not to reflect on either the goodness or wisdom of God.

It may be confidently asserted that no man chooses evil, because it is evil; he only mistakes it for happiness, the good he seeks. And the desire of rectifying these mistakes, is the noble ambition of an enlightened understanding, the impulse of feelings that Philosophy invigo-

rates. To endeavour to make unhappy men resigned to their fate, is the
tender endeavour of short-sighted benevolence, of transient yearnings
of humanity; but to labour to increase human happiness by extirpating
error, is a masculine godlike affection. This remark may be carried still
further. Men who possess uncommon sensibility, whose quick emotions
shew how closely the eye and heart are connected, soon forget the most
forcible sensations. Not tarrying long enough in the brain to be subject
to reflection, the next sensations, of course, obliterate them. Memory,
however, treasures up these proofs of native goodness; and the being
who is not spurred on to any virtuous act, still thinks itself of consequence, and boasts of its feelings. Why? Because the sight of distress,
or an affecting narrative, made its blood flow with more velocity, and
the heart, literally speaking, beat with sympathetic emotion. We ought
to beware of confounding mechanical instinctive sensations with emotions that reason deepens, and justly terms the feelings of *humanity*.
This word discriminates the active exertions of virtue from the vague
declamation of sensibility. . . .

I know, indeed, that there is often something disgusting in the distresses of poverty, at which the imagination revolts, and starts back to
exercise itself in the more attractive Arcadia of fiction. The rich man
builds a house, art and taste give it the highest finish. His gardens are
planted, and the trees grow to recreate the fancy of the planter, though
the temperature of the climate may rather force him to avoid the dangerous damps they exhale, than seek the umbrageous retreat. Every
thing on the estate is cherished but man;—yet, to contribute to the happiness of man, is the most sublime of all enjoyments. But if, instead of
sweeping pleasure-grounds, obelisks, temples, and elegant cottages, as
objects for the eye, the heart was allowed to beat true to nature, decent
farms would be scattered over the estate, and plenty smile around. Instead of the poor being subject to the griping hand of an avaricious
steward, they would be watched over with fatherly solicitude, by the
man whose duty and pleasure it was to guard their happiness, and shield
from rapacity the beings who, by the sweat of their brow, exalted him
above his fellows.

I could almost imagine I see a man thus gathering blessings as he
mounted the hill of life; or consolation, in those days when the spirits
lag, and the tired heart finds no pleasure in them. It is not by squander-
ing alms that the poor can be relieved, or improved—it is the fostering
sun of kindness, the wisdom that finds them employments calculated to
give them habits of virtue, that meliorates their condition. Love is only
the fruit of love; condescension and authority may produce the obedi-

ence you applaud; but he has lost his heart of flesh who can see a fellow-creature humbled before him, and trembling at the frown of a being, whose heart is supplied by the same vital current, and whose pride ought to be checked by a consciousness of having the same infirmities.

What salutary dews might not be shed to refresh this thirsty land, if men were more *enlightened!* Smiles and premiums might encourage cleanliness, industry, and emulation.—A garden more inviting than Eden would then meet the eye, and springs of joy murmur on every side. The clergyman would superintend his own flock, the shepherd would then love the sheep he daily tended; the school might rear its decent head, and the buzzing tribe, let loose to play, impart a portion of their vivacious spirits to the heart that longed to open their minds, and lead them to taste the pleasures of men. Domestic comfort, the civilizing relations of husband, brother, and father, would soften labour, and render life contented.

Returning once from a despotic country to a part of England well cultivated, but not very picturesque—with what delight did I not observe the poor man's garden!—The homely palings and twining woodbine, with all the rustic contrivances of simple, unlettered taste, was a sight which relieved the eye that had wandered indignant from the stately palace to the pestiferous hovel, and turned from the awful contrast into itself to mourn the fate of man, and curse the arts of civilization!

Why cannot large estates be divided into small farms? these dwellings would indeed grace our land. Why are huge forests still allowed to stretch out with idle pomp and all the indolence of Eastern grandeur? Why does the brown waste meet the traveller's view, when men want work? But commons cannot be enclosed without *acts of parliament* to increase the property of the rich! Why might not the industrious peasant be allowed to steal a farm from the heath?* This sight I have seen; —the cow that supported the children grazed near the hut, and the cheerful poultry were fed by the chubby babes, who breathed a bracing air, far from the diseases and the vices of cities. Domination blasts all these prospects; virtue can only flourish amongst equals, and the man who submits to a fellow-creature, because it promotes his worldly interest, and he who relieves only because it is his duty to lay up a treasure in heaven, are much on a par, for both are radically degraded by the habits of their life.

In this great city [London], that proudly rears its head, and boasts

* Wollstonecraft is here referring to the controversial agricultural practice of enclosing common land for cattle or crops. Enclosure required an act of parliament and consequently was available primarily to the richer farmers.—Editor.

of its population and commerce, how much misery lurks in pestilential corners, whilst idle mendicants assail, on every side, the man who hates to encourage impostors, or repress, with angry frown, the plaints of the poor! How many mechanics, by a flux of trade or fashion, lose their employment; whom misfortunes, not to be warded off, lead to the idleness that vitiates their character and renders them afterwards averse to honest labour! Where is the eye that marks these evils, more gigantic than any of the infringements of property, which you piously deprecate? Are these remediless evils? And is the humane heart satisfied with turning the poor over to *another* world, to receive the blessings this could afford? If society was regulated on a more enlarged plan; if man was contented to be the friend of man, and did not seek to bury the sympathies of humanity in the servile appellation of master; if, turning his eyes from ideal regions of taste and elegance, he laboured to give the earth he inhabited all the beauty it is capable of receiving, and was ever on the watch to shed abroad all the happiness which human nature can enjoy;—he who, respecting the rights of men, wishes to convince or persuade society that this is true happiness and dignity, is not the cruel *oppressor* of the poor, nor a short-sighted philosopher—HE fears God and loves his fellow-creatures.—Behold the whole duty of man!—the citizen who acts differently is a sophisticated being.

Surveying civilized life, and seeing, with undazzled eye, the polished vices of the rich, their insincerity, want of natural affections, with all the specious train that luxury introduces, I have turned impatiently to the poor, to look for man undebauched by riches or power—but, alas! what did I see? a being scarcely above the brutes, over which he tyrannized; a broken spirit, worn-out body, and all those gross vices which the example of the rich, rudely copied, could produce. Envy built a wall of separation, that made the poor hate, whilst they bent to their superiors; who, on their part, stepped aside to avoid the loathsome sight of human misery.

What were the outrages of a day* to these continual miseries? Let those sorrows hide their diminished head before the tremendous mountain of woe that thus defaces our globe! Man preys on man; and you mourn for the idle tapestry that decorated a gothic pile, and the dronish bell that summoned the fat priest to prayer. You mourn for the empty pageant of a name, when slavery flaps her wing, and the sick heart retires to die in lonely wilds, far from the abodes of men. Did the pangs you felt for insulted nobility, the anguish that rent your heart when the

---

* The 6th of October, 1789, the people's march to Versailles, which led to the King's forced removal to Paris. Burke condemned the events of this day, as did Wollstonecraft in her history of the French Revolution (1794).—Editor.

gorgeous robes were torn off the idol human weakness had set up, deserve to be compared with the long-drawn sigh of melancholy reflection, when misery and vice are thus seen to haunt our steps, and swim on the top of every cheering prospect? Why is our fancy to be appalled by terrific perspectives of a hell beyond the grave?—Hell stalks abroad;—the lash resounds on the slave's naked sides; and the sick wretch, who can no longer earn the sour bread of unremitting labour, steals to a ditch to bid the world a long good night—or, neglected in some ostentatious hospital, breathes his last amidst the laugh of mercenary attendants.

Such misery demands more than tears—

A Vindication of the Rights of Woman*

Wollstonecraft's major work was written in 1791 and published in 1792. It is a response both to her experience as a woman and to the prevailing English literary tradition of ridicule and scorn for women. Except for Catherine Macaulay, Wollstonecraft makes no mention of earlier writers who supported women's right to education and social equality, but she devotes many pages to the works that systematically denigrate women, from the Bible to Milton's *Paradise Lost* and Pope's *Moral Essays*. Above all she combats Rousseau's *Émile,* which she felt stated women's inferiority in a particularly seductive and humiliating way.

The *Rights of Woman* sold well and before the year was out a second, corrected edition was issued. The reaction to the work was widespread and, in the journals, predictable. The radical ones, such as the *Analytical Review* of 1792, were laudatory; others such as the *Anti-Jacobin* were scathing. The book was burlesqued and parodied in numerous works with titles such as *A Vindication of the Rights of Brutes,* while at the same time it evoked high praise from women like Mary Hays who found it expressing much that they had long and deeply felt. Of Wollstonecraft and her book, Hays wrote: "In the cause of half the human race she stood forth, deprecating and exposing, in a tone of impassioned eloquence, the various means and arts by which woman had been forcibly subjugated, flattered into imbecility, and invariably held in bondage" (*Annual Necrology for 1797–98*).

from the
INTRODUCTION

AFTER CONSIDERING the historic page, and viewing the living world with anxious solicitude, the most melancholy emotions of sorrowful in-

* The text follows the second edition of 1792.—Editor.

dignation have depressed my spirits, and I have sighed when obliged to confess, that either nature has made a great difference between man and man, or that the civilization which has hitherto taken place in the world has been very partial. I have turned over various books written on the subject of education,* and patiently observed the conduct of parents and the management of schools; but what has been the result? —a profound conviction that the neglected education of my fellow-creatures is the grand source of the misery I deplore; and that women, in particular, are rendered weak and wretched by a variety of concurring causes, originating from one hasty conclusion. The conduct and manners of women, in fact, evidently prove that their minds are not in a healthy state; for, like the flowers which are planted in too rich a soil, strength and usefulness are sacrificed to beauty; and the flaunting leaves, after having pleased a fastidious eye, fade, disregarded on the stalk, long before the season when they ought to have arrived at maturity.—One cause of this barren blooming I attribute to a false system of education, gathered from the books written on this subject by men who, considering females rather as women than human creatures, have been more anxious to make them alluring mistresses than affectionate wives and rational mothers; and the understanding of the sex has been so bubbled by this specious homage, that the civilized women of the present century, with a few exceptions, are only anxious to inspire love, when they ought to cherish a nobler ambition, and by their abilities and virtues exact respect. . . .

Yet, because I am a woman, I would not lead my readers to suppose that I mean violently to agitate the contested question respecting the equality or inferiority of the sex, but as the subject lies in my way, and I cannot pass it over without subjecting the main tendency of my reasoning to misconstruction, I shall stop a moment to deliver, in a few words, my opinion.—In the government of the physical world it is observable that the female in point of strength is, in general, inferior to the male. This is the law of nature; and it does not appear to be suspended or abrogated in favour of woman. A degree of physical superiority cannot, therefore, be denied—and it is a noble prerogative.† But not content with this natural pre-eminence, men endeavour to sink us still lower, merely to render us alluring objects for a moment; and

* Wollstonecraft is referring to such popular works as Dr. John Gregory's *Father's Legacy to His Daughters* (1774) and Dr. James Fordyce's *Sermons to Young Women* (1765). She discusses both works in her book.—Editor.

† In the first edition Wollstonecraft was more emphatic: "the female, in general, is inferior to the male. The male pursues, the female yields—this is the law of nature; and it does not appear to be suspended or abrogated in favour of woman. This physical superiority cannot be denied—and it is a noble prerogative!"—Editor.

women, intoxicated by the adoration which men, under the influence of their senses, pay them, do not seek to obtain a durable interest in their hearts, or to become the friends of the fellow creatures who find amusement in their society.

I am aware of an obvious inference:—from every quarter have I heard exclamations against masculine women; but where are they to be found? If by this appellation men mean to inveigh against their ardour in hunting, shooting, and gaming, I shall most cordially join in the cry; but if it be against the imitation of manly virtues, or, more properly speaking, the attainment of those talents and virtues, the exercise of which ennobles the human character, and which raise females in the scale of animal being, when they are comprehensively termed mankind; —all those who view them with a philosophic eye must, I should think, wish with me, that they may every day grow more and more masculine. . . .

My own sex, I hope, will excuse me, if I treat them like rational creatures, instead of flattering their *fascinating* graces, and viewing them as if they were in a state of perpetual childhood, unable to stand alone. I earnestly wish to point out in what true dignity and human happiness consists—I wish to persuade women to endeavour to acquire strength, both of mind and body, and to convince them that the soft phrases, susceptibility of heart, delicacy of sentiment, and refinement of taste, are almost synonymous with epithets of weakness, and that those beings who are only the objects of pity and that kind of love, which has been termed its sister, will soon become objects of contempt. . . .

The education of women has, of late, been more attended to than formerly; yet they are still reckoned a frivolous sex, and ridiculed or pitied by the writers who endeavour by satire or instruction to improve them. It is acknowledged that they spend many of the first years of their lives in acquiring a smattering of accomplishments; meanwhile strength of body and mind are sacrificed to libertine notions of beauty, to the desire of establishing themselves,—the only way women can rise in the world,—by marriage. And this desire making mere animals of them, when they marry they act as such children may be expected to act:— they dress; they paint, and nickname God's creatures.—Surely these weak beings are only fit for a seraglio!—Can they be expected to govern a family with judgment, or take care of the poor babes whom they bring into the world?

If then it can be fairly deduced from the present conduct of the sex, from the prevalent fondness for pleasure which takes place of ambition and those nobler passions that open and enlarge the soul; that the instruction which women have hitherto received has only tended, with the constitution of civil society, to render them insignificant objects of desire—mere propagators of fools!—if it can be proved that in aiming to accomplish them, without cultivating their understandings, they are taken out of their sphere of duties, and made ridiculous and useless when the short-lived bloom of beauty is over,* I presume that *rational* men will excuse me for endeavouring to persuade them to become more masculine and respectable.

Indeed the word masculine is only a bugbear: there is little reason to fear that women will acquire too much courage or fortitude; for their apparent inferiority with respect to bodily strength, must render them, in some degree, dependent on men in the various relations of life; but why should it be increased by prejudices that give a sex to virtue, and confound simple truths with sensual reveries?

Women are, in fact, so much degraded by mistaken notions of female excellence, that I do not mean to add a paradox when I assert, that this artificial weakness produces a propensity to tyrannize, and gives birth to cunning, the natural opponent of strength, which leads them to play off those contemptible infantine airs that undermine esteem even whilst they excite desire. Let men become more chaste and modest, and if women do not grow wiser in the same ratio, it will be clear that they have weaker understandings. It seems scarcely necessary to say, that I now speak of the sex in general. Many individuals have more sense than their male relatives; and, as nothing preponderates where there is a constant struggle for an equilibrium, without it has naturally more gravity, some women govern their husbands without degrading themselves, because intellect will always govern.

from Chapter II
THE PREVAILING OPINION OF A
SEXUAL CHARACTER DISCUSSED

To account for, and excuse the tyranny of man, many ingenious arguments have been brought forward to prove, that the two sexes, in the acquirement of virtue, ought to aim at attaining a very different character: or, to speak explicitly, women are not allowed to have sufficient strength of mind to acquire what really deserves the name of virtue. Yet it should seem, allowing them to have souls, that there is but one way appointed by Providence to lead *mankind* to either virtue or happiness.

---

* A lively writer, I cannot recollect his name, asks what business women turned of forty have to do in the world?—Wollstonecraft.

If then women are not a swarm of ephemeron triflers, why should they be kept in ignorance under the specious name of innocence? Men complain, and with reason, of the follies and caprices of our sex, when they do not keenly satirize our headstrong passions and groveling vices. —Behold, I should answer, the natural effect of ignorance! The mind will ever be unstable that has only prejudices to rest on, and the current will run with destructive fury when there are no barriers to break its force. Women are told from their infancy, and taught by the example of their mothers, that a little knowledge of human weakness, justly termed cunning, softness of temper, *outward* obedience, and a scrupulous attention to a puerile kind of propriety, will obtain for them the protection of man; and should they be beautiful, every thing else is needless, for, at least, twenty years of their lives. . . .

. . . the most perfect education, in my opinion, is such an exercise of the understanding as is best calculated to strengthen the body and form the heart. Or, in other words, to enable the individual to attain such habits of virtue as will render it independent. In fact, it is a farce to call any being virtuous whose virtues do not result from the exercise of its own reason. This was Rousseau's opinion respecting men: I extend it to women, and confidently assert that they have been drawn out of their sphere by false refinement, and not by an endeavour to acquire masculine qualities. Still the regal homage which they receive is so intoxicating, that till the manners of the times are changed, and formed on more reasonable principles, it may be impossible to convince them that the illegitimate power, which they obtain, by degrading themselves, is a curse, and that they must return to nature and equality, if they wish to secure the placid satisfaction that unsophisticated affections impart. But for this epoch we must wait—wait, perhaps, till kings and nobles, enlightened by reason, and, preferring the real dignity of man to childish state, throw off their gaudy hereditary trappings: and if then women do not resign the arbitrary power of beauty—they will prove that they have *less* mind than man. . . .

Many are the causes that, in the present corrupt state of society, contribute to enslave women by cramping their understandings and sharpening their senses. One, perhaps, that silently does more mischief than all the rest, is their disregard of order.

To do every thing in an orderly manner, is a most important precept, which women, who, generally speaking, receive only a disorderly kind of education, seldom attend to with that degree of exactness that men, who from their infancy are broken into method, observe. This negligent kind of guess-work, for what other epithet can be used to point out the random exertions of a sort of instinctive common sense, never brought to the test of reason? prevents their generalizing matters of fact—so they do to-day, what they did yesterday, merely because they did it yesterday.

This contempt of the understanding in early life has more baneful consequences than is commonly supposed; for the little knowledge which women of strong minds attain, is, from various circumstances, of a more desultory kind than the knowledge of men, and it is acquired more by sheer observations on real life, than from comparing what has been individually observed with the results of experience generalized by speculation. Led by their dependent situation and domestic employments more into society, what they learn is rather by snatches; and as learning is with them, in general, only a secondary thing, they do not pursue any one branch with that persevering ardour necessary to give vigour to the faculties, and clearness to the judgment. In the present state of society, a little learning is required to support the character of a gentleman; and boys are obliged to submit to a few years of discipline. But in the education of women, the cultivation of the understanding is always subordinate to the acquirement of some corporeal accomplishment; even while enervated by confinement and false notions of modesty, the body is prevented from attaining that grace and beauty which relaxed half-formed limbs never exhibit. Besides, in youth their faculties are not brought forward by emulation; and having no serious scientific study, if they have natural sagacity it is turned too soon on life and manners. They dwell on effects, and modifications, without tracing them back to causes; and complicated rules to adjust behaviour are a weak substitute for simple principles.

As a proof that education gives this appearance of weakness to females, we may instance the example of military men, who are, like them, sent into the world before their minds have been stored with knowledge or fortified by principles. The consequences are similar; soldiers acquire a little superficial knowledge, snatched from the muddy current of conversation, and, from continually mixing with society, they gain, what is termed a knowledge of the world; and this acquaintance with manners and customs has frequently been confounded with a knowledge of the human heart. But can the crude fruit of casual observation, never brought to the test of judgment, formed by comparing speculation and experience, deserve such a distinction? Soldiers, as well as women, practice the minor virtues with punctilious politeness. Where is then the sexual difference, when the education has been the same? All the difference that I can discern, arises from the superior advantage of liberty, which enables the former to see more of life. . . .

Let it not be concluded that I wish to invert the order of things; I have already granted, that, from the constitution of their bodies, men seem to be designed by Providence to attain a greater degree of virtue. I speak collectively of the whole sex; but I see not the shadow of a reason to conclude that their virtues should differ in respect to their nature. In fact, how can they, if virtue has only one eternal standard? I must therefore, if I reason consequentially, as strenuously maintain that they have the same simple direction, as that there is a God.

It follows then that cunning should not be opposed to wisdom, little cares to great exertions, or insipid softness, varnished over with the name of gentleness, to that fortitude which grand views alone can inspire.

I shall be told that woman would then lose many of her peculiar graces, and the opinion of a well known poet might be quoted to refute my unqualified assertion. For Pope has said, in the name of the whole male sex,

'Yet ne'er so sure our passion to create,
'As when she touch'd the brink of all we hate.' [Moral Essays, II]

In what light this sally places men and women, I shall leave to the judicious to determine; meanwhile I shall content myself with observing, that I cannot discover why, unless they are mortal, females should always be degraded by being made subservient to love or lust.

To speak disrespectfully of love is, I know, high treason against sentiment and fine feelings; but I wish to speak the simple language of truth, and rather to address the head than the heart. To endeavour to reason love out of the world, would be to out Quixote Cervantes, and equally offend against common sense; but an endeavour to restrain this tumultuous passion, and to prove that it should not be allowed to dethrone superior powers, or to usurp the sceptre which the understanding should ever coolly wield, appears less wild.

Youth is the season for love in both sexes; but in those days of thoughtless enjoyment provision should be made for the more important years of life, when reflection takes place of sensation. But Rousseau, and most of the male writers who have followed his steps, have warmly inculcated that the whole tendency of female education ought to be directed to one point:—to render them pleasing.

Let me reason with the supporters of this opinion who have any knowledge of human nature, do they imagine that marriage can eradicate the habitude of life? The woman who has only been taught to please will soon find that her charms are oblique sunbeams, and that they cannot have much effect on her husband's heart when they are seen every day, when the summer is passed and gone. Will she then have sufficient native energy to look into herself for comfort, and cultivate her dormant faculties? or, is it not more rational to expect that she will try to please other men; and, in the emotions raised by the expectation of new conquests, endeavour to forget the mortification her love or pride has received? When the husband ceases to be a lover—and the time will inevitably come, her desire of pleasing will then grow languid, or become a spring of bitterness; and love, perhaps, the most evanescent of all passions, gives place to jealousy or vanity.

I now speak of women who are restrained by principle or prejudice; such women, though they would shrink from an intrigue with real abhorrence, yet, nevertheless, wish to be convinced by the homage of gallantry that they are cruelly neglected by their husbands; or, days and weeks are spent in dreaming of the happiness enjoyed by congenial souls till their health is undermined and their spirits broken by discontent. How then can the great art of pleasing be such a necessary study? it is only useful to a mistress; the chaste wife, and serious mother, should only consider her power to please as the polish of her virtues, and the affection of her husband as one of the comforts that render her task less difficult and her life happier.—But, whether she be loved or neglected, her first wish should be to make herself respectable, and not to rely for all her happiness on a being subject to like infirmities with herself. . . .

. . . avoiding, as I have hitherto done, any direct comparison of the two sexes collectively, or frankly acknowledging the inferiority of woman, according to the present appearance of things, I shall only insist that men have increased that inferiority till women are almost sunk below the standard of rational creatures. Let their faculties have room to unfold, and their virtues to gain strength, and then determine where the whole sex must stand in the intellectual scale. Yet let it be remembered, that for a small number of distinguished women I do not ask a place.

It is difficult for us purblind mortals to say to what height human discoveries and improvements may arrive when the gloom of despotism subsides, which makes us stumble at every step; but, when morality shall be settled on a more solid basis, then, without being gifted with a prophetic spirit, I will venture to predict that woman will be either the friend or slave of man. We shall not, as at present, doubt whether she is a moral agent, or the link which unites man with brutes. But, should it then appear, that like the brutes they were principally created for the use of man, he will let them patiently bite the bridle, and not mock them with empty praise; or, should their rationality be proved, he will not impede their improvement merely to gratify his sensual appetites. He will not, with all the graces of rhetoric, advise them to submit implicitly their understanding to the guidance of man. He will not, when he treats of the education of women, assert that they ought never to have the free use of reason, nor would he recommend cunning and dissimulation to beings who are acquiring, in like manner as himself, the virtues of humanity.

from Chapter III
THE SAME SUBJECT CONTINUED

Women, as well as despots, have now, perhaps, more power than they would have if the world, divided and subdivided into kingdoms and families, were governed by laws deduced from the exercise of reason; but in obtaining it, to carry on the comparison, their character is degraded, and licentiousness spread through the whole aggregate of society. The many become pedestal to the few. I, therefore, will venture to assert, that till women are more rationally educated, the progress of human virtue and improvement in knowledge must receive continual checks. And if it be granted that woman was not created merely to gratify the appetite of man, or to be the upper servant, who provides his meals and takes care of his linen, it must follow, that the first care of those mothers or fathers, who really attend to the education of females, should be, if not to strengthen the body, at least, not to destroy the constitution by mistaken notions of beauty and female excellence; nor should girls ever be allowed to imbibe the pernicious notion that a defect can, by any chemical process of reasoning, become an excellence. . . .

To preserve personal beauty, woman's glory! the limbs and faculties are cramped with worse than Chinese bands,* and the sedentary life which they are condemned to live, whilst boys frolic in the open air, weakens the muscles and relaxes the nerves.—As for Rousseau's remarks, which have since been echoed by several writers, that they have naturally, that is from their birth, independent of education, a fondness for dolls, dressing, and talking†—they are so puerile as not to merit a serious refutation. That a girl, condemned to sit for hours together listening to the idle chat of weak nurses, or to attend at her mother's toilet, will endeavour to join the conversation, is, indeed, very natural;

---

* A reference to the Chinese custom, only recently discontinued, of binding girls' feet so that they remain small and delicate.—Editor.

† "Even the tiniest little girls love finery. . . . The doll is the girl's special plaything; this shows her instinctive bent towards her life's work. . . . Women have ready tongues; they talk earlier, more easily, and more pleasantly than men. They are also said to talk more," *Émile.*—Editor.

and that she will imitate her mother or aunts, and amuse herself by adorning her lifeless doll, as they do in dressing her, poor innocent babe! is undoubtedly a most natural consequence. For men of the greatest abilities have seldom had sufficient strength to rise above the surrounding atmosphere; and, if the page of genius have always been blurred by the prejudices of the age, some allowance should be made for a sex, who, like kings, always see things through a false medium.

Pursuing these reflections, the fondness for dress, conspicuous in women, may be easily accounted for, without supposing it the result of a desire to please the sex on which they are dependent. The absurdity, in short, of supposing that a girl is naturally a coquette, and that a desire connected with the impulse of nature to propagate the species,* should appear even before an improper education has, by heating the imagination, called it forth prematurely, is so unphilosophical, that such a sagacious observer as Rousseau would not have adopted it, if he had not been accustomed to make reason give way to his desire of singularity, and truth to a favourite paradox. . . .

I have, probably, had an opportunity of observing more girls in their infancy than J. J. Rousseau—I can recollect my own feelings, and I have looked steadily around me; yet, so far from coinciding with him in opinion respecting the first dawn of the female character, I will venture to affirm, that a girl, whose spirits have not been damped by inactivity, or innocence tainted by false shame, will always be a romp, and the doll will never excite attention unless confinement allows her no alternative. Girls and boys, in short, would play harmlessly together, if the distinction of sex was not inculcated long before nature makes any difference.—I will go further, and affirm, as an indisputable fact, that most of the women, in the circle of my observation, who have acted like rational creatures, or shewn any vigour of intellect, have accidentally been allowed to run wild—as some of the elegant formers of the fair sex would insinuate. . . .

Birth, riches, and every extrinsic advantage that exalt a man above his fellows, without any mental exertion, sink him in reality below them. In proportion to his weakness, he is played upon by designing men, till the bloated monster has lost all traces of humanity. And that tribes of men, like flocks of sheep, should quietly follow such a leader, is a solecism that only a desire of present enjoyment and narrowness of understanding can solve. Educated in slavish dependence, and ener-

* "Woman is a coquette by profession, but her coquetry varies with her aims; let these aims be in accordance with those of nature, and a woman will receive a fitting education," *Émile*.—Editor.

Jean-Jacques Rousseau composing *Émile* in the valley of Montmorency.

vated by luxury and sloth, where shall we find men who will stand forth to assert the rights of man;—or claim the privilege of moral beings, who should have but one road to excellence? Slavery to monarchs and ministers, which the world will be long in freeing itself from, and whose deadly grasp stops the progress of the human mind, is not yet abolished.

Let not men then in the pride of power, use the same arguments that tyrannic kings and venal ministers have used, and fallaciously assert that woman ought to be subjected because she has always been so.—But, when man, governed by reasonable laws, enjoys his natural freedom, let him despise woman, if she do not share it with him; and, till that glorious period arrives, in descanting on the folly of the sex, let him not overlook his own. . . .

I here throw down my gauntlet, and deny the existence of sexual virtues, not excepting modesty. For man and woman, truth, if I understand the meaning of the word, must be the same; yet the fanciful female character, so prettily drawn by poets and novelists, demanding the sacrifice of truth and sincerity, virtue becomes a relative idea, having no other foundation than utility, and of that utility men pretend arbitrarily to judge, shaping it to their own convenience.

Women, I allow, may have different duties to fulfil; but they are *human* duties, and the principles that should regulate the discharge of them, I sturdily maintain, must be the same. . . .

In the superior ranks of life how seldom do we meet with a man of superior abilities, or even common acquirements? The reason appears to me clear, the state they are born in was an unnatural one. The human character has ever been formed by the employments the individual, or class, pursues; and if the faculties are not sharpened by necessity, they must remain obtuse. The argument may fairly be extended to women; for, seldom occupied by serious business, the pursuit of pleasure gives that insignificancy to their character which renders the society of the *great* so insipid. The same want of firmness, produced by a similar cause, forces them both to fly from themselves to noisy pleasures, and artificial passions, till vanity takes place of every social affection, and the characteristics of humanity can scarcely be discerned. Such are the blessings of civil governments, as they are at present organized, that wealth and female softness equally tend to debase mankind, and are produced by the same cause; but allowing women to be rational creatures, they should be incited to acquire virtues which they may call their own, for how can a rational being be ennobled by any thing that is not obtained by its *own* exertions?

from Chapter IV
OBSERVATIONS ON THE STATE
OF DEGRADATION TO WHICH WOMAN
IS REDUCED BY VARIOUS CAUSES

Pleasure is the business of woman's life, according to the present modification of society, and while it continues to be so, little can be expected from such weak beings. Inheriting, in a lineal descent from the first fair defect in nature,* the sovereignty of beauty, they have, to maintain their power, resigned the natural rights, which the exercise of reason might have procured them, and chosen rather to be short-lived queens than labour to obtain the sober pleasures that arise from equality. Exalted by their inferiority (this sounds like a contradiction), they constantly demand homage as women, though experience should teach them that the men who pride themselves upon paying this arbitrary insolent respect to the sex, with the most scrupulous exactness, are most inclined to tyrannize over, and despise, the very weakness they cherish. . . .

Ah! why do women, I write with affectionate solicitude, condescend to receive a degree of attention and respect from strangers, different from that reciprocation of civility which the dictates of humanity and the politeness of civilization authorise between man and man? And, why do they not discover, when 'in the noon of beauty's power,' that they are treated like queens only to be deluded by hollow respect, till they are led to resign, or not assume, their natural prerogatives? Confined then in cages like the feathered race, they have nothing to do but to plume themselves, and stalk with mock majesty from perch to perch. It is true they are provided with food and raiment, for which they neither toil nor spin; but health, liberty, and virtue, are given in exchange. But, where, amongst mankind, has been found sufficient strength of mind to enable a being to resign these adventitious prerogatives; one who, rising with the calm dignity of reason above opinion, dared to be proud of the privileges inherent in man? And it is vain to expect it whilst hereditary power chokes the affections and nips reason in the bud.

The passions of men have thus placed women on thrones, and, till mankind become more reasonable, it is to be feared that women will avail themselves of the power which they attain with the least exertion,

* Milton calls woman "this fair defect/Of nature," *Paradise Lost.*—Editor.

and which is the most indisputable. They will smile,—yes, they will smile, though told that—

> 'In beauty's empire is no mean,
> 'And woman, either slave or queen,
> 'Is quickly scorn'd when not ador'd.'
> ["Song" by Anna Laetitia Barbauld]

But the adoration comes first, and the scorn is not anticipated. . . .

I lament that women are systematically degraded by receiving the trivial attentions, which men think it manly to pay to the sex, when, in fact, they are insultingly supporting their own superiority. It is not condescension to bow to an inferior. So ludicrous, in fact, do these ceremonies appear to me, that I scarcely am able to govern my muscles, when I see a man start with eager, and serious solicitude, to lift a handkerchief, or shut a door, when the *lady* could have done it herself, had she only moved a pace or two.

A wild wish has just flown from my heart to my head, and I will not stifle it though it may excite a horse-laugh.—I do earnestly wish to see the distinction of sex confounded in society, unless where love animates the behaviour. For this distinction is, I am firmly persuaded, the foundation of the weakness of character ascribed to woman; is the cause why the understanding is neglected, whilst accomplishments are acquired with sedulous care: and the same cause accounts for their preferring the graceful before the heroic virtues. . . .

. . . women, in general, as well as the rich of both sexes, have acquired all the follies and vices of civilization, and missed the useful fruit. It is not necessary for me always to premise, that I speak of the condition of the whole sex, leaving exceptions out of the question. Their senses are inflamed, and their understandings neglected, consequently they become the prey of their senses, delicately termed sensibility, and are blown about by every momentary gust of feeling. Civilized women are, therefore, so weakened by false refinement, that, respecting morals, their condition is much below what it would be were they left in a state nearer to nature. Ever restless and anxious, their over exercised sensibility not only renders them uncomfortable themselves, but troublesome, to use a soft phrase, to others. All their thoughts turn on things calculated to excite emotion; and feeling, when they should reason, their conduct is unstable, and their opinions are wavering—not the wavering produced by deliberation or progressive views, but by contradictory emotions. By fits and starts they are warm

in many pursuits; yet this warmth, never concentrated into persever-
ance, soon exhausts itself; exhaled by its own heat, or meeting with
some other fleeting passion, to which reason has never given any specific gravity, neutrality ensues. Miserable, indeed, must be that being
whose cultivation of mind has only tended to inflame its passions! A distinction should be made between inflaming and strengthening them.
The passions thus pampered, whilst the judgment is left unformed,
what can be expected to ensue?—Undoubtedly, a mixture of madness
and folly!

This observation should not be confined to the *fair* sex; however,
at present, I only mean to apply it to them.

Novels, music, poetry, and gallantry, all tend to make women the
creatures of sensation, and their character is thus formed in the mould
of folly during the time they are acquiring accomplishments, the only
improvement they are excited, by their station in society, to acquire.
This overstretched sensibility naturally relaxes the other powers of the
mind, and prevents intellect from attaining that sovereignty which it
ought to attain to render a rational creature useful to others, and content with its own station: for the exercise of the understanding, as life
advances, is the only method pointed out by nature to calm the passions.

Satiety has a very different effect, and I have often been forcibly
struck by an emphatical description of damnation:—when the spirit is
represented as continually hovering with abortive eagerness round the
defiled body, unable to enjoy any thing without the organs of sense.
Yet, to their senses, are women made slaves, because it is by their sensibility that they obtain present power.

And will moralists pretend to assert, that this is the condition in
which one half of the human race should be encouraged to remain
with listless inactivity and stupid acquiescence? Kind instructors! what
were we created for? To remain, it may be said, innocent; they mean
in a state of childhood.—We might as well never have been born, unless it were necessary that we should be created to enable man to acquire the noble privilege of reason, the power of discerning good from
evil, whilst we lie down in the dust from whence we were taken, never
to rise again.—

It would be an endless task to trace the variety of meannesses, cares,
and sorrows, into which women are plunged by the prevailing opinion,
that they were created rather to feel than reason, and that all the power
they obtain, must be obtained by their charms and weakness:

'Fine by defect, and amiably weak!'*

* Pope wrote "Fine by defect, and delicately weak," *Moral Essays*, II.—Editor.

And, made by this amiable weakness entirely dependent, excepting what they gain by illicit sway, on man, not only for protection, but advice, is it surprising that, neglecting the duties that reason alone points out, and shrinking from trials calculated to strengthen their minds, they only exert themselves to give their defects a graceful covering, which may serve to heighten their charms in the eye of the voluptuary, though it sink them below the scale of moral excellence?

Fragile in every sense of the word, they are obliged to look up to man for every comfort. In the most trifling dangers they cling to their support, with parasitical tenacity, piteously demanding succour; and their *natural* protector extends his arm, or lifts up his voice, to guard the lovely trembler—from what? Perhaps the frown of an old cow, or the jump of a mouse; a rat, would be a serious danger. In the name of reason, and even common sense, what can save such beings from contempt; even though they be soft and fair? . . .

. . . highly as I respect marriage, as the foundation of almost every social virtue, I cannot avoid feeling the most lively compassion for those unfortunate females who are broken off from society, and by one error torn from all those affections and relationships that improve the heart and mind. It does not frequently even deserve the name of error; for many innocent girls become the dupes of a sincere, affectionate heart, and still more are, as it may emphatically be termed, *ruined* before they know the difference between virtue and vice:—and thus prepared by their education for infamy, they become infamous. Asylums and Magdalenes* are not the proper remedies for these abuses. It is justice, not charity, that is wanting in the world!

A woman who has lost her honour, imagines that she cannot fall lower, and as for recovering her former station, it is impossible; no exertion can wash this stain away. Losing thus every spur, and having no other means of support, prostitution becomes her only refuge, and the character is quickly depraved by circumstances over which the poor wretch has little power, unless she possesses an uncommon portion of sense and loftiness of spirit. Necessity never makes prostitution the business of men's lives; though numberless are the women who are thus rendered systematically vicious. This, however, arises, in a great degree, from the state of idleness in which women are educated, who are always taught to look up to man for a maintenance, and to consider their persons as the proper return for his exertions to support them. Meretricious airs, and the whole science of wantonness, have then a

* Homes for the reformation of prostitutes.—Editor.

more powerful stimulus than either appetite or vanity; and this remark gives force to the prevailing opinion, that with chastity all is lost that is respectable in woman. Her character depends on the observance of one virtue, though the only passion fostered in her heart—is love. Nay, the honour of a woman is not made even to depend on her will.

When Richardson* makes Clarissa tell Lovelace that he had robbed her of her honour, he must have had strange notions of honour and virtue.† For, miserable beyond all names of misery is the condition of a being, who could be degraded without its own consent!

from Chapter IX
OF THE PERNICIOUS EFFECTS WHICH ARISE FROM THE UNNATURAL DISTINCTIONS ESTABLISHED IN SOCIETY

From the respect paid to property flow, as from a poisoned fountain, most of the evils and vices which render this world such a dreary scene to the contemplative mind. For it is in the most polished society that noisome reptiles and venomous serpents lurk under the rank herbage; and there is voluptuousness pampered by the still sultry air, which relaxes every good disposition before it ripens into virtue.

One class presses on another; for all are aiming to procure respect on account of their property: and property, once gained, will procure the respect due only to talents and virtue. Men neglect the duties incumbent on man, yet are treated like demi-gods; religion is also separated from morality by a ceremonial veil, yet men wonder that the world is almost, literally speaking, a den of sharpers or oppressors.

There is a homely proverb, which speaks a shrewd truth, that whoever the devil finds idle he will employ. And what but habitual idleness can hereditary wealth and titles produce? For man is so constituted that he can only attain a proper use of his faculties by exercising them, and will not exercise them unless necessity, of some kind, first set the wheels in motion. Virtue likewise can only be acquired by the discharge of relative duties; but the importance of these sacred duties will scarcely be felt by the being who is cajoled out of his humanity by the flattery of sycophants. There must be more equality established in society, or

---

* Dr. [Edward] Young supports the same opinion, in his plays, when he talks of the misfortune that shunned the light of day.—Wollstonecraft.

† In Samuel Richardson's *Clarissa*, Lovelace rapes Clarissa; she subsequently dies. —Editor.

morality will never gain ground, and this virtuous equality will not rest firmly even when founded on a rock, if one half of mankind be chained to its bottom by fate, for they will be continually undermining it through ignorance or pride.

It is vain to expect virtue from women till they are, in some degree, independent of men; nay, it is vain to expect that strength of natural affection, which would make them good wives and mothers. Whilst they are absolutely dependent on their husbands they will be cunning, mean, and selfish, and the men who can be gratified by the fawning fondness of spaniel-like affection, have not much delicacy, for love is not to be bought, in any sense of the words, its silken wings are instantly shrivelled up when any thing beside a return in kind is sought. Yet whilst wealth enervates men; and women live, as it were, by their personal charms, how can we expect them to discharge those ennobling duties which equally require exertion and self-denial. Hereditary property sophisticates the mind, and the unfortunate victims to it, if I may so express myself, swathed from their birth, seldom exert the locomotive faculty of body or mind; and, thus viewing every thing through one medium, and that a false one, they are unable to discern in what true merit and happiness consist. False, indeed, must be the light when the drapery of situation hides the man, and makes him stalk in masquerade, dragging from one scene of dissipation to another the nerveless limbs that hang with stupid listlessness, and rolling round the vacant eye which plainly tells us that there is no mind at home.

I mean, therefore, to infer that the society is not properly organized which does not compel men and women to discharge their respective duties, by making it the only way to acquire that countenance from their fellow-creatures, which every human being wishes some way to attain. The respect, consequently, which is paid to wealth and mere personal charms, is a true north-east blast, that blights the tender blossoms of affection and virtue. Nature has wisely attached affections to duties, to sweeten toil, and to give that vigour to the exertions of reason which only the heart can give. But, the affection which is put on merely because it is the appropriated insignia of a certain character, when its duties are not fulfilled, is one of the empty compliments which vice and folly are obliged to pay to virtue and the real nature of things.

To illustrate my opinion, I need only observe, that when a woman is admired for her beauty, and suffers herself to be so far intoxicated by the admiration she receives, as to neglect to discharge the indispensable duty of a mother, she sins against herself by neglecting to cultivate an affection that would equally tend to make her useful and happy. True happiness, I mean all the contentment, and virtuous satisfaction, that can be snatched in this imperfect state, must arise from well regulated affections; and an affection includes a duty. Men are not aware of the misery they cause, and the vicious weakness they cherish, by only inciting women to render themselves pleasing; they do not consider that they thus make natural and artificial duties clash, by sacrificing the comfort and respectability of a woman's life to voluptuous notions of beauty, when in nature they all harmonize. . . .

Women . . . must be considered as only the wanton solace of men, when they become so weak in mind and body, that they cannot exert themselves, unless to pursue some frothy pleasure, or to invent some frivolous fashion. What can be a more melancholy sight to a thinking mind, than to look into the numerous carriages that drive helter-skelter about this metropolis in a morning full of pale-faced creatures who are flying from themselves. I have often wished, with Dr. Johnson, to place some of them in a little shop with half a dozen children looking up to their languid countenances for support. I am much mistaken, if some latent vigour would not soon give health and spirit to their eyes, and some lines drawn by the exercise of reason on the blank cheeks, which before were only undulated by dimples, might restore lost dignity to the character, or rather enable it to attain the true dignity of its nature. Virtue is not to be acquired even by speculation, much less by the negative supineness that wealth naturally generates.

Besides, when poverty is more disgraceful than even vice, is not morality cut to the quick? Still to avoid misconstruction, though I consider that women in the common walks of life are called to fulfil the duties of wives and mothers, by religion and reason, I cannot help lamenting that women of a superiour cast have not a road open by which they can pursue more extensive plans of usefulness and independence. I may excite laughter, by dropping an hint, which I mean to pursue, some future time, for I really think that women ought to have representatives, instead of being arbitrarily governed without having any direct share allowed them in the deliberations of government.

But, as the whole system of representation is now, in this country, only a convenient handle for despotism, they need not complain, for they are as well represented as a numerous class of hard working mechanics, who pay for the support of royalty when they can scarcely stop their children's mouths with bread. How are they represented whose very sweat supports the splendid stud of an heir apparent, or varnishes the chariot of some female favourite who looks down on shame? Taxes on the very necessaries of life, enable an endless tribe of idle princes and princesses to pass with stupid pomp before a gaping crowd, who almost worship the very parade which costs them so dear. This is mere gothic grandeur, something like the barbarous useless parade of having sentinels on horseback at Whitehall,* which I could never view without a mixture of contempt and indignation.

How strangely must the mind be sophisticated when this sort of state impresses it! But, till these monuments of folly are levelled by virtue, similar follies will leaven the whole mass. For the same character, in some degree, will prevail in the aggregate of society: and the refinements of luxury, or the vicious repinings of envious poverty, will equally banish virtue from society, considered as the characteristic of that society, or only allow it to appear as one of the stripes of the harlequin coat, worn by the civilized man.

In the superiour ranks of life, every duty is done by deputies, as if duties could ever be waved, and the vain pleasures which consequent idleness forces the rich to pursue, appear so enticing to the next rank, that the numerous scramblers for wealth sacrifice every thing to tread on their heels. The most sacred trusts are then considered as sinecures, because they were procured by interest, and only sought to enable a man to keep *good company*. Women, in particular, all want to be ladies. Which is simply to have nothing to do, but listlessly to go they scarcely care where, for they cannot tell what.

But what have women to do in society? I may be asked, but to loiter with easy grace; surely you would not condemn them all to suckle fools and chronicle small beer! No. Women might certainly study the art of healing, and be physicians as well as nurses. And midwifery, decency seems to allot to them, though I am afraid the word midwife, in our dictionaries, will soon give place to *accoucheur*,† and one proof of the former delicacy of the sex be effaced from the language.

They might, also, study politics, and settle their benevolence on the broadest basis; for the reading of history will scarcely be more useful than the perusal of romances, if read as mere biography; if the character of the times, the political improvements, arts, &c. be not observed. In short, if it be not considered as the history of man; and not of particular men, who filled a niche in the temple of fame, and dropped into the black rolling stream of time, that silently sweeps all before it, into the shapeless void called—eternity.—For shape, can it be called, 'that shape hath none?'

Business of various kinds, they might likewise pursue, if they were educated in a more orderly manner, which might save many from

* The Horse Guards who mount guard before the government offices of Whitehall.—Editor.

† A male physician dealing with childbirth.—Editor.

common and legal prostitution. Women would not then marry for a support, as men accept of places under government, and neglect the implied duties; nor would an attempt to earn their own subsistence, a most laudable one! sink them almost to the level of those poor abandoned creatures who live by prostitution. For are not milliners and mantua-makers* reckoned the next class? The few employments open to women, so far from being liberal, are menial; and when a superiour education enables them to take charge of the education of children as governesses, they are not treated like the tutors of sons, though even clerical tutors are not always treated in a manner calculated to render them respectable in the eyes of their pupils, to say nothing of the private comfort of the individual. But as women educated like gentlewomen, are never designed for the humiliating situation which necessity sometimes forces them to fill; these situations are considered in the light of a degradation; and they know little of the human heart, who need to be told, that nothing so painfully sharpens sensibility as such a fall in life.

Some of these women might be restrained from marrying by a proper spirit or delicacy, and others may not have had it in their power to escape in this pitiful way from servitude; is not that government then very defective, and very unmindful of the happiness of one half of its members, that does not provide for honest, independent women, by encouraging them to fill respectable stations?

from Chapter XI
DUTY TO PARENTS

A great proportion of the misery that wanders, in hideous forms, around the world, is allowed to rise from the negligence of parents; and still these are the people who are most tenacious of what they term a natural right, though it be subversive of the birth-right of man, the right of acting according to the direction of his own reason.

I have already very frequently had occasion to observe, that vicious or indolent people are always eager to profit by enforcing arbitrary privileges; and, generally, in the same proportion as they neglect the discharge of the duties which alone render the privileges reasonable. This is at the bottom a dictate of common sense, or the instinct of self-defence, peculiar to ignorant weakness; resembling that instinct, which makes a fish muddy the water it swims in to elude its enemy, instead of boldly facing it in the clear stream. . . .

Why should the minds of children be warped as they just begin to

* Dressmakers.—Editor.

expand, only to favour the indolence of parents, who insist on a privilege without being willing to pay the price fixed by nature? I have before had occasion to observe, that a right always includes a duty, and I think it may, likewise, fairly be inferred, that they forfeit the right, who do not fulfil the duty.

It is easier, I grant, to command than reason; but it does not follow from hence that children cannot comprehend the reason why they are made to do certain things habitually: for, from a steady adherence to a few simple principles of conduct flows that salutary power which a judicious parent gradually gains over a child's mind. And this power becomes strong indeed, if tempered by an even display of affection brought home to the child's heart. For, I believe, as a general rule, it must be allowed that the affection which we inspire always resembles that we cultivate; so that natural affections, which have been supposed almost distinct from reason, may be found more nearly connected with judgment than is commonly allowed. Nay, as another proof of the necessity of cultivating the female understanding, it is but just to observe, that the affections seem to have a kind of animal capriciousness when they merely reside in the heart.

It is the irregular exercise of parental authority that first injures the mind, and to these irregularities girls are more subject than boys. The will of those who never allow their will to be disputed, unless they happen to be in a good humour, when they relax proportionally, is almost always unreasonable. To elude this arbitrary authority girls very early learn the lessons which they afterwards practise on their husbands; for I have frequently seen a little sharp-faced miss rule a whole family, excepting that now and then mamma's anger will burst out of some accidental cloud;—either her hair was ill dressed,* or she had lost more money at cards, the night before, than she was willing to own to her husband; or some such moral cause of anger.

After observing sallies of this kind, I have been led into a melancholy train of reflection respecting females, concluding that when their first affection must lead them astray, or make their duties clash till they rest on mere whims and customs, little can be expected from them as they advance in life. How indeed can an instructor remedy this evil? for to teach them virtue on any solid principle is to teach them to despise their parents. Children cannot, ought not, to be taught to make allowance for the faults of their parents, because every such allowance

* "I myself heard a little girl once say to a servant, 'My mamma has been scolding me finely this morning, because her hair was not dressed to please her.' Though this remark was pert, it was just. And what respect could a girl acquire for such a parent without doing violence to reason?'—Wollstonecraft.

weakens the force of reason in their minds, and makes them still more indulgent to their own. It is one of the most sublime virtues of maturity that leads us to be severe with respect to ourselves, and forbearing to others; but children should only be taught the simple virtues, for if they begin too early to make allowance for human passions and manners, they wear off the fine edge of the criterion by which they should regulate their own, and become unjust in the same proportion as they grow indulgent.

The affections of children, and weak people, are always selfish; they love their relatives, because they are beloved by them, and not on account of their virtues. Yet, till esteem and love are blended together in the first affection, and reason made the foundation of the first duty, morality will stumble at the threshold. But, till society is very differently constituted, parents, I fear, will still insist on being obeyed, because they will be obeyed, and constantly endeavour to settle that power on a Divine right which will not bear the investigation of reason.

from Chapter XII
ON NATIONAL EDUCATION

True taste is ever the work of the understanding employed in observing natural effects; and till women have more understanding, it is vain to expect them to possess domestic taste. Their lively senses will ever be at work to harden their hearts, and the emotions struck out of them will continue to be vivid and transitory, unless a proper education store their mind with knowledge.

It is the want of domestic taste, and not the acquirement of knowledge, that takes women out of their families, and tears the smiling babe from the breast that ought to afford it nourishment. Women have been allowed to remain in ignorance, and slavish dependence, many, very many years, and still we hear of nothing but their fondness of pleasure and sway, their preference of rakes and soldiers, their childish attachment to toys, and the vanity that makes them value accomplishments more than virtues.

History brings forward a fearful catalogue of the crimes which their cunning has produced, when the weak slaves have had sufficient address to over-reach their masters. In France, and in how many other countries, have men been the luxurious despots, and women the crafty ministers?—Does this prove that ignorance and dependence domesticate them? Is not their folly the by-word of the libertines, who relax in their society; and do not men of sense continually lament that an immoderate fondness for dress and dissipation carries the mother of a family for ever from home? Their hearts have not been debauched by knowledge, or their minds led astray by scientific pursuits; yet, they do not fulfil the peculiar duties which as women they are called upon by nature to fulfil. On the contrary, the state of warfare which subsists between the sexes, makes them employ those wiles, that often frustrate the more open designs of force.

When, therefore, I call women slaves, I mean in a political and civil sense; for, indirectly they obtain too much power, and are debased by their exertions to obtain illicit sway.

Let an enlightened nation* then try what effect reason would have to bring them back to nature, and their duty; and allowing them to share the advantages of education and government with man, see whether they will become better, as they grow wiser and become free. They cannot be injured by the experiment; for it is not in the power of man to render them more insignificant than they are at present.

To render this practicable, day schools, for particular ages, should be established by government, in which boys and girls might be educated together. The school for the younger children, from five to nine years of age, ought to be absolutely free and open to all classes.† A sufficient number of masters should also be chosen by a select committee, in each parish, to whom any complaint of negligence, &c. might be made, if signed by six of the children's parents. . . .

. . . to prevent any of the distinctions of vanity, [the children] should be dressed alike, and all obliged to submit to the same discipline, or leave the school. The school-room ought to be surrounded by a large piece of ground, in which the children might be usefully exercised, for at this age they should not be confined to any sedentary employment for more than an hour at a time. But these relaxations might all be rendered a part of elementary education, for many things improve and amuse the senses, when introduced as a kind of show, to the principles of which, dryly laid down, children would turn a deaf ear. For instance, botany, mechanics, and astronomy. Reading, writing, arithmetic, natural history, and some simple experiments in natural philosophy, might fill up the day; but these pursuits should never encroach on gymnastic plays in the open air. The elements of religion, history, the history of man, and politics, might also be taught by conversations, in the socratic form.

After the age of nine, girls and boys, intended for domestic employ-

---

* France.—Wollstonecraft.

† Treating this part of the subject, I have borrowed some hints from a very sensible pamphlet, written by the late bishop of Autun [Talleyrand] on Public Education. —Wollstonecraft.

ments, or mechanical trades, ought to be removed to other schools, and receive instruction, in some measure appropriated to the destination of each individual, the two sexes being still together in the morning; but in the afternoon, the girls should attend a school, where plain-work, mantua-making, millinery, &c. would be their employment.

The young people of superior abilities, or fortune, might now be taught, in another school, the dead and living languages, the elements of science, and continue the study of history and politics, on a more extensive scale, which would not exclude polite literature.

Girls and boys still together? I hear some readers ask: yes. And I should not fear any other consequence than that some early attachment might take place; which, whilst it had the best effect on the moral character of the young people, might not perfectly agree with the views of the parents, for it will be a long time, I fear, before the world will be so far enlightened that parents, only anxious to render their children virtuous, shall allow them to choose companions for life themselves.

Besides, this would be a sure way to promote early marriages, and from early marriages the most salutary physical and moral effects naturally flow. What a different character does a married citizen assume from the selfish coxcomb, who lives, but for himself, and who is often afraid to marry lest he should not be able to live in a certain style. Great emergencies excepted, which would rarely occur in a society of which equality was the basis, a man can only be prepared to discharge the duties of public life, by the habitual practice of those inferiour ones which form the man. . . .

I have already inveighed against the custom of confining girls to their needle, and shutting them out from all political and civil employments; for by thus narrowing their minds they are rendered unfit to fulfil the peculiar duties which nature has assigned them.

Only employed about the little incidents of the day, they necessarily grow up cunning. My very soul has often sickened at observing the sly tricks practised by women to gain some foolish thing on which their silly hearts were set. Not allowed to dispose of money, or call any thing their own, they learn to turn the market penny; or, should a husband offend, by staying from home, or give rise to some emotions of jealousy—a new gown, or any pretty bawble, smooths Juno's angry brow.*

But these *littlenesses* would not degrade their character, if women were led to respect themselves, if political and moral subjects were opened to them; and, I will venture to affirm, that this is the only way

---

* Juno, wife of Jupiter, degenerated in mythology from the powerful goddess to the jealous, nagging wife.—Editor.

to make them properly attentive to their domestic duties.—An active mind embraces the whole circle of its duties, and finds time enough for all. It is not, I assert, a bold attempt to emulate masculine virtues; it is not the enchantment of literary pursuits, or the steady investigation of scientific subjects, that leads women astray from duty. No, it is indolence and vanity—the love of pleasure and the love of sway, that will reign paramount in an empty mind. I say empty emphatically, because the education which women now receive scarcely deserves the name. For the little knowledge that they are led to acquire, during the important years of youth, is merely relative to accomplishments; and accomplishments without a bottom, for unless the understanding be cultivated, superficial and monotonous is every grace. Like the charms of a made up face, they only strike the senses in a crowd; but at home, wanting mind, they want variety. The consequence is obvious; in gay scenes of dissipation we meet the artificial mind and face, for those who fly from solitude dread, next to solitude, the domestic circle; not having it in their power to amuse or interest, they feel their own insignificance, or find nothing to amuse or interest themselves. . . .

Make [women] free, and they will quickly become wise and virtuous, as men become more so; for the improvement must be mutual, or the injustice which one half of the human race are obliged to submit to, retorting on their oppressors, the virtue of men will be worm-eaten by the insect whom he keeps under his feet.

Let men take their choice, man and woman were made for each other, though not to become one being;* and if they will not improve women, they will deprave them!

I speak of the improvement and emancipation of the whole sex, for I know that the behaviour of a few women, who, by accident, or following a strong bent of nature, have acquired a portion of knowledge superiour to that of the rest of their sex, has often been overbearing; but there have been instances of women who, attaining knowledge, have not discarded modesty, nor have they always pedantically appeared to despise the ignorance which they laboured to disperse in their own

---

* Wollstonecraft criticized the kind of thinking that subsumed the woman into the man after marriage. It is well illustrated by William Blackstone, an immensely influential legal commentator of the eighteenth century, who believed that a woman forfeited her legal identity after marrying: "By marriage, the husband and the wife are one person in law; that is, the very being or legal existence of the woman is suspended during the marriage, or at least is incorporated and consolidated into that of the husband; under whose wing, protection, and cover, she performs everything," *Commentaries on the Laws of England.*—Editor.

minds. The exclamations then which any advice respecting female learning, commonly produces, especially from pretty women, often arise from envy. When they chance to see that even the lustre of their eyes, and the flippant sportiveness of refined coquetry will not always secure them attention, during a whole evening, should a woman of a more cultivated understanding endeavour to give a rational turn to the conversation, the common source of consolation is, that such women seldom get husbands. What arts have I not seen silly women use to interrupt by *flirtation*, a very significant word to describe such a manoeuvre, a rational conversation which made the men forget that they were pretty women.

But, allowing what is very natural to man, that the possession of rare abilities is really calculated to excite over-weening pride, disgusting in both men and women—in what a state of inferiority must the female faculties have rusted when such a small portion of knowledge as those women attained, who have sneeringly been termed learned women, could be singular?—Sufficiently so to puff up the possessor, and excite envy in her contemporaries, and some of the other sex. Nay, has not a little rationality exposed many women to the severest censure? I advert to well known facts, for I have frequently heard women ridiculed, and every little weakness exposed, only because they adopted the advice of some medical men, and deviated from the beaten track in their mode of treating their infants.* I have actually heard this barbarous aversion to innovation carried still further, and a sensible woman stigmatized as an unnatural mother, who has thus been wisely solicitous to preserve the health of her children, when in the midst of her care she has lost one by some of the casualties of infancy, which no prudence can ward off. Her acquaintance have observed, that this was the consequence of new-fangled notions—the new-fangled notions of ease and cleanliness. And those who pretending to experience, though they have long adhered to prejudices that have, according to the opinion of the most sagacious physicians, thinned the human race, almost rejoiced at the disaster that gave a kind of sanction to prescription.

Indeed, if it were only on this account, the national education of women is of the utmost consequence, for what a number of human sacrifices are made to that moloch prejudice! And in how many ways are children destroyed by the lasciviousness of man? The want of natural affection, in many women, who are drawn from their duty by the admiration of men, and the ignorance of others, render the infancy of

---

* Probably an allusion to women who suckled their babies instead of employing wet-nurses.—Editor.

man a much more perilous state than that of brutes; yet men are unwilling to place women in situations proper to enable them to acquire
sufficient understanding to know how even to nurse their babes.

So forcibly does this truth strike me, that I would rest the whole
tendency of my reasoning upon it, for whatever tends to incapacitate
the maternal character, takes woman out of her sphere. . . .

In public schools women, to guard against the errors of ignorance,
should be taught the elements of anatomy and medicine, not only to
enable them to take proper care of their own health, but to make them
rational nurses of their infants, parents, and husbands; for the bills of
mortality* are swelled by the blunders of self-willed old women, who
give nostrums of their own without knowing any thing of the human
frame. It is likewise proper only in a domestic view, to make women
acquainted with the anatomy of the mind, by allowing the sexes to associate together in every pursuit; and by leading them to observe the
progress of the human understanding in the improvement of the sciences and arts; never forgetting the science of morality, or the study of
the political history of mankind.

A man has been termed a microcosm; and every family might also
be called a state. States, it is true, have mostly been governed by arts
that disgrace the character of man; and the want of a just constitution,
and equal laws, have so perplexed the notions of the worldly wise, that
they more than question the reasonableness of contending for the rights
of humanity. Thus morality, polluted in the national reservoir, sends
off streams of vice to corrupt the constituent parts of the body politic;
but should more noble, or rather, more just principles regulate the laws,
which ought to be the government of society, and not those who exe-
cute them, duty might become the rule of private conduct.

Besides, by the exercise of their bodies and minds women would
acquire that mental activity so necessary in the maternal character,
united with the fortitude that distinguishes steadiness of conduct from
the obstinate perverseness of weakness. For it is dangerous to advise the
indolent to be steady, because they instantly become rigorous, and to
save themselves trouble, punish with severity faults that the patient
fortitude of reason might have prevented.

But fortitude presupposes strength of mind; and is strength of mind
to be acquired by indolent acquiescence? by asking advice instead of
exerting the judgment? by obeying through fear, instead of practising
the forbearance, which we all stand in need of ourselves?—The con-

* Lists of deaths in a parish.—Editor.

clusion which I wish to draw, is obvious; make women rational creatures, and free citizens, and they will quickly become good wives, and
mothers; that is—if men do not neglect the duties of husbands and
fathers.*

from Chapter XIII
SOME INSTANCES OF THE FOLLY
WHICH THE IGNORANCE OF WOMEN
GENERATES; WITH CONCLUDING
REFLECTIONS ON THE MORAL
IMPROVEMENT THAT A REVOLUTION
IN FEMALE MANNERS MIGHT
NATURALLY BE EXPECTED
TO PRODUCE

Moralists have unanimously agreed, that unless virtue be nursed by
liberty, it will never attain due strength—and what they say of man I
extend to mankind, insisting that in all cases morals must be fixed on
immutable principles; and, that the being cannot be termed rational or
virtuous, who obeys any authority, but that of reason.

To render women truly useful members of society, I argue that they
should be led, by having their understandings cultivated on a large
scale, to acquire a rational affection for their country, founded on
knowledge, because it is obvious that we are little interested about what
we do not understand. And to render this general knowledge of due
importance, I have endeavoured to shew that private duties are never
properly fulfilled unless the understanding enlarges the heart; and that
public virtue is only an aggregate of private. But, the distinctions established in society undermine both, by beating out the solid gold of virtue,
till it becomes only the tinsel-covering of vice; for whilst wealth renders
a man more respectable than virtue, wealth will be sought before virtue; and, whilst women's persons are caressed, when a childish simper
shews an absence of mind—the mind will lie fallow. Yet, true voluptuousness must proceed from the mind—for what can equal the sensations produced by mutual affection, supported by mutual respect? What
are the cold, or feverish caresses of appetite, but sin embracing death,
compared with the modest overflowings of a pure heart and exalted
imagination? Yes, let me tell the libertine of fancy when he despises
understanding in woman—that the mind, which he disregards, gives

---

* In *Émile* Rousseau made the rather different point: "When women become good
mothers, men will be good husbands and fathers."—Editor.

life to the enthusiastic affection from which rapture, short-lived as it is, alone can flow! And, that, without virtue, a sexual attachment must expire, like a tallow candle in the socket, creating intolerable disgust. To prove this, I need only observe, that men who have wasted great part of their lives with women, and with whom they have sought for pleasure with eager thirst, entertain the meanest opinion of the sex.— Virtue, true refiner of joy!—if foolish men were to fright thee from earth, in order to give loose to all their appetites without a check—some sensual wight of taste would scale the heavens to invite thee back, to give a zest to pleasure!

That women at present are by ignorance rendered foolish or vicious, is, I think, not to be disputed; and, that the most salutary effects tending to improve mankind might be expected from a REVOLUTION in female manners, appears, at least, with a face of probability, to rise out of the observation. For as marriage has been termed the parent of those endearing charities which draw man from the brutal herd, the corrupting intercourse that wealth, idleness, and folly, produce between the sexes, is more universally injurious to morality than all the other vices of mankind collectively considered. To adulterous lust the most sacred duties are sacrificed, because before marriage, men, by a promiscuous intimacy with women, learned to consider love as a selfish gratification —learned to separate it not only from esteem, but from the affection merely built on habit, which mixes a little humanity with it. Justice and friendship are also set at defiance, and that purity of taste is vitiated which would naturally lead a man to relish an artless display of affection rather than affected airs. But that noble simplicity of affection, which dares to appear unadorned, has few attractions for the libertine, though it be the charm, which by cementing the matrimonial tie, secures to the pledges of a warmer passion the necessary parental attention; for children will never be properly educated till friendship subsists between parents. Virtue flies from a house divided against itself—and a whole legion of devils take up their residence there.

The affection of husbands and wives cannot be pure when they have so few sentiments in common, and when so little confidence is established at home, as must be the case when their pursuits are so different. That intimacy from which tenderness should flow, will not, cannot subsist between the vicious.

Contending, therefore, that the sexual distinction which men have so warmly insisted upon, is arbitrary, I have dwelt on an observation, that several sensible men, with whom I have conversed on the subject, allowed to be well founded; and it is simply this, that the little chastity to be found amongst men, and consequent disregard of modesty, tend to degrade both sexes; and further, that the modesty of women, characterized as such, will often be only the artful veil of wantonness instead of being the natural reflection of purity, till modesty be universally respected.

From the tyranny of man, I firmly believe, the greater number of female follies proceed; and the cunning, which I allow makes at present a part of their character, I likewise have repeatedly endeavoured to prove, is produced by oppression. . . .

Asserting the rights which women in common with men ought to contend for, I have not attempted to extenuate their faults; but to prove them to be the natural consequence of their education and station in society. If so, it is reasonable to suppose that they will change their character, and correct their vices and follies, when they are allowed to be free in a physical, moral, and civil sense.*

Let woman share the rights and she will emulate the virtues of man; for she must grow more perfect when emancipated, or justify the authority that chains such a weak being to her duty.—If the latter, it will be expedient to open a fresh trade with Russia for whips; a present which a father should always make to his son-in-law on his wedding day, that a husband may keep his whole family in order by the same means; and without any violation of justice reign, wielding this sceptre, sole master of his house, because he is the only being in it who has reason:—the divine, indefeasible earthly sovereignty breathed into man by the Master of the universe. Allowing this position, women have not any inherent rights to claim; and, by the same rule, their duties vanish, for rights and duties are inseparable.

Be just then, O ye men of understanding! and mark not more severely what women do amiss, than the vicious tricks of the horse or the ass for whom ye provide provender—and allow her the privileges of ignorance, to whom ye deny the rights of reason, or ye will be worse than Egyptian task-masters, expecting virtue where nature has not given understanding!

---

* I had further enlarged on the advantages which might reasonably be expected to result from an improvement in female manners, towards the general reformation of society; but it appeared to me that such reflections would more properly close the last volume.—Wollstonecraft. This volume was never written.—Editor.

Review of Catherine Macaulay's

Letters on Education

This review appeared in the November 1790 issue of the *Analytical Review*. In it Wollstonecraft quotes extensively from *Letters on Education* (1790), emphasizing its pious and humanitarian ideas and applauding its melancholy picture of female education.

Catherine Macaulay (1731–1791) was a famous and notorious woman in her time. She wrote histories, topical political works, and educational manuals, among which were *The History of England*, published in eight volumes between 1763 and 1783, and *Letters on Education*. Her works and liberal principles gained her much attention, both hostile and admiring; for Dr. Johnson she was argumentative and insufficiently feminine, while for Mary Hays her talent and courage were exemplary. In *A Vindication of the Rights of Woman* Mary Wollstonecraft described her glowingly as "the woman of the greatest abilities, undoubtedly, that this country ever produced."

Late in life, Macaulay shocked public opinion by marrying a man twenty-six years her junior; her literary reputation seems to have declined with her personal one. She died in 1791, just before the publication of *The Rights of Woman*.

'MORALS MUST be taught on immutable principles.' From which position Mrs. M[acaulay] infers—'That true wisdom, which is never found at variance with rectitude, is as useful to women as to men; because it is necessary to the highest degree of happiness, which can never exist with ignorance.' Again, 'it would be paying you a bad compliment, were I to answer all the frivolous objections which prejudice has framed against the giving a learned education to women; for I know of no learning, worth having, that does not tend to free the mind from error, and enlarge our stock of useful knowledge.'

No characteristic difference in sex. The observations on this subject might have been carried much farther, if Mrs. M[acaulay]'s object had not been a general system of education.

'The situation and education of women,' she observes, 'is precisely that which must necessarily tend to corrupt and debilitate both the powers of mind and body. From a false notion of beauty and delicacy, their system of nerves is depraved before they come out of their nursery; and this kind of depravity has more influence over the mind, and consequently over morals, than is commonly apprehended. But it would be well if such causes only acted towards the debasement of the sex; their moral education is, if possible, more absurd than their physical. The principles and nature of virtue, which is never properly explained to boys, is kept quite a mystery to girls. They are told indeed, that they must abstain from those vices which are contrary to their personal happiness, or they will be regarded as criminals, both by God and man; but all the higher parts of rectitude, every thing that ennobles our being, and that renders us innoxious and useful, is either not taught, or is taught in such a manner as to leave no proper impression on the mind. This is so obvious a truth, that the defects of female education have ever been a fruitful topic of declamation for the moralist; but not one of this class of writers have laid down any judicious rules for amendment.'

Coquetry. Its baneful effects on the moral character of women, are explained with great perspicuity.

Flattery.—Chastity.—Male Rakes. The reflections on female chastity are just; but they required further explanation; for till the minds of women are more enlarged, we should not weaken the salutary prejudices which serve as a substitute, a weak one we own, for rational principles. . . .

[*Letters on Education*], which we warmly recommend to parents, adds new lustre to Mrs. M[acaulay]'s character as an historian and a moralist, and displays a degree of sound reason and profound thought which either through defective organs, or a mistaken education, seldom appears in female productions.

Part III

Works of Commentary

The selections in "Works of Commentary" are taken primarily from Wollstonecraft's writings on France and Scandinavia. The letter to her publisher, Joseph Johnson, the "Letter on the Present Character of the French Nation," and *An Historical and Moral View of the Origin and Progress of the French Revolution* follow her shifting attitudes toward the French nation and the Revolution; they also record her struggle to reaffirm her political faith in humanity. *Letters Written . . . in Sweden, Norway, and Denmark*, her work on Scandinavia, continues her statement of political faith in France and all countries, and ratifies her belief in the significance of every human being, from Swedish servant girls to the Hanoverian princess Caroline Matilda. The work speaks eloquently of Wollstonecraft's love of nature, her belief in its healing power and in the mind's ability to expand through its contemplation. Nature and the aesthetic appreciation of humanity form the subject of the two final selections: "On Poetry and Our Relish for the Beauties of Nature" and the paragraphs from "Hints."

Although the works in this section differ in many ways in interest and theme, they are related in time; they were probably written during the same years, between 1792 and 1797, and they are among her final literary works. They reflect their late date; in them Wollstonecraft shows the effect of her sorrowful period with Gilbert Imlay and the testing of the rationalist and imaginative theories she had earlier held on trust. The works are her most mature reflections on the questions of society and progress, life and death.

Letter to Joseph Johnson

The work is a personal letter written to Joseph Johnson from Paris in December 1792, immediately after Wollstonecraft arrived in the city. It describes the passing of Louis XVI to his trial, although Wollstonecraft has him going to his death. Perhaps she was confused or perhaps she anticipated the outcome of the trial. The letter was first published in *Posthumous Works* in 1798.

[Paris, December 26, 1792.]

I SHOULD immediately on the receipt of your letter, my dear friend, have thanked you for your punctuality, for it highly gratified me, had I not wished to wait till I could tell you that this day was not stained with blood. Indeed the prudent precautions taken by the National Convention to prevent a tumult, made me suppose that the dogs of faction would not dare to bark, much less to bite, however true to their scent; and I was not mistaken; for the citizens, who were all called out, are returning home with composed countenances, shouldering their arms. About nine o'clock this morning, the king passed by my window, moving silently along (excepting now and then a few strokes on the drum, which rendered the stillness more awful) through empty streets, surrounded by the national guards, who, clustering round the carriage, seemed to deserve their name. The inhabitants flocked to their windows, but the casements were all shut, not a voice was heard, nor did I see any thing like an insulting gesture.—For the first time since I entered France, I bowed to the majesty of the people, and respected the propriety of behaviour so perfectly in unison with my own feelings. I can scarcely tell you why, but an association of ideas made the tears flow insensibly from my eyes, when I saw Louis sitting, with more dignity than I expected from his character, in a hackney coach, going to meet death, where so many of his race have triumphed. My fancy instantly brought Louis XIV before me, entering the capital with all his pomp, after one of the victories most flattering to his pride, only to see the sunshine of prosperity overshadowed by the sublime gloom of misery. I have been alone ever since; and, though my mind is calm, I cannot dismiss the lively images that have filled my imagination all the day.—Nay, do not smile, but pity me; for, once or twice, lifting my eyes from the paper, I have seen eyes glare through a glass-door opposite my chair and bloody hands shook at me. Not the distant sound of a footstep can I hear.—My apartments are remote from those of the servants, the only persons who sleep with me in an immense hotel, one folding door opening after another.*—I wish I had even kept the cat with me!—I want to see something alive; death in so many frightful shapes has taken hold of my fancy.—I am going to bed—and, for the first time in my life, I cannot put out the candle.

* Wollstonecraft had arranged to stay with a French family in Paris. She found them out of the city when she arrived and she had to stay in their house without them. —Editor.

"Letter on the Present Character of the French Nation"

The work was written early in 1793 and sent to Joseph Johnson for publication. It was intended as the first of a series of letters from France detailing events and commenting on them. Johnson must have sensed that its despair was a passing phase and he did not publish the work until after Wollstonecraft's death, when it appeared in *Posthumous Works*.

BEFORE I CAME to France, I cherished, you know, an opinion, that strong virtues might exist with the polished manners produced by the progress of civilization; and I even anticipated the epoch, when, in the course of improvement, men would labour to become virtuous, without being goaded on by misery. But now, the perspective of the golden age, fading before the attentive eye of observation, almost eludes my sight; and, losing thus in part my theory of a more perfect state, start not, my friend, if I bring forward an opinion, which at the first glance seems to be levelled against the existence of God! I am not become an Atheist, I assure you, by residing at Paris: yet I begin to fear that vice, or, if you will, evil, is the grand mobile of action, and that, when the passions are justly poized, we become harmless, and in the same proportion useless.

The wants of reason are very few; and, were we to consider dispassionately the real value of most things, we should probably rest satisfied with the simple gratification of our physical necessities, and be content with negative goodness: for it is frequently, only that wanton, the Imagination, with her artful coquetry, who lures us forward, and makes us run over a rough road, pushing aside every obstacle merely to catch a disappointment.

The desire also of being useful to others, is continually damped by experience; and, if the exertions of humanity were not in some measure their own reward, who would endure misery, or struggle with care, to make some people ungrateful, and others idle?

You will call these melancholy effusions, and guess that, fatigued by the vivacity, which has all the bustling folly of childhood, without the innocence which renders ignorance charming, I am too severe in my strictures. It may be so; and I am aware that the good effects of the revolution will be last felt at Paris; where surely the soul of Epicurus has long been at work to root out the simple emotions of the heart, which, being natural, are always moral. Rendered cold and artificial by the selfish enjoyments of the senses, which the government fostered, is it surprising that simplicity of manners, and singleness of heart, rarely appear, to recreate me with the wild odour of nature, so passing sweet?

Seeing how deep the fibres of mischief have shot, I sometimes ask, with a doubting accent. Whether a nation can go back to the purity of manners which has hitherto been maintained unsullied only by the keen air of poverty, when, emasculated by pleasure, the luxuries of prosperity are become the wants of nature? I cannot yet give up the hope, that a fairer day is dawning on Europe, though I must hesitatingly observe, that little is to be expected from the narrow principle of commerce which seems every where to be shoving aside *the point of honour* of the *noblesse*. I can look beyond the evils of the moment, and do not expect muddied water to become clear before it has had time to stand; yet, even for the moment, it is the most terrific of all sights, to see men vicious without warmth—to see the order that should be the superscription of virtue, cultivated to give security to crimes which only thoughtlessness could palliate. Disorder is, in fact the very essence of vice, though with the wild wishes of a corrupt fancy humane emotions often kindly mix to soften their atrocity. Thus humanity, generosity, and even self-denial, sometimes render a character grand, and even useful, when hurried away by lawless passions; but what can equal the turpitude of a cold calculator who lives for himself alone, and considering his fellow-creatures merely as machines of pleasure, never forgets that honesty is the best policy? Keeping ever within the pale of the law, he crushes his thousands with impunity; but it is with that degree of management, which makes him, to borrow a significant vulgarism, a villain *in grain*. The very excess of his depravation preserves him, whilst the more respectable beast of prey, who prowls about like the lion, and roars to announce his approach, falls into a snare.

You may think it too soon to form an opinion of the future government, yet it is impossible to avoid hazarding some conjectures, when every thing whispers me, that names, not principles, are changed, and when I see that the turn of the tide has left the dregs of the old system to corrupt the new. For the same pride of office, the same desire of power are still visible; with this aggravation, that, fearing to return to obscurity after having but just acquired a relish for distinction, each hero, or philosopher, for all are dubbed with these new titles, endeavours to make hay while the sun shines; and every petty municipal officer, become the idol, or rather the tyrant of the day, stalks like a cock on a dunghil.

An Historical and Moral View
of the Origin and Progress
of the French Revolution
and the Effect it has Produced in Europe

Like the "Letter on the Present Character of the French Nation," this work was the only one completed of a projected series. Although written between late 1793 and April 1794, it describes the events only of the early part of the Revolution in 1789, the debates and decisions of the National Assembly, the character and actions of leaders such as Necker, Mirabeau, and Lafayette, the storming of the Bastille, and the people's march to Versailles in October.

The French Revolution is a mingling of description of historical events with personal opinions, a combination severely condemned by *The Critical Review* in 1796. The main source of the historical facts is the *New Annual Register*, a contemporary record written from an English liberal standpoint. The reviewer of *The British Critic* of 1795 was much struck by the resemblance of Wollstonecraft's history to its source; with some justification, if the book is read solely for its account of events, the reviewer concluded that it was "an abridgement of the history of the French revolution given in the *New Annual Register*."

Several reviews were favorable, among them the one in Johnson's *Analytical Review* of 1794, which praises the work less as history than as commentary. The reviewer of *The Monthly Review* of 1795 notes Wollstonecraft's impartiality of comment and approves of her balanced view of revolutionary France, while the reviewer of the *New Annual Register* of 1794 commends the judicious and philosophical reflections in the work. Most reviewers, however, had some reservations about the style of the book, especially its use of excessive metaphorical language.

On the whole, *The French Revolution* seems to have been fairly well received and a second edition appeared in 1795. Its influence on attitudes is difficult to gauge but it was read by many students of the

French Revolution, including John Adams and Percy Bysshe Shelley, both of whom seem to have been struck by its call for mental as well as political change and by its analysis of revolutionary violence.

PREFACE

THE REVOLUTION in France exhibits a scene, in the political world, not less novel and interesting than the contrast is striking between the narrow opinions of superstition, and the enlightened sentiments of masculine and improved philosophy.

To mark the prominent features of this revolution, requires a mind, not only unsophisticated by old prejudices, and the inveterate habits of degeneracy; but an amelioration of temper, produced by the exercise of the most enlarged principles of humanity.

The rapid changes, the violent, the base, and nefarious assassinations, which have clouded the vivid prospect that began to spread a ray of joy and gladness over the gloomy horizon of oppression, cannot fail to chill the sympathizing bosom, and palsy intellectual vigour. To sketch these vicissitudes is a task so arduous and melancholy, that, with a heart trembling to the touches of nature, it becomes necessary to guard against the erroneous inferences of sensibility; and reason beaming on the grand theatre of political changes, can prove the only sure guide to direct us to a favourable or just conclusion.

This important conclusion, involving the happiness and exaltation of the human character, demands serious and mature consideration; as it must ultimately sink the dignity of society into contempt, and its members into greater wretchedness; or elevate it to a degree of grandeur not hitherto anticipated, but by the most enlightened statesmen and philosophers.

Contemplating then these stupendous events with the cool eye of observation, the judgement, difficult to be preserved unwarped under the pressure of the calamitous horrours produced by desperate and enraged factions, will continually perceive that it is the uncontaminated mass of the French nation, whose minds begin to grasp the sentiments of freedom, that has secured the equilibrium of the state; often tottering on the brink of annihilation; in spite of the folly, selfishness, madness, treachery, and more fatal mock patriotism, the common result of depraved manners, the concomitant of that servility and voluptuousness which for so long a space of time has embruted the higher orders of this celebrated nation.

By thus attending to circumstances, we shall be able to discern clearly that the revolution was neither produced by the abilities or intrigues of a few individuals; nor was the effect of sudden and short-lived enthusiasm; but the natural consequence of intellectual improvement, gradually proceeding to perfection in the advancement of communities, from a state of barbarism to that of polished society, till now arrived at the point when sincerity of principles seems to be hastening the overthrow of the tremendous empire of superstition and hypocrisy, erected upon the ruins of gothic brutality and ignorance.

from
BOOK I, CHAPTER I

We must get entirely clear of all the notions drawn from the wild traditions of original sin: the eating of the apple, the theft of Prometheus, the opening of Pandora's box, and the other fables, too tedious to enumerate, on which priests have erected their tremendous structures of imposition, to persuade us, that we are naturally inclined to evil: we shall then leave room for the expansion of the human heart, and, I trust, find, that men will insensibly render each other happier as they grow wiser. It is indeed the necessity of stifling many of its most spontaneous desires, to obtain the factitious virtues of society, that makes man vicious, by depriving him of that dignity of character, which rests only on truth. For it is not paradoxical to assert, that the social virtues are nipt in the bud by the very laws of society. One principal of action is sufficient—Respect thyself—whether it be termed fear of God—religion; love of justice—morality; or, self-love—the desire of happiness. Yet, how can a man respect himself; and if not, how believe in the existence of virtue; when he is practising the daily shifts, which do not come under the cognisance of the law, in order to obtain a respectable situation in life? It seems, in fact, to be the business of a civilized man, to harden his heart, that on it he may sharpen the wit; which, assuming the appellation of sagacity, or cunning, in different characters, is only a proof, that the head is clear, because the heart is cold.

Besides, one great cause of misery in the present imperfect state of society is, that the imagination, continually tantalized, becomes the inflated wen of the mind, draining off the nourishment from the vital parts. Nor would it, I think, be stretching the inference too far, to insist, that men become vicious in the same proportion as they are obliged,

by the defects of society, to submit to a kind of self-denial, which ignorance, not morals, prescribes.

But these evils are passing away; a new spirit has gone forth, to
organise the body-politic; and where is the criterion to be found, to estimate the means, by which the influence of this spirit can be confined,
now enthroned in the hearts of half the inhabitants of the globe? Reason has, at last, shown her captivating face, beaming with benevolence;
and it will be impossible for the dark hand of despotism again to obscure
its radiance, or the lurking dagger of subordinate tyrants to reach her
bosom. The image of God implanted in our nature is now more rapidly
expanding; and, as it opens, liberty with maternal wing seems to be
soaring to regions far above vulgar annoyance, promising to shelter all
mankind.

It is a vulgar errour, built on a superficial view of the subject, though
it seems to have the sanction of experience, that civilization can only
go as far as it has hitherto gone, and then must necessarily fall back into
barbarism. Yet thus much appears certain, that a state will infallibly
grow old and feeble, if hereditary riches support hereditary rank, under
any description. But when courts and primogeniture are done away,
and simple equal laws are established, what is to prevent each generation from retaining the vigour of youth?—What can weaken the body
or mind, when the great majority of society must exercise both, to earn
a subsistence, and acquire respectability?

from
BOOK II, CHAPTER II

The courtly, dignified politeness of the queen,* with all those com-
placent graces which dance round flattered beauty, whose every charm
is drawn forth by the consciousness of pleasing, promised all that a sanguine fancy had pourtrayed of future happiness and peace. From her
fascinating smiles, indeed, was caught the careless hope, that, expanding the heart, makes the animal spirits vibrate, in every nerve, with
pleasure:—yet, she smiled but to deceive; or, if she felt some touches of
sympathy, it was only the unison of the moment.

It is certain, that education, and the atmosphere of manners in
which a character is formed, change the natural laws of humanity;
otherwise it would be unaccountable, how the human heart can be so
dead to the tender emotions of benevolence, which most forcibly teach

* Marie Antoinette (1755–1793), Queen of France and daughter of Maria The-
resa, Empress of Austria.—Editor.

us, that real or lasting felicity flows only from a love of virtue, and the practice of sincerity.

The unfortunate queen of France, beside the advantages of birth and station, possessed a very fine person; and her lovely face, sparkling with vivacity, hid the want of intelligence. Her complexion was dazzlingly clear; and, when she was pleased, her manners were bewitching; for she happily mingled the most insinuating voluptuous softness and affability, with an air of grandeur, bordering on pride, that rendered the contrast more striking. Independence also, of whatever kind, always gives a degree of dignity to the mien; so that monarchs and nobles, with most ignoble souls, from believing themselves superiour to others, have actually acquired a look of superiority.

But her opening faculties were poisoned in the bud; for before she came to Paris, she had already been prepared, by a corrupt, supple abbé, for the part she was to play;* and, young as she was, became so firmly attached to the aggrandizement of her house, that, though plunged deep in pleasure, she never omitted sending immense sums to her brother, on every occasion. The person of the king, in itself very disgusting, was rendered more so by gluttony, and a total disregard of delicacy, and even decency in his apartments; and, when jealous of the queen, for whom he had a kind of devouring passion, he treated her with great brutality, till she acquired sufficient finesse to subjugate him. Is it then surprizing, that a very desirable woman, with a sanguine constitution, should shrink abhorrent from his embraces; or that an empty mind should be employed only to vary the pleasures, which emasculated her circean court? And, added to this, the histories of the Julias and Messalinas of antiquity,† convincingly prove, that there is no end to the vagaries of the imagination, when power is unlimited, and reputation set at defiance.

Lost then in the most luxurious pleasures, or managing court intrigues, the queen became a profound dissembler; and her heart hardened by sensual enjoyments to such a degree, that when her family and favourites stood on the brink of ruin, her little portion of mind was employed only to preserve herself from danger. As a proof of the justness of this assertion, it is only necessary to observe, that, in the general wreck, not a scrap of her writing has been found to criminate her; neither has she suffered a word to escape her to exasperate the people, even

* The Abbé de Vermond was sent as Marie Antoinette's tutor to ease her transition from Austria to France; he was noted for his hypocrisy and intrigue.—Editor.

† Julia was the daughter of the Emperor Augustus and wife of the Emperor Tiberius; Messalina was the wife of the Emperor Claudius. Both women were proverbial for their profligacy.—Editor.

when burning with rage, and contempt. The effect that adversity may have on her choked understanding time will show;* but during her prosperity, the moments of languor, that glide into the interstices of enjoyment, were passed in the most childish manner; without the appearance of any vigour of mind, to palliate the wanderings of the imagination.—Still she was a woman of uncommon address; and though her conversation was insipid, her compliments were so artfully adapted to flatter the person she wished to please or dupe, and so eloquent is the beauty of a queen, in the eyes even of superiour men, that she seldom failed to carry her point when she endeavoured to gain an ascendancy over the mind of an individual. Over that of the king she acquired unbounded sway, when, managing the disgust she had for his person, she made him pay a kingly price for her favours. A court is the best school in the world for actors; it was very natural then for her to become a complete actress, and an adept in all the arts of coquetry that debauch the mind, whilst they render the person alluring. . . .

How silent is now Versailles!†—The solitary foot, that mounts the sumptuous stair-case, rests on each landing-place, whilst the eye traverses the void, almost expecting to see the strong images of fancy burst into life.—The train of the Louises, like the posterity of the Banquoes,‡ pass in solemn sadness, pointing at the nothingness of grandeur, fading away on the cold canvass, which covers the nakedness of the spacious walls—whilst the gloominess of the atmosphere gives a deeper shade to the gigantic figures, that seem to be sinking into the embraces of death.

Warily entering the endless apartments, half shut up, the fleeting shadow of the pensive wanderer, reflected in long glasses, that vainly gleam in every direction, slacken the nerves, without appalling the heart; through lascivious pictures, in which grace varnishes voluptuousness, no longer seductive, strike continually home to the bosom the melancholy moral, that anticipates the frozen lesson of experience. The very air is chill, seeming to clog the breath; and the wasting dampness of destruction appears to be stealing into the vast pile, on every side.

The oppressed heart seeks for relief in the garden; but even there the same images glide along the wide neglected walks—all is fearfully still; and, if a little rill creeping through the gathering moss down the

---

* This was written some months before the death of the Queen.—Wollstonecraft.

† Wollstonecraft either visited or imagined visiting the royal palace after the downfall of the King.—Editor.

‡ An allusion to Shakespeare's *Macbeth* where the ghost of Banquo points to the ghostly kings who will come after him.—Editor.

Marie Antoinette by Madame Vigée-Lebrun. Arrayed in splendid dress and elaborate coiffure, the French Queen represented the type of trivial and privileged woman Wollstonecraft most abhorred.

cascade, over which it used to rush, bring to mind the description of the grand water works, it is only to excite a languid smile at the futile attempt to equal nature.

Lo! this was the palace of the great king!—the abode of magnificence! Who has broken the charm?—Why does it now inspire only pity?—Why;—because nature, smiling around, presents to the imagination materials to build farms, and hospitable mansions, where, without raising idle admiration, that gladness will reign, which opens the heart to benevolence, and that industry, which renders innocent pleasure sweet.

Weeping—scarcely conscious that I weep, O France! over the vestiges of thy former oppression; which, separating man from man with a fence of iron, sophisticated all, and made many completely wretched; I tremble, lest I should meet some unfortunate being, fleeing from the despotism of licentious freedom, hearing the snap of the *guillotine* at his heels; merely because he was once noble, or has afforded an asylum to those, whose only crime is their name—and, if my pen almost bound with eagerness to record the day, that levelled the Bastille with the dust, making the towers of despair tremble to their base; the recollection, that still the abbey* is appropriated to hold the victims of revenge and suspicion, palsies the hand that would fain do justice to the assault, which tumbled into heaps of ruins walls that seemed to mock the resistless force of time.—Down fell the temple of despotism; but—despotism has not been buried in its ruins!—Unhappy country!—when will thy children cease to tear thy bosom?—When will a change of opinion, producing a change of morals, render thee truly free?—When will truth give life to real magnanimity, and justice place equality on a stable seat?—When will thy sons trust, because they deserve to be trusted; and private virtue become the guarantee of patriotism? Ah!—when will thy government become the most perfect, because thy citizens are the most virtuous!

from
BOOK V, CHAPTER II

The Parisians were now continually brooding over the wrongs they had heretofore only enumerated in a song; and changing ridicule into invective, all called for redress, looking for a degree of public happiness immediately, which could not be attained, and ought not to have been

---

* Probably a reference to the Abbaye prison in Paris, to which some of Wollstonecraft's French acquaintances were taken in the Fall of 1793.—Editor.

expected, before an alteration in the national character seconded the new system of government.*

From the enjoyment of more freedom than the women of other parts of the world, those of France have acquired more independence of spirit than any others; it has, therefore, been the scheme of designing men very often since the revolution, to lurk behind them as a kind of safeguard, working them up to some desperate act, and then terming it a folly, because merely the rage of women, who were supposed to be actuated only by the emotions of the moment. Early then on the fifth of October a multitude of women by some impulse were collected together; and hastening to the *hôtel-de-ville* obliged every female they met to accompany them, even entering many houses to force others to follow in their train.

The concourse, at first, consisted mostly of market women, and the lowest refuse of the streets, women who had thrown off the virtues of one sex without having power to assume more than the vices of the other. A number of men also followed them, armed with pikes, bludgeons, and hatchets; but they were strictly speaking a mob, affixing all the odium to the appellation it can possibly import; and not to be confounded with the honest multitude, who took the Bastille.—In fact, such a rabble has seldom been gathered together; and they quickly showed, that their movement was not the effect of public spirit.

They first talked of addressing the committee appointed by the municipality to superintend the operations necessary to obtain provision for the city, and to remonstrate respecting their inattention or indifference to the public calamity. Mean time a new cord was fixed to the notorious lamp-iron, where the amusement of death was first tolerated.†
The national guards, forming a hedge of bayonets to prevent the women from entering the hotel, kept them in suspense a few moments.—
When, uttering a loud and general cry, they hurled a volley of stones at the soldiers, who, unwilling, or ashamed, to fire on women, though with the appearance of furies, retreated into the hall, and left the passage free. They then sought for arms; and breaking open the doors of the magazines, soon procured fusils, cannons, and ammunition; and even took advantage of the confusion to carry off money and notes belonging to the public. In the interim some went to search for the volunteers of the Bastille, and chose a commander from among them to con-

---

* This is the beginning of Wollstonecraft's description of the events of early October 1789, the march to Versailles which ended with the King's removal to Paris.—Editor.

† A lamp-iron was a projecting iron rod from which hung a lamp; it was used as a gallows during the Revolution.—Editor.

duct the party to Versailles; whilst others tied cords to the carriages of the cannons to drag them along.—But these, being mostly marine artillery, did not follow with the alacrity necessary to accord with their wishes; they, therefore, stopped several coaches, forcing the men to get out and the ladies to join them; fastening the cannons behind, on which a number of the most furious mounted, brandishing whatever weapon they had found, or the matches of the cannons. Some drove the horses, and others charged themselves with the care of the powder and ball, falling into ranks to facilitate their march. They took the road by the *Champs Elisées* about noon, to the number of four thousand, escorted by four or five hundred men, armed with every thing on which they could lay their hands.

from
BOOK V, CHAPTER III

It is allowed by all parties, that civilization is a blessing, so far as it gives security to person and property, and the milder graces of taste to society and manners. If, therefore, the polishing of man, and the improvement of his intellect, become necessary to secure these advantages, it follows, of course, that the more general such improvement grows, the greater the extension of human happiness.

In a savage state man is distinguished only by superiority of genius, prowess, and eloquence. I say eloquence, for I believe, that in this stage of society he is most eloquent, because most natural. For it is only in the progress of governments, that hereditary distinctions, cruelly abridging rational liberty, have prevented man from rising to his just point of elevation, by the exercise of his improveable faculties.

That there is a superiority of natural genius among men does not admit of dispute; and that in countries the most free there will always be distinctions proceeding from superiority of judgment, and the power of acquiring more delicacy of taste, which may be the effect of the peculiar organization, or whatever cause produces it, is an incontestible truth. But it is a palpable errour to suppose, that men of every class are not equally susceptible of common improvement: if therefore it be the contrivance of any government, to preclude from a chance of improvement the greater part of the citizens of the state, it can be considered in no other light than as a monstrous tyranny, a barbarous oppression, equally injurious to the two parties, though in different ways. For all the advantages of civilization cannot be felt, unless it pervades the whole mass, humanizing every description of men—and then it is the first of blessings, the true perfection of man.

from
BOOK V, CHAPTER IV

Every political good carried to the extreme must be productive of evil; yet every poison has its antidote: and there is a pitch of luxury and refinement, which, when reached, will overturn all the absolute governments in the world. The ascertainment of these antidotes is a task the most difficult; and whilst it remains imperfect, a number of men will continue to be the victims of mistaken applications. Like the empirics,* who bled a patient to death to prevent a mortification from becoming fatal, the tyrants of the earth have had recourse to cutting off the heads, or torturing the bodies, of those persons who have attempted to check their sway, or doubt their omnipotence. But, though thousands have perished the victims of empirics, and of despots, yet the improvements made both in medicine and moral philosophy have kept a sure, though gradual pace.—And, if men have not clearly discovered a specific remedy for every evil, physical, moral, and political, it is to be presumed, that the accumulation of experimental facts will greatly tend to lessen them in future.

Whilst, therefore, the sumptuous galas of the court of France were the grand source of the refinement of the arts, taste became the antidote to *ennui*; and when sentiment had taken place of chivalrous and gothic tournaments, the reign of philosophy succeeded that of the imagination. And though the government, enveloped in precedents, adjusted still the idle ceremonials, which were no longer imposing, blind to the imperceptible change of things and opinions, as if their faculties were bound by an eternal frost, the progress was invariable; till, reaching a certain point, Paris, which from the particular formation of the empire had been such an useful head to it, began to be the cause of dreadful calamities, extending from individuals to the nation, and from the nation to Europe. Thus it is, that we are led to blame those, who insist, that, because a state of things has been productive of good, it is always respectable; when, on the contrary, the endeavouring to keep alive any hoary establishment, beyond its natural date, is often pernicious and always useless.

In the infancy of governments, or rather of civilization, courts seem to be necessary to accelerate the improvement of arts and manners, to lead to that of science and morals. Large capitals are the obvious consequences of the riches and luxury of courts; but as, after they have

* Physicians.—Editor.

arrived at a certain magnitude and degree of refinement, they become dangerous to the freedom of the people, and incompatible with the safety of a republican government, it may be questioned whether Paris will not occasion more disturbance in settling the new order of things, than is equivalent to the good she produced by accelerating the epocha of the revolution.

However, it appears very certain, that should a republican government be consolidated, Paris must rapidly crumble into decay. Its rise and splendour were owing chiefly, if not entirely, to the old system of government; and since the foundation of its luxury has been shaken, and it is not likely that the disparting* structure will ever again rest securely on its basis, we may fairly infer, that, in proportion as the charms of solitary reflection and agricultural recreations are felt, the people, by leaving the villages and cities, will give a new complexion to the face of the country—and we may then look for a turn of mind more solid, principles more fixed, and a conduct more consistent and virtuous.

The occupations and habits of life have a wonderful influence on the forming mind; so great, that the superinductions of art stop the growth of the spontaneous shoots of nature, till it is difficult to distinguish natural from factitious morals and feelings; and as the energy of thinking will always proceed, in a great measure, either from our education or manner of living, the frivolity of the French character may be accounted for, without taking refuge in the old hiding place of ignorance—occult causes.

When it is the object of education to prepare the pupil to please every body, and of course to deceive, accomplishments are the one thing needful; and the desire to be admired ever being uppermost, the passions are subjugated, or all drawn into the whirlpool of egotism.† This gives to each person, however different the temper, a tincture of vanity, and that weak vacillation of opinion, which is incompatible with what we term character.

Thus a Frenchman, like most women, may be said to have no character distinguishable from that of the nation; unless little shades, and casual lights, be allowed to constitute an essential characteristic. What then could have been expected, when their ambition was mostly confined to dancing gracefully, entering a room with easy assurance, and smiling on and complimenting the very persons whom they meant to ridicule at the next fashionable assembly? The learning to fence

* Separating and dissolving.—Editor.

† I use this word according to the French acceptation, because we have not one to express so forcibly the same signification.—Wollstonecraft.

with skill, it is true, was useful to a people, whose false notions of honour required that at least a drop of blood should atone for the shadow of an affront. The knack also of uttering sprightly repartees became a necessary art, to supply the place of that real interest only to be nourished in the affectionate intercourse of domestic intimacy, where confidence enlarges the heart it opens. Besides, the desire of eating of every dish at table, no matter if there were fifty, and the custom of separating immediately after the repast, destroy the social affections, reminding a stranger of the vulgar saying—'every man for himself, and God for us all.' After these cursory observations, it is not going too far to advance, that the French were in some respects the most unqualified of any people in Europe to undertake the important work in which they are embarked.

Whilst pleasure was the sole object of living among the higher orders of society, it was the business of the lower to give life to their joys, and convenience to their luxury. This cast-like division, by destroying all strength of character in the former, and debasing the latter to machines, taught Frenchmen to be more ingenious in their contrivances for pleasure and show, than the men of any other country; whilst, with respect to the abridgment of labour in the mechanic arts, or to promote the comfort of common life, they were far behind. They had never, in fact, acquired an idea of that independent, comfortable situation, in which contentment is sought rather than happiness; because the slaves of pleasure or power can be roused only by lively emotions and extravagant hopes. Indeed they have no word in their vocabulary to express *comfort*—that state of existence, in which reason renders serene and useful the days, which passion would only cheat with flying dreams of happiness.

A change of character cannot be so sudden as some sanguine calculators expect: yet by the destruction of the rights of primogeniture, a greater degree of equality of property is sure to follow; and as Paris cannot maintain its splendour, but by the trade of luxury, which can never be carried to the same height it was formerly, the opulent having strong motives to induce them to live more in the country, they must acquire new inclinations and opinions.—As a change also of the system of education and domestic manners will be a natural consequence of the revolution, the French will insensibly rise to a dignity of character far above that of the present race; and then the fruit of their liberty, ripening gradually, will have a relish not to be expected during its crude and forced state.

The late arrangement of things seems to have been the common effect of an absolute government, a domineering priesthood, and a great inequality of fortune; and whilst it completely destroyed the most important end of society, the comfort and independence of the people, it generated the most shameful depravity and weakness of intellect; so that we have seen the French engaged in a business the most sacred to mankind, giving, by their enthusiasm, splendid examples of their fortitude at one moment, and at another, by their want of firmness and deficiency of judgment, affording the most glaring and fatal proofs of the just estimate, which all nations have formed of their character.

Men so thoroughly sophisticated, it was to be supposed, would never conduct any business with steadiness and moderation: but it required a knowledge of the nation and their manners, to form a distinct idea of their disgusting conceit and wretched egotism; so far surpassing all the calculations of reason, that, perhaps, should not a faithful picture be now sketched, posterity would be at loss to account for their folly; and attribute to madness, what arose from imbecility.

The natural feelings of man seldom become so contaminated and debased as not sometimes to let escape a gleam of the generous fire, an ethereal spark of the soul; and it is these glowing emotions, in the inmost recesses of the heart, which have continued to feed feelings, that on sudden occasions manifest themselves with all their pristine purity and vigour. But, by the habitual slothfulness of rusty intellects, or the depravity of the heart, lulled into hardness on the lascivious couch of pleasure, those heavenly beams are obscured, and man appears either an hideous monster, a devouring beast; or a spiritless reptile, without dignity or humanity.

Those miserable wretches who crawl under the feet of others are seldom to be found among savages, where men accustomed to exercise and temperance are, in general, brave, hospitable, and magnanimous; and it is only as they surrender their rights, that they lose those noble qualities of the heart. The ferocity of the savage is of a distinct nature from that of the degenerate slaves of tyrants. One murders from mistaken notions of courage; yet he respects his enemy in proportion to his fortitude, and contempt of death: the other assassinates without remorse, whilst his trembling nerves betray the weakness of his affrighted soul at every appearance of danger. Among the former, men are respected according to their abilities; consequently idle drones are driven out of this society; but among the latter, men are raised to honours and employments in proportion as a talent for intrigue, the sure proof of littleness of mind, has rendered them servile. The most melancholy reflections are produced by a retrospective glance over the rise and progress of the governments of different countries, when we are compelled to remark, that flagrant follies and atrocious crimes have been more common under the governments of modern Europe, than in any of the ancient nations, if we except the Jews. Sanguinary tortures, insidious poisonings, and dark assassinations, have alternately exhibited a race of monsters in human shape, the contemplation of whose ferocity chills the blood, and darkens every enlivening expectation of humanity: but we ought to observe, to reanimate the hopes of benevolence, that the perpetration of these horid deeds has arisen from a despotism in the government, which reason is teaching us to remedy. Sometimes, it is true, restrained by an iron police, the people appear peaceable, when they are only stunned; so that we find, whenever the mob has broken loose, the fury of the populace has been shocking and calamitous. These considerations account for the contradictions in the French character, which must strike a stranger: for robberies are very rare in France, where daily frauds and sly pilfering prove, that the lower class have as little honesty as sincerity. Besides, murder and cruelty almost always show the dastardly ferocity of fear in France; whilst in England, where the spirit of liberty has prevailed, it is usual for an highwayman, demanding your money, not only to avoid barbarity, but to behave with humanity, and even complaisance.

Degeneracy of morals, with polished manners, produces the worst of passions, which floating through the social body, the genial current of natural feelings has been poisoned; and, committing crimes with trembling inquietude, the culprits have not only drawn on themselves the vengeance of the law, but thrown an odium on their nature, that has blackened the face of humanity. And whilst its temple has been sacrilegiously profaned by the drops of blood, which have issued from the very hearts of the sad victims of their folly; a hardness of temper, under the veil of sentiment, calling it vice, has prevented our sympathy from leading us to examine into the sources of the atrocity of our species, and obscured the true cause of disgraceful and vicious habits.

Since the existence of courts, whose aggrandisement has been conspicuous in the same degree as the miseries of the debased people have accumulated, the convenience and comfort of men have been sacrificed to the ostentatious display of pomp and ridiculous pageantry. For every order of men, from the beggar to the king, has tended to introduce that extravagance into society, which equally blasts domestic virtue and happiness. The prevailing custom of living beyond their income has had the most baneful effect on the independence of individuals of every class in England, as well as in France; so that whilst they have lived in habits of idleness, they have been drawn into excesses, which, proving ruinous, produced consequences equally pernicious to the community, and degrading to the private character. Extravagance forces the peer to prostitute his talents and influence for a place, to repair his broken fortune; and the country gentleman becomes venal in the senate, to enable himself to live on a par with him, or reimburse himself for the expences of electioneering, into which he was led by sheer vanity. The professions, on the same account, become equally un-principled. The one, whose characteristic ought to be integrity, de-scends to chicanery; whilst another trifles with the health, of which it knows all the importance. The merchant likewise enters into specula-tions so closely bordering on fraudulency, that common straight for-ward minds can scarcely distinguish the devious art of selling any thing for a price far beyond that necessary to ensure a just profit, from sheer dishonesty, aggravated by hard-heartedness, when it is to take advan-tage of the necessities of the indigent.

The destructive influence of commerce, it is true, carried on by men who are eager by overgrown riches to partake of the respect paid to nobility, is felt in a variety of ways. The most pernicious, perhaps, is its producing an aristocracy of wealth, which degrades mankind, by making them only exchange savageness for tame servility, instead of acquiring the urbanity of improved reason. Commerce also, overstock-ing a country with people, obliges the majority to become manufac-turers rather than husbandmen; and then the division of labour, solely to enrich the proprietor, renders the mind entirely inactive. The time which, a celebrated writer says, is sauntered away, in going from one part of an employment to another, is the very time that preserves the man from degenerating into a brute; for every one must have observed how much more intelligent are the blacksmiths, carpenters, and masons in the country, than the journeymen in great towns; and, respecting morals, there is no making a comparison. The very gait of the man, who is his own master, is so much more steady than the slouching step of the servant of a servant, that it is unnecessary to ask which proves by his actions he has the most independence of character.

The acquiring of a fortune is likewise the least arduous road to pre-eminence, and the most sure: thus are whole knots of men turned into machines, to enable a keen speculator to become wealthy; and every noble principle of nature is eradicated by making a man pass his life in stretching wire, pointing a pin, heading a nail, or spreading a sheet of paper on a plain surface. Besides, it is allowed, that all asso-ciations of men render them sensual, and consequently selfish; and whilst lazy friars are driven out of their cells as stagnate bodies that corrupt society, it may admit of a doubt whether large work-shops do not contain men equally, tending to impede that gradual progress of improvement, which leads to the perfection of reason, and the estab-lishment of rational equality.

The deprivation of natural, equal, civil and political rights, reduced the most cunning of the lower orders to practise fraud, and the rest to habits of stealing, audacious robberies, and murders. And why? because the rich and poor were separated into bands of tyrants and slaves, and the retaliation of slaves is always terrible. In short, every sacred feeling, moral and divine, has been obliterated, and the dignity of man sullied, by a system of policy and jurisprudence as repugnant to reason, as at variance with humanity.

The only excuse that can be made for the ferocity of the Parisians is then simply to observe, that they had not any confidence in the laws, which they had always found to be merely cobwebs to catch small flies. Accustomed to be punished themselves for every trifle, and often for only being in the way of the rich, or their parasites; which, in fact, had the Parisians seen the execution of a noble, or priest, though convicted of crimes beyond the daring of vulgar minds?—When justice, or the law, is so partial, the day of retribution will come with the red sky of vengeance, to confound the innocent with the guilty. The mob were barbarous beyond the tiger's cruelty: for how could they trust a court that had so often deceived them, or expect to see its agents punished, when the same measures were pursuing?

Let us cast our eyes over the history of man, and we shall scarcely find a page that is not tarnished by some foul deed, or bloody transaction. Let us examine the catalogue of the vices of men in a savage state, and contrast them with those of men civilized; we shall find, that a barbarian, considered as a moral being, is an angel, compared with the refined villain of artificial life. Let us investigate the causes which have produced this degeneracy, and we shall discover, that they are those unjust plans of government, which have been formed by peculiar circumstances in every part of the globe.—Then let us coolly and impartially contemplate the improvements, which are gaining ground in the formation of principles of policy; and I flatter myself it will be allowed by every humane and considerate being, that a political system more simple than has hitherto existed would effectually check those aspiring follies, which, by imitation, leading to vice, have banished from governments the very shadow of justice and magnanimity.

Thus had France grown up, and sickened on the corruption of a state diseased. But, as in medicine there is a species of complaint in the bowels which works its own cure, and, leaving the body healthy, gives an invigorated tone to the system, so there is in politics: and whilst the agitation of its regeneration continues, the excrementitious humours exuding from the contaminated body will excite a general dislike and contempt for the nation; and it is only the philosophical eye, which looks into the nature and weighs the consequences of human actions, that will be able to discern the cause, which has produced so many dreadful effects.

Letters Written during a Short Residence in Sweden, Norway, and Denmark

The work started as semi-public letters sent to Gilbert Imlay during Wollstonecraft's Scandinavian journey, which lasted from June to September of 1795. On her return she took back her letters, which she reworked into a travel book; it was published by Joseph Johnson in 1796. As a record of Wollstonecraft's feelings during the summer of 1795, it can be augmented by the personal letters she wrote for Imlay alone.

The epistolary travel work was a common genre for women in the eighteenth century and it was practised with success by such notable writers as Lady Mary Wortley Montagu. An immediate model for Wollstonecraft was provided by Helen Maria Williams, her friend in Paris and fellow chronicler of the revolutionary events. During many years Williams wrote down descriptions of her movements in France and Switzerland in the desultory form of the letter, which allowed her to mingle political commentary, anecdote, and self-revelation in a manner similar to Wollstonecraft in her Scandinavian work.

Letters Written . . . in Sweden was one of the few firsthand accounts of Scandinavia written in English in the eighteenth century. It was much liked by critics. The reviewer of the *Analytical Review* of 1796 singled out for praise its spontaneity, and Mary Hays in the *Monthly Magazine* of 1796 noted the acuteness of observation and poignancy of feeling. Several reviewers commented on the character of the author as it emerged from the work. The critic of the *New Annual Register* of 1796 mentioned her melancholy and the reviewer in the *British Critic*, usually hostile to Wollstonecraft, found that she had been much improved by her experiences of marriage and motherhood. *Letters Written . . . in Sweden* was widely read in England, Europe, and America. Among its readers were the English Romantic poets, Robert Southey and Samuel Taylor Coleridge.

from
LETTER I

ELEVEN DAYS of weariness on board a vessel not intended for the accommodation of passengers have so exhausted my spirits, to say nothing
of the other causes, with which you are already sufficiently acquainted,
that it is with some difficulty I adhere to my determination of giving
you my observations, as I travel through new scenes, whilst warmed
with the impression they have made on me.

The captain, as I mentioned to you, promised to put me on shore
at Arendall,* or Gothenburg, in his way to Elsineur; but contrary winds
obliged us to pass both places during the night. In the morning, however, after we had lost sight of the entrance of the latter bay, the vessel
was becalmed; and the captain, to oblige me, hanging out a signal for
a pilot, bore down towards the shore.

My attention was particularly directed to the light-house; and you
can scarcely imagine with what anxiety I watched two long hours for
a boat to emancipate me—still no one appeared. Every cloud that flitted
on the horizon was hailed as a liberator, till approaching nearer, like
most of the prospects sketched by hope, it dissolved under the eye into
disappointment.

Weary of expectation, I then began to converse with the captain
on the subject; and, from the tenour of the information my questions
drew forth, I soon concluded, that, if I waited for a boat, I had little
chance of getting on shore at this place. Despotism, as is usually the
case, I found had here cramped the industry of man. The pilots being
paid by the king, and scantily, they will not run into any danger, or
even quit their hovels, if they can possibly avoid it, only to fulfil what
is termed their duty. How different is it on the English coast, where,
in the most stormy weather, boats immediately hail you, brought out
by the expectation of extraordinary profit.

Disliking to sail for Elsineur, and still more to lie at anchor, or cruise
about the coast for several days, I exerted all my rhetoric to prevail on
the captain to let me have the ship's boat; and though I added the most
forcible of arguments, I for a long time addressed him in vain.

It is a kind of rule at sea, not to send out a boat. The captain was a
good-natured man; but men with common minds seldom break through
general rules. Prudence is ever the resort of weakness; and they rarely
go as far as they may in any undertaking, who are determined not to

* In Norway—Wollstonecraft.

go beyond it on any account. If, however, I had some trouble with the captain, I did not lose much time with the sailors; for they, all alacrity, hoisted out the boat, the moment I obtained permission, and promised to row me to the light-house.

I did not once allow myself to doubt of obtaining a conveyance from thence round the rocks—and then away for Gothenburg—confinement is so unpleasant.

The day was fine; and I enjoyed the water till, approaching the little island, poor Marguerite,* whose timidity always acts as a feeler before her adventuring spirit, began to wonder at our not seeing any inhabitants. I did not listen to her. But when, on landing, the same silence prevailed, I caught the alarm, which was not lessened by the sight of two old men, whom we forced out of their wretched hut. Scarcely human in their appearance, we with difficulty obtained an intelligible reply to our questions—the result of which was, that they had no boat, and were not allowed to quit their post, on any pretence. But, they informed us, that there was at the other side, eight or ten miles over, a pilot's dwelling; two guineas tempted the sailors to risk the captain's displeasure, and once more embark to row me over.

The weather was pleasant, and the appearance of the shore so grand, that I should have enjoyed the two hours it took to reach it, but for the fatigue which was too visible in the countenances of the sailors who, instead of uttering a complaint, were, with the thoughtless hilarity peculiar to them, joking about the possibility of the captain's taking advantage of a slight westerly breeze, which was springing up, to sail without them. Yet, in spite of their good humour, I could not help growing uneasy when the shore, receding, as it were, as we advanced, seemed to promise no end to their toil. This anxiety increased when, turning into the most picturesque bay I ever saw, my eyes sought in vain for the vestige of a human habitation. Before I could determine what step to take in such a dilemma, for I could not bear to think of returning to the ship, the sight of a barge relieved me, and we hastened towards it for information. We were immediately directed to pass some jutting rocks when we should see a pilot's hut.

There was a solemn silence in this scene, which made itself be felt. The sun-beams that played on the ocean, scarcely ruffled by the lightest breeze, contrasted with the huge, dark rocks, that looked like the rude materials of creation forming the barrier of unwrought space, forcibly struck me; but I should not have been sorry if the cottage had not ap-

---

* The French nursemaid Wollstonecraft had brought on her travels to take care of Fanny, her baby daughter.—Editor.

peared equally tranquil Approaching a retreat where strangers, especially women, so seldom appeared, I wondered that curiosity did not bring the beings who inhabited it to the windows or door. I did not immediately recollect that men who remain so near the brute creation, as only to exert themselves to find the food necessary to sustain life, have little or no imagination to call forth the curiosity necessary to fructify the faint glimmerings of mind which entitles them to rank as lords of the creation.—Had they either, they could not contentedly remain rooted in the clods they so indolently cultivate.

Whilst the sailors went to seek for the sluggish inhabitants, these conclusions occurred to me; and, recollecting the extreme fondness which the Parisians ever testify for novelty, their very curiosity appeared to me a proof of the progress they had made in refinement. Yes; in the art of living—in the art of escaping from the cares which embarrass the first steps towards the attainment of the pleasures of social life.

The pilots informed the sailors that they were under the direction of a lieutenant retired from the service, who spoke English; adding, that they could do nothing without his orders; and even the offer of money could hardly conquer their laziness, and prevail on them to accompany us to his dwelling. They would not go with me alone which I wanted them to have done, because I wished to dismiss the sailors as soon as possible. Once more we rowed off, they following tardily, till, turning round another bold protuberance of the rocks, we saw a boat making towards us, and soon learnt that it was the lieutenant himself, coming with some earnestness to see who we were.

To save the sailors any further toil, I had my baggage instantly removed into his boat; for, as he could speak English, a previous parley was not necessary; though Marguerite's respect for me could hardly keep her from expressing the fear, strongly marked on her countenance, which my putting ourselves into the power of a strange man excited. He pointed out his cottage; and, drawing near to it, I was not sorry to see a female figure, though I had not, like Marguerite, been thinking of robberies, murders, or the other evil which instantly, as the sailors would have said, runs foul of a woman's imagination.

On entering, I was still better pleased to find a clean house, with some degree of rural elegance. The beds were of muslin, coarse it is true, but dazzlingly white; and the floor was strewed over with little sprigs of juniper (the custom, as I afterwards found, of the country), which formed a contrast with the curtains and produced an agreeable sensation of freshness, to soften the ardour of noon. Still nothing was so pleasing as the alacrity of hospitality—all that the house afforded was quickly spread on the whitest linen.—Remember I had just left the vessel, where, without being fastidious, I had continually been disgusted. Fish, milk, butter, and cheese, and I am sorry to add, brandy, the bane of this country, were spread on the board. After we had dined, hospitality made them, with some degree of mystery, bring us some excellent coffee. I did not then know that it was prohibited.*

The good man of the house apologized for coming in continually, but declared that he was so glad to speak English, he could not stay out. He need not have apologized; I was equally glad of his company. With the wife I could only exchange smiles; and she was employed observing the make of our clothes. My hands, I found, had first led her to discover that I was the lady. I had, of course, my quantum of reverences; for the politeness of the north seems to partake of the coldness of the climate, and the rigidity of its iron sinewed rocks. Amongst the peasantry, there is, however, so much of the simplicity of the golden age in this land of flint—so much overflowing of heart, and fellow-feeling, that only benevolence, and the honest sympathy of nature, diffused smiles over my countenance when they kept me standing, regardless of my fatigue, whilst they dropt courtesy after courtesy.

The situation of this house was beautiful, though chosen for convenience. The master being the officer who commanded all the pilots on the coast, and the person appointed to guard wrecks, it was necessary for him to fix on a spot that would overlook the whole bay. As he had seen some service, he wore, not without a pride I thought becoming, a badge to prove that he had merited well of his country. It was happy, I thought, that he had been paid in honour; for the stipend he received was little more than twelve pounds a year.—I do not trouble myself or you with the calculation of Swedish ducats. Thus, my friend, you perceive the necessity of *perquisites*. This same narrow policy runs through every thing. I shall have occasion further to animadvert on it.

Though my host amused me with an account of himself, which gave me an idea of the manners of the people I was about to visit, I was eager to climb the rocks to view the country, and see whether the honest tars had regained their ship. With the help of the lieutenant's telescope I saw the vessel underway with a fair though gentle gale. The sea was calm, playful even as the most shallow stream, and on the vast bason† I did not see a dark speck to indicate the boat. My conductors were consequently arrived.

* Owing to the poor economic situation of Sweden toward the end of the eighteenth century, many imports, including coffee, were forbidden or highly taxed.—Editor.

† A variant of "basin."—Editor.

Straying further, my eye was attracted by the sight of some heart's-ease* that peeped through the rocks. I caught at it as a good omen, and going to preserve it in a letter that had not conveyed balm to my heart, a cruel remembrance suffused my eyes; but it passed away like an April shower. If you are deep read in Shakspeare, you will recollect that this was the little western flower tinged by love's dart, which "maidens call love in idleness." The gaiety of my babe was unmixed; regardless of omens or sentiments, she found a few wild strawberries more grateful than flowers or fancies.

The lieutenant informed me that this was a commodious bay. Of that I could not judge, though I felt its picturesque beauty. Rocks were piled on rocks, forming a suitable bulwark to the ocean. Come no further, they emphatically said, turning their dark sides to the waves to augment the idle roar. The view was sterile: still little patches of earth, of the most exquisite verdure, enamelled with the sweetest wild flowers, seemed to promise the goats and a few straggling cows luxurious herbage. How silent and peaceful was the scene. I gazed around with rapture, and felt more of that spontaneous pleasure which gives credibility to our expectation of happiness, than I had for a long, long time before. I forgot the horrors I had witnessed in France, which had cast a gloom over all nature, and suffering the enthusiasm of my character, too often, gracious God! damped by the tears of disappointed affection, to be lighted up afresh, care took wing while simple fellow feeling expanded my heart.

To prolong this enjoyment, I readily assented to the proposal of our host to pay a visit to a family, the master of which spoke English, who was the drollest dog in the country, he added, repeating some of his stories, with a hearty laugh.

I walked on, still delighted with the rude beauties of the scene; for the sublime often gave place imperceptibly to the beautiful, dilating the emotions which were painfully concentrated.

When we entered this abode, the largest I had yet seen, I was introduced to a numerous family; but the father, from whom I was led to expect so much entertainment, was absent. The lieutenant consequently was obliged to be the interpreter of our reciprocal compliments. The phrases were awkwardly transmitted, it is true; but looks and gestures were sufficient to make them intelligible and interesting. The girls were all vivacity, and respect for me could scarcely keep them from romping with my host, who, asking for a pinch of snuff, was presented with a box, out of which an artificial mouse, fastened to the bottom,

* A wild form of pansy.—Editor.

sprung. Though this trick had doubtless been played time out of mind, yet the laughter it excited was not less genuine.

They were overflowing with civility; but to prevent their almost killing my babe with kindness, I was obliged to shorten my visit; and two or three of the girls accompanied us, bringing with them a part of whatever the house afforded to contribute towards rendering my supper more plentiful; and plentiful in fact it was, though I with difficulty did honour to some of the dishes, not relishing the quantity of sugar and spices put into every thing. At supper my host told me bluntly that I was a woman of observation, for I asked him *men's questions.*

The arrangements for my journey were quickly made; I could only have a car with post-horses, as I did not chuse to wait till a carriage could be sent for to Gothenburg. The expense of my journey, about one or two and twenty English miles, I found would not amount to more than eleven or twelve shillings, paying, he assured me, generously. I gave him a guinea and a half. But it was with the greatest difficulty that I could make him take so much, indeed any thing for my lodging and fare. He declared that it was next to robbing me, explaining how much I ought to pay on the road. However, as I was positive, he took the guinea for himself; but, as a condition, insisted on accompanying me, to prevent my meeting with any trouble or imposition on the way.

I then retired to my apartment with regret. The night was so fine, that I would gladly have rambled about much longer; yet recollecting that I must rise very early, I reluctantly went to bed: but my senses had been so awake, and my imagination still continued so busy, that I sought for rest in vain. Rising before six, I scented the sweet morning air; I had long before heard the birds twittering to hail the dawning day, though it could scarcely have been allowed to have departed.

Nothing, in fact, can equal the beauty of the northern summer's evening and night; if night it may be called that only wants the glare of day, the full light, which frequently seems so impertinent; for I could write at midnight very well without a candle. I contemplated all nature at rest; the rocks, even grown darker in their appearance, looked as if they partook of the general repose, and reclined more heavily on their foundation.—What, I exclaimed, is this active principle which keeps me still awake?—Why fly my thoughts abroad when every thing around me appears at home? My child was sleeping with equal calmness—innocent and sweet as the closing flowers.—Some recollections, attached to the idea of home, mingled with reflections respecting the state of society I had been contemplating that evening, made a tear drop on the rosy cheek I had just kissed; and emotions that trembled on the brink of extacy and agony gave a poignancy to my sensations, which made me feel more alive than usual.

What are these imperious sympathies? How frequently has melancholy and even mysanthropy taken possession of me, when the world has disgusted me, and friends have proved unkind. I have then considered myself as a particle broken off from the grand mass of mankind;—I was alone, till some involuntary sympathetic emotion, like the attraction of adhesion, made me feel that I was still a part of a mighty whole, from which I could not sever myself—not, perhaps, for the reflection has been carried very far, by snapping the thread of an existence which loses its charms in proportion as the cruel experience of life stops or poisons the current of the heart. Futurity, what hast thou not to give to those who know that there is such a thing as happiness! I speak not of philosophical contentment, though pain has afforded them the strongest conviction of it.

from
LETTER III

The population of Sweden has been estimated from two millions and a half to three millions; a small number for such an immense tract of country: of which only so much is cultivated, and that in the simplest manner, as is absolutely necessary to supply the necessaries of life; and near the seashore, from whence herrings are easily procured, there scarcely appears a vestige of cultivation. The scattered huts that stand shivering on the naked rocks, braving the pitiless elements, are formed of logs of wood, rudely hewn; and so little pains are taken with the craggy foundation, that nothing like a pathway points out the door.

Gathered into himself by the cold, lowering his visage to avoid the cutting blast, is it surprising that the churlish pleasure of drinking drams takes place of social enjoyments amongst the poor, especially if we take into the account, that they mostly live on high-seasoned provisions and rye bread? Hard enough, you may imagine, as it is only baked once a year. The servants also, in most families, eat this kind of bread, and have a different kind of food from their masters, which, in spite of all the arguments I have heard to vindicate the custom, appears to me a remnant of barbarism.

In fact, the situation of the servants in every respect, particularly that of the women, shews how far the Swedes are from having a just conception of rational equality. They are not *termed* slaves; yet a man may strike a man with impunity because he pays him wages; though these wages are so low, that necessity must teach them to pilfer, whilst servility renders them false and boorish. Still the men stand up for the dignity of man, by oppressing the women. The most menial, and even laborious offices, are therefore left to these poor drudges. Much of this I have seen. In the winter, I am told, they take the linen down to the river, to wash it in the cold water; and though their hands, cut by the ice, are cracked and bleeding, the men, their fellow servants, will not disgrace their manhood by carrying a tub to lighten their burden.

You will not be surprised to hear that they do not wear shoes or stockings, when I inform you that their wages are seldom more than twenty or thirty shillings per annum. It is the custom, I know, to give them a new year's gift, and a present at some other period; but can it all amount to a just indemnity for their labour? The treatment of servants in most countries, I grant, is very unjust; and in England, that boasted land of freedom, it is often extremely tyrannical. I have frequently, with indignation, heard gentlemen declare that they would never allow a servant to answer them; and ladies of the most exquisite sensibility, who were continually exclaiming against the cruelty of the vulgar to the brute creation, have in my presence forgot that their attendants had human feelings, as well as forms. I do not know a more agreeable sight than to see servants part of a family. By taking an interest, generally speaking, in their concerns, you inspire them with one for yours. We must love our servants, or we shall never be sufficiently attentive to their happiness; and how can those masters be attentive to their happiness, who living above their fortunes, are more anxious to outshine their neighbours than to allow their household the innocent enjoyments they earn.

It is, in fact, much more difficult for servants who are tantalized by seeing and preparing the dainties of which they are not to partake, to remain honest, than the poor, whose thoughts are not led from their homely fare; so that, though the servants here are commonly thieves, you seldom hear of house-breaking, or robbery on the highway. The country is, perhaps, too thinly inhabited to produce many of that description of thieves termed footpads, or highwaymen. They are usually the spawn of great cities; the effect of the spurious desires generated by wealth, rather than the desperate struggles of poverty to escape from misery. . . .

I am, my friend, more and more convinced that a metropolis, or an abode absolutely solitary, is the best calculated for the improvement of the heart, as well as the understanding; whether we desire to become acquainted with man, nature, or ourselves. Mixing with mankind, we are obliged to examine our prejudices, and often imperceptibly lose, as we analyze them. And in the country, growing intimate with nature, a thousand little circumstances, unseen by vulgar eyes, give birth to sentiments dear to the imagination, and inquiries which expand the soul, particularly when cultivation has not smoothed into insipidity all its originality of character.

I love the country; yet whenever I see a picturesque situation chosen on which to erect a dwelling, I am always afraid of the improvements. It requires uncommon taste to form a whole, and to introduce accommodations and ornaments analogous with the surrounding scene.*

I visited, near Gothenburg, a house with improved land about it, with which I was particularly delighted. It was close to a lake embosomed in pine clad rocks. In one part of the meadows, your eye was directed to the broad expanse; in another, you were led into a shade, to see a part of it, in the form of a river, rush amongst the fragments of rocks and roots of trees; nothing seemed forced. One recess, particularly grand and solemn, amongst the towering cliffs, had a rude stone table, and seat, placed in it, that might have served for a druid's haunt; whilst a placid stream below enlivened the flowers on its margin, where light-footed elves would gladly have danced their airy rounds.

Here the hand of taste was conspicuous, though not obtrusive, and formed a contrast with another abode in the same neighbourhood, on which much money had been lavished: where Italian colonades were placed to excite the wonder of the rude craggs; and a stone staircase, to threaten with destruction a wooden house. Venuses and Apollos condemned to lie hid in snow three parts of the year, seemed equally dis-

---

* With respect to gardening in England, I think we often make an egregious blunder by introducing too much shade; not considering that the shade which our climate requires need not be very thick. If it keep off the intense heat of the sun, and afford a solitary retirement, it is sufficient. But in many great gardens, or pleasure-grounds, the sun's rays can scarcely ever penetrate. These may amuse the eye; yet they are not *home walks* to which the owner can retire to enjoy air and solitude; for, excepting during an extraordinary dry summer, they are damp and chill. For the same reason, grottoes are absurd in this temperate climate. An umbrageous tree will afford sufficient shelter from the most ardent heat, that we ever feel. To speak explicitly, the usefulness of a garden ought to be conspicuous, because it ought not to be planted for the season when nature wantons in her prime; for the whole country is then a garden—far sweeter. If not very extensive, I think a garden should contain more shrubs and flowers than lofty trees; and in order to admit the sun-beams to enliven our spring, autumn and winter, serpentine walks, the rage for the line of beauty, should be made to submit to convenience. Yet, in this country, a broad straight gravel walk is a great convenience for those who wish to take exercise in all seasons, after rain particularly. When the weather is fine, the meadows offer winding paths, far superior to the formal turnings that interrupt reflection, without amusing the fancy.—Wollstonecraft.

placed, and called the attention off from the surrounding sublimity, without inspiring any voluptuous sensations. Yet even these abortions of vanity have been useful. Numberless workmen have been employed, and the superintending artist has improved the labourers whose unskilfulness tormented him, by obliging them to submit to the discipline of rules. Adieu!

from
LETTER IV

The severity of the long Swedish winter tends to render the people sluggish; for, though this season has its peculiar pleasures, too much time is employed to guard against its inclemency. Still, as warm cloathing is absolutely necessary, the women spin, and the men weave, and by these exertions get a fence to keep out the cold. I have rarely passed a knot of cottages without seeing cloth laid out to bleach; and when I entered, always found the women spinning or knitting.

A mistaken tenderness, however, for their children, makes them, even in summer, load them with flannels; and, having a sort of natural antipathy to cold water, the squalid appearance of the poor babes, not to speak of the noxious smell which flannel and rugs retain, seems a reply to a question I had often asked—Why I did not see more children in the villages I passed through? Indeed the children appear to be nipt in the bud, having neither the graces nor charms of their age. And this, I am persuaded, is much more owing to the ignorance of the mothers than to the rudeness of the climate. Rendered feeble by the continual perspiration they are kept in, whilst every pore is absorbing unwholesome moisture, they give them, even at the breast, brandy, salt fish, and every other crude substance, which air and exercise enables the parent to digest.

The women of fortune here, as well as every where else, have nurses to suckle their children; and the total want of chastity in the lower class of women frequently renders them very unfit for the trust.*

You have sometimes remarked to me the difference of the manners of the country girls in England and in America; attributing the reserve of the former to the climate—to the absence of genial suns. But it must be their stars, not the zephyrs gently stealing on their senses, which here lead frail women astray.—Who can look at these rocks, and allow the voluptuousness of nature to be an excuse for gratifying the desires

---

* Wollstonecraft is referring to the possibility of venereal disease in promiscuous women.—Editor.

it inspires? We must, therefore, find some other cause beside voluptuousness, I believe, to account for the conduct of the Swedish and American country girls; for I am led to conclude, from all the observations I
have made, that there is always a mixture of sentiment and imagination
in voluptuousness, to which neither of them have much pretension.

The country girls of Ireland and Wales equally feel the first impulse of nature, which, restrained in England by fear or delicacy, proves
that society is there in a more advanced state. Besides, as the mind is
cultivated, and taste gains ground, the passions become stronger, and
rest on something more stable than the casual sympathies of the moment.
Health and idleness will always account for promiscuous amours; and
in some degree I term every person idle, the exercise of whose mind
does not bear some proportion to that of the body.

The Swedish ladies exercise neither sufficiently; of course, grow
very fat at an early age; and when they have not this downy appearance, a comfortable idea, you will say, in a cold climate, they are not
remarkable for fine forms. They have, however, mostly fine complex-
ions; but indolence makes the lily soon displace the rose. The quantity
of coffee, spices, and other things of that kind, with want of care, almost universally spoil their teeth, which contrast but ill with their
ruby lips.

The manners of Stockholm are refined, I hear, by the introduction
of gallantry; but in the country, romping and coarse freedoms, with
coarser allusions, keep the spirits awake. In the article of cleanliness,
the women, of all descriptions, seem very deficient; and their dress
shews that vanity is more inherent in women than taste.

The men appear to have paid still less court to the graces. They are
a robust, healthy race, distinguished for their common sense and turn
for humour, rather than for wit or sentiment. I include not, as you may
suppose, in this general character, some of the nobility and officers,
who having travelled, are polite and well informed.

I must own to you, that the lower class of people here amuse and
interest me much more than the middling, with their apish good breed-
ing and prejudices. The sympathy and frankness of heart conspicuous
in the peasantry produces even a simple gracefulness of deportment,
which has frequently struck me as very picturesque; I have often also
been touched by their extreme desire to oblige me, when I could not
explain my wants, and by their earnest manner of expressing that desire. There is such a charm in tenderness!—It is so delightful to love our
fellow-creatures, and meet the honest affections as they break forth.
Still, my good friend, I begin to think that I should not like to live
continually in the country, with people whose minds have such a nar-

row range. My heart would frequently be interested; but my mind would languish for more companionable society.

The beauties of nature appear to me now even more alluring than in my youth, because my intercourse with the world has formed, without vitiating my taste. But, with respect to the inhabitants of the country, my fancy has probably, when disgusted with artificial manners, solaced itself by joining the advantages of cultivation with the interesting sincerity of innocence, forgetting the lassitude that ignorance will naturally produce. I like to see animals sporting, and sympathize in their pains and pleasures. Still I love sometimes to view the human face divine, and trace the soul, as well as the heart, in its varying lineaments.

from
LETTER V*

Arriving at Fredericshall, at the siege of which Charles XII lost his life,† we had only time to take a transient view of it, wilst they were preparing us some refreshment.

Poor Charles! I thought of him with respect. I have always felt the same for Alexander; with whom he has been classed as a madman, by several writers, who have reasoned superficially, confounding the morals of the day with the few grand principles on which unchangeable morality rests. Making no allowance for the ignorance and prejudices of the period, they do not perceive how much they themselves are indebted to general improvement for the acquirements, and even the virtues, which they would not have had the force of mind to attain, by their individual exertions in a less advanced state of society.

The evening was fine, as is usual at this season; and the refreshing odour of the pine woods became more perceptible; for it was nine o'clock when we left Fredericshall. At the ferry we were detained by a dispute relative to our Swedish passport, which we did not think of getting countersigned in Norway. Midnight was coming on; yet it might with such propriety have been termed the noon of night, that had Young ever travelled towards the north, I should not have wondered at his becoming enamoured of the moon.‡ But it is not the queen

---

* By this stage Wollstonecraft was traveling alone; she had left Marguerite and Fanny at Gothenburg, expecting the next section of her journey to be hazardous.—Editor.

† Charles XII of Sweden (1682–1718), a renowned military commander, was killed at the siege of Fredrikshald during his invasion of Norway, at that time ruled by Denmark.—Editor.

‡ Edward Young's *Night Thoughts* (1742–1745) contains an invocation to the moon.—Editor.

of night alone who reigns here in all her splendor, though the sun, loitering just below the horizon, decks her with a golden tinge from his car, illuminating the cliffs that hide him; the heavens also, of a clear softened blue, throw her forward, and the evening star appears a lesser moon to the naked eye. The huge shadows of the rocks, fringed with firs, concentrating the views, without darkening them, excited that tender melancholy which, sublimating the imagination, exalts, rather than depresses the mind.

My companions fell asleep:—fortunately they did not snore; and I contemplated, fearless of idle questions, a night such as I had never before seen or felt to charm the senses, and calm the heart. The very air was balmy, as it freshened into morn, producing the most voluptuous sensations. A vague pleasurable sentiment absorbed me, as I opened my bosom to the embraces of nature; and my soul rose to its author, with the chirping of the solitary birds, which began to feel, rather than see, advancing day. I had leisure to mark its progress. The grey morn, streaked with silvery rays, ushered in the orient beams,— how beautifully varying into purple!—yet, I was sorry to lose the soft watry clouds which preceded them, exciting a kind of expectation that made me almost afraid to breathe, lest I should break the charm. I saw the sun—and sighed.

One of my companions, now awake, perceiving that the postillion had mistaken the road, began to swear at him, and roused the other two, who reluctantly shook off sleep.

We had immediately to measure back our steps, and did not reach Stromstad before five in the morning.

The wind had changed in the night, and my boat was ready.

A dish of coffee, and fresh linen, recruited my spirits; and I directly set out again for Norway; purposing to land much higher up the coast.

Wrapping my great coat round me, I lay down on some sails at the bottom of the boat, its motion rocking me to rest, till a discourteous wave interrupted my slumbers, and obliged me to rise and feel a solitariness which was not so soothing as that of the past night.

from
LETTER VI

As the Norwegians do not frequently see travellers, they are very curious to know their business, and who they are—so curious that I was half tempted to adopt Dr. Franklin's plan, when travelling in America, where they are equally prying, which was to write on a paper, for public inspection, my name, from whence I came, where I was going, and what was my business. But if I were importuned by their curiosity, their friendly gestures gratified me. A woman, coming alone, interested them. And I know not whether my weariness gave me a look of peculiar delicacy; but they approached to assist me, and enquire after my wants, as if they were afraid to hurt, and wished to protect me. The sympathy I inspired, thus dropping down from the clouds in a strange land, affected me more than it would have done, had not my spirits been harassed by various causes—by much thinking—musing almost to madness—and even by a sort of weak melancholy that hung about my heart at parting with my daughter for the first time.

You know that as a female I am particularly attached to her—I feel more than a mother's fondness and anxiety, when I reflect on the dependent and oppressed state of her sex. I dread lest she should be forced to sacrifice her heart to her principles, or principles to her heart. With trembling hand I shall cultivate sensibility, and cherish delicacy of sentiment, lest, whilst I lend fresh blushes to the rose, I sharpen the thorns that will wound the breast I would fain guard—I dread to unfold her mind, lest it should render her unfit for the world she is to inhabit—Hapless woman! what a fate is thine!

But whither am I wandering? I only meant to tell you that the impression the kindness of the simple people made visible on my countenance increased my sensibility to a painful degree. I wished to have had a room to myself; for their attention, and rather distressing observation, embarrassed me extremely. Yet, as they would bring me eggs, and make my coffee, I found I could not leave them without hurting their feelings of hospitality.

It is customary here for the host and hostess to welcome their guests as master and mistress of the house.

My clothes, in their turn, attracted the attention of the females; and I could not help thinking of the foolish vanity which makes many women so proud of the observation of strangers as to take wonder very gratuitously for admiration. This error they are very apt to fall into; when arrived in a foreign country, the populace stare at them as they pass: yet the make of a cap, or the singularity of a gown, is often the cause of the flattering attention, which afterwards supports a fantastic superstructure of self-conceit. . . .

Amongst the Norwegians I had the arrangement of my own time; and I determined to regulate it in such a manner, that I might enjoy as much of their sweet summer as I possibly could;—short, it is true; but "passing sweet."

I never endured a winter in this rude clime; consequently it was not the contrast, but the real beauty of the season which made the present summer appear to me the finest I had ever seen. Sheltered from the north and eastern winds, nothing can exceed the salubrity, the soft freshness of the western gales. In the evening they also die away; the aspen leaves tremble into stillness, and reposing nature seems to be warmed by the moon, which here assumes a genial aspect: and if a light shower has chanced to fall with the sun, the juniper the under-wood of the forest, exhales a wild perfume, mixed with a thousand nameless sweets, that, soothing the heart, leave images in the memory which the imagination will ever hold dear.

Nature is the nurse of sentiment,—the true source of taste;—yet what misery, as well as rapture, is produced by a quick perception of the beautiful and sublime, when it is exercised in observing animated nature, when every beauteous feeling and emotion excites responsive sympathy, and the harmonized soul sinks into melancholy, or rises to extasy, just as the chords are touched, like the aeolian harp agitated by the changing wind. But how dangerous is it to foster these sentiments in such an imperfect state of existence; and how difficult to eradicate them when an affection for mankind, a passion for an individual, is but the unfolding of that love which embraces all that is great and beautiful.

When a warm heart has received strong impressions, they are not to be effaced. Emotions become sentiments; and the imagination renders even transient sensations permanent, by fondly retracing them. I cannot, without a thrill of delight, recollect views I have seen, which are not to be forgotten,—nor looks I have felt in every nerve which I shall never more meet. The grave has closed over a dear friend, the friend of my youth;* still she is present with me, and I hear her soft voice warbling as I stray over the heath. Fate has separated me from another, the fire of whose eyes, tempered by infantine tenderness, still warms my breast; even when gazing on these tremendous cliffs, sublime emotions absorb my soul. And, smile not, if I add, that the rosy tint of morning reminds me of a suffusion, which will never more charm my senses, unless it reappears on the cheeks of my child. Her sweet blushes I may yet hide in my bosom, and she is still too young to ask why starts the tear, so near akin to pleasure and pain?

I cannot write any more at present. Tomorrow we will talk of Tonsberg.

from
LETTER VII

The Norwegians are fond of music; and every little church has an organ. In the church I have mentioned, there is an inscription import-

* Fanny Blood.—Editor.

ing that a king,* James the sixth, of Scotland, and first of England, who came with more than princely gallantry, to escort his bride home, stood there, and heard divine service.

There is a little recess full of coffins, which contains bodies embalmed long since—so long, that there is not even a tradition to lead to a guess at their names.

A desire of preserving the body seems to have prevailed in most countries of the world, futile as it is to term it a preservation, when the noblest parts are immediately sacrificed merely to save the muscles, skin and bone from rottenness. When I was shewn these human petrifactions, I shrunk back with disgust and horror. "Ashes to ashes!" thought I—"Dust to dust!"—If this be not dissolution, it is something worse than natural decay. It is treason against humanity, thus to lift up the awful veil which would fain hide its weakness. The grandeur of the active principle is never more strongly felt than at such a sight; for nothing is so ugly as the human form when deprived of life, and thus dried into stone, merely to preserve the most disgusting image of death. The contemplation of noble ruins produces a melancholy that exalts the mind.—We take a retrospect of the exertions of man, the fate of empires and their rulers; and marking the grand destruction of ages, it seems the necessary change of time leading to improvement.—Our very soul expands, and we forget our littleness; how painfully brought to our recollection by such vain attempts to snatch from decay what is destined so soon to perish. Life, what art thou? Where goes this breath? this I, so much alive? In what element will it mix, giving or receiving fresh energy?—What will break the enchantment of animation?—For worlds, I would not see a form I loved—embalmed in my heart—thus sacrilegiously handled!—Pugh! my stomach turns.—Is this all the distinction of the rich in the grave?—They had better quietly allow the scythe of

---

* "Anno 1589, St. Martin's Day, which was the 11th Day of November, on a Tuesday, came the high-born Prince and Lord Jacob Stuart, King in Scotland, to this Town, and the 25th Sunday after Trinity (Sunday:) which was the 16th Day of November, stood his Grace in this Pew, and heard Scotch Preaching from the 23d Psalm, 'The Lord is my Shepherd,' &c. which M. David Lentz, Preacher in Lith, then preached between 10 and 12."

The above is an inscription which stands in St. Mary's church, in Tonsberg [Norway].

It is known that king James the sixth went to Norway, to marry Princess Anna, the daughter of Frederick the second, and sister to Christian the fourth; and that the wedding was performed at Opslo (now Christiania), where the princess, by contrary winds, was detained; but that the king, during this voyage, was at Tonsberg, nobody would have known, if an inscription, in remembrance of it, had not been placed in this church.—Wollstonecraft.

equality to mow them down with the common mass, than struggle to
become a monument of the instability of human greatness.

The teeth, nails and skin were whole, without appearing black like
the Egyptian mummies; and some silk, in which they had been wrapt,
still preserved its colour, pink, with tolerable freshness.

I could not learn how long the bodies had been in this state, in
which they bid fair to remain till the day of judgment, if there is to be
such a day; and before that time, it will require some trouble to make
them fit to appear in company with angels, without disgracing humanity.—God bless you! I feel a conviction that we have some perfectible
principle in our present vestment, which will not be destroyed just as
we begin to be sensible of improvement; and I care not what habit it
next puts on, sure that it will be wisely formed to suit a higher state of
existence. Thinking of death makes us tenderly cling to our affections
—with more than usual tenderness, I therefore assure you that I am
yours, wishing that the temporary death of absence may not endure
longer than is absolutely necessary.

from
LETTER VIII

Tonsberg was formerly the residence of one of the little sovereigns
of Norway; and on an adjacent mountain the vestiges of a fort remain,
which was battered down by the Swedes; the entrance of the bay lying
close to it.

Here I have frequently strayed, sovereign of the waste, I seldom met
any human creature; and sometimes, reclining on the mossy down, under the shelter of a rock, the prattling of the sea amongst the pebbles
has lulled me to sleep—no fear of any rude satyr's approaching to interrupt my repose. Balmy were the slumbers, and soft the gales, that re-
freshed me, when I awoke to follow, with an eye vaguely curious, the
white sails, as they turned the cliffs, or seemed to take shelter under
the pines which covered the little islands that so gracefully rose to render the terrific ocean beautiful. The fishermen were calmly casting their
nets; whilst the seagulls hovered over the unruffled deep. Every thing
seemed to harmonize into tranquillity—even the mournful call of the
bittern was in cadence with the tinkling bells on the necks of the cows,
that, pacing slowly one after the other, along an inviting path in the
vale below, were repairing to the cottages to be milked. With what ineffable pleasure have I not gazed—and gazed again, losing my breath
through my eyes—my very soul diffused itself in the scene—and, seeming to become all senses, glided in the scarcely-agitated waves, melted

in the freshening breeze, or, taking its flight with fairy wing, to the misty mountains which bounded the prospect, fancy tript over new lawns, more beautiful even than the lovely slopes on the winding shore before me.—I pause, again breathless, to trace, with renewed delight, sentiments which entranced me, when, turning my humid eyes from the expanse below to the vault above, my sight pierced the fleecy clouds that softened the azure brightness; and, imperceptibly recalling the reveries of childhood, I bowed before the awful throne of my Creator, whilst I rested on its footstool.

You have sometimes wondered, my dear friend, at the extreme affection of my nature—But such is the temperature of my soul—It is not the vivacity of youth, the hey-day of existence. For years have I endeavoured to calm an impetuous tide—labouring to make my feelings take an orderly course.—It was striving against the stream.—I must love and admire with warmth, or I sink into sadness. Tokens of love which I have received have rapt me in elysium—purifying the heart they enchanted. —My bosom still glows.—Do not saucily ask, repeating Sterne's question, "Maria, is it still so warm?"* Sufficiently, O my God! has it been chilled by sorrow and unkindness—still nature will prevail—and if I blush at recollecting past enjoyment, it is the rosy hue of pleasure heightened by modesty; for the blush of modesty and shame are as distinct as the emotions by which they are produced.

I need scarcely inform you, after telling you of my walks, that my constitution has been renovated here; and that I have recovered my activity, even whilst attaining a little *embonpoint*.† My imprudence last winter, and some untoward accidents just at the time I was weaning my child, had reduced me to a state of weakness which I never before experienced. A slow fever preyed on me every night, during my residence in Sweden, and after I arrived at Tonsberg. By chance I found a fine rivulet filtered through the rocks, and confined in a bason for the cattle. It tasted to me like a chalybeat;‡ at any rate it was pure; and the good effect of the various waters which invalids are sent to drink, depends, I believe, more on the air, exercise and change of scene, than on their medicinal qualities. I therefore determined to turn my morning walks towards it, and seek for health from the nymph of the fountain; partaking of the beverage offered to the tenants of the shade.

* In Laurence Sterne's *Sentimental Journey*, the traveler Yorick cries so profusely over Maria's misfortunes that he drenches his handkerchief. She says she will dry it in her bosom, to which Yorick replies, "And is your heart still so warm, Maria?"— Editor.

† Plumpness.—Editor.

‡ Mineral water impregnated with iron, often used as a tonic.—Editor.

Chance likewise led me to discover a new pleasure, equally bene-
ficial to my health. I wished to avail myself of my vicinity to the sea,
and bathe; but it was not possible near the town; there was no convenience. The young woman whom I mentioned to you, proposed row-
ing me across the water, amongst the rocks; but as she was pregnant, I
insisted on taking one of the oars, and learning to row. It was not difficult; and I do not know a pleasanter exercise. I soon became expert, and
my train of thinking kept time, as it were, with the oars, or I suffered
the boat to be carried along by the current, indulging a pleasing forgetfulness, or fallacious hopes.—How fallacious! yet, without hope, what
is to sustain life, but the fear of annihilation—the only thing of which
I have ever felt dread—I cannot bear to think of being no more—of
losing myself—though existence is often but a painful consciousness
of misery; nay, it appears to me impossible that I should cease to exist,
or that this active, restless spirit, equally alive to joy and sorrow, should
only be organized dust—ready to fly abroad the moment the spring
snaps, or the spark goes out, which kept it together. Surely something
resides in this heart that is not perishable—and life is more than a
dream.

Sometimes, to take up my oar, once more, when the sea was calm,
I was amused by disturbing the innumerable young star fish which
floated just below the surface: I had never observed them before; for
they have not a hard shell, like those which I have seen on the sea-shore.
They look like thickened water, with a white edge; and four purple
circles, of different forms, were in the middle, over an incredible number of fibres, or white lines. Touching them, the cloudy substance
would turn or close, first on one side, then on the other, very gracefully;
but when I took one of them up in the ladle with which I heaved the
water out of the boat, it appeared only a colourless jelly.

I did not see any of the seals, numbers of which followed our boat
when we landed in Sweden; for though I like to sport in the water, I
should have had no desire to join in their gambols.

from
LETTER IX

As the farmers cut away the wood, they clear the ground. Every
year, therefore, the country is becoming fitter to support the inhabitants. Half a century ago the Dutch, I am told, only paid for the cutting
down of the wood, and the farmers were glad to get rid of it without
giving themselves any trouble. At present they form a just estimate of
its value; nay, I was surprised to find even fire wood so dear, when it

appears to be in such plenty. The destruction, or gradual reduction, of their forests, will probably meliorate the climate; and their manners will naturally improve in the same ratio as industry requires ingenuity. It is very fortunate that men are, a long time, but just above the brute creation, or the greater part of the earth would never have been rendered habitable; because it is the patient labour of men, who are only seeking for a subsistence, which produces whatever embellishes existence, affording leisure for the cultivation of the arts and sciences, that lift man so far above his first state. I never, my friend, thought so deeply of the advantages obtained by human industry as since I have been in Norway. The world requires, I see, the hand of man to perfect it; and as this task naturally unfolds the faculties he exercises, it is physically impossible that he should have remained in Rousseau's golden age of stupidity.* And, considering the question of human happiness, where, oh! where does it reside? Has it taken up its abode with unconscious ignorance, or with the high-wrought mind? Is it the offspring of thoughtless animal spirits, or the elve of fancy continually flitting round the expected pleasure?

The increasing population of the earth must necessarily tend to its improvement, as the means of existence are multiplied by invention.

You have probably made similar reflections in America, where the face of the country, I suppose, resembles the wilds of Norway.† I am delighted with the romantic views I daily contemplate, animated by the purest air; and I am interested by the simplicity of manners which reigns around me. Still nothing so soon wearies out the feelings as unmarked simplicity. I am, therefore, half convinced, that I could not live very comfortably exiled from the countries where mankind are so much further advanced in knowledge, imperfect as it is, and unsatisfactory to the thinking mind. Even now I begin to long to hear what you are doing in England and France. My thoughts fly from this wilderness to the polished circles of the world, till recollecting its vices and follies, I bury myself in the woods, but find it necessary to emerge again, that I may not lose sight of the wisdom and virtue which exalts my nature.

What a long time it requires to know ourselves; and yet almost every one has more of this knowledge than he is willing to own, even to him-

---

* Wollstonecraft is mocking what she takes to be Jean-Jacques Rousseau's idea of the state of nature, in which a person was free and alone, without limitation by social institutions and customs. Rousseau in fact did not treat such a state as a reality; rather, it was a hypothesis, against which actual societies could be measured.—Editor.

† Although Imlay was born and raised in New Jersey, he claimed to have passed his childhood "in the back parts of America."—Editor.

self. I cannot immediately determine whether I ought to rejoice at having turned over in this solitude a new page in the history of my own heart, though I may venture to assure you that a further acquaintance with mankind only tends to increase my respect for your judgment, and esteem for your character.

from
LETTER XI

The view of this wild coast, as we sailed along it, afforded me a continual subject for meditation. I anticipated the future improvement of the world, and observed how much man had still to do, to obtain of the earth all it could yield. I even carried my speculations so far as to advance a million or two of years to the moment when the earth would perhaps be so perfectly cultivated, and so completely peopled, as to render it necessary to inhabit every spot; yes; these bleak shores. Imagination went still farther, and pictured the state of man when the earth could no longer support him. Where was he to fly to from universal famine? Do not smile: I really became distressed for these fellow creatures, yet unborn. The images fastened on me, and the world appeared a vast prison. I was soon to be in a smaller one—for no other name can I give to Rusoer. It would be difficult to form an idea of the place, if you have never seen one of these rocky coasts.

We were a considerable time entering amongst the islands, before we saw about two hundred houses crowded together, under a very high rock—still higher appearing above. Talk not of bastilles! To be born here, was to be bastilled by nature—shut out from all that opens the understanding, or enlarges the heart. Huddled one behind another, not more than a quarter of the dwellings even had a prospect of the sea. A few planks formed passages from house to house, which you must often scale, mounting steps like a ladder, to enter.

The only road across the rocks leads to a habitation, sterile enough, you may suppose, when I tell you that the little earth on the adjacent ones was carried there by the late inhabitant. A path, almost impracticable for a horse, goes on to Arendall, still further to the westward.

I enquired for a walk, and mounting near two hundred steps made round a rock, walked up and down for about a hundred yards, viewing the sea, to which I quickly descended by steps that cheated the declivity. The ocean, and these tremendous bulwarks, enclosed me on every side. I felt the confinement, and wished for wings to reach still loftier cliffs, whose slippery sides no foot was so hardy as to tread; yet what was it to see?—only a boundless waste of water—not a glimpse of smiling nature—not a patch of lively green to relieve the aching sight, or vary the objects of meditation.

I felt my breath oppressed, though nothing could be clearer than the atmosphere. Wandering there alone, I found the solitude desirable; my mind was stored with ideas, which this new scene associated with astonishing rapidity. But I shuddered at the thought of receiving existence, and remaining here, in the solitude of ignorance, till forced to leave a world of which I had seen so little; for the character of the inhabitants is as uncultivated, if not as picturesquely wild, as their abode.

Having no employment but traffic, of which a contraband trade makes the basis of their profit, the coarsest feelings of honesty are quickly blunted. You may suppose that I speak in general terms; and that, with all the disadvantages of nature and circumstances, there are still some respectable exceptions, the more praiseworthy, as tricking is a very contagious mental disease that dries up all the generous juices of the heart. Nothing genial, in fact, appears around this place, or within the circle of its rocks. And, now I recollect, it seems to me that the most genial and humane characters I have met with in life, were most alive to the sentiments inspired by tranquil country scenes. What, indeed, is to humanise these beings, who rest shut up, for they seldom even open their windows, smoking, drinking brandy, and driving bargains? I have been almost stifled by these smokers. They begin in the morning, and are rarely without their pipe till they go to bed. Nothing can be more disgusting than the rooms and men towards the evening: breath, teeth, clothes, and furniture, all are spoilt. It is well that the women are not very delicate, or they would only love their husbands because they were their husbands. Perhaps, you may add, that the remark need not be confined to so small a part of the world; and, *entre nous,* I am of the same opinion. You must not term this inuendo fancy, for it does not come home.*

If I had not determined to write, I should have found my confinement here, even for three or four days, tedious. I have no books; and to pace up and down a small room, looking at tiles, overhung by rocks, soon becomes wearisome. I cannot mount two hundred steps, to walk a hundred yards, many times in the day. Besides, the rocks, retaining the heat of the sun, are intolerably warm. I am nevertheless very well; for though there is a shrewdness in the character of these people, depraved by a sordid love of money which repels me, still the comparisons

* Wollstonecraft regarded Imlay as her husband.—Editor.

they force me to make keep my heart calm, by exercising my understanding.

Every where wealth commands too much respect; but here, almost
exclusively; and it is the only object pursued—not through brake and
briar, but over rocks and waves—yet of what use would riches be to me?
I have sometimes asked myself, were I confined to live in such a spot. I
could only relieve a few distressed objects, perhaps render them idle,
and all the rest of life would be a blank.

My present journey has given fresh force to my opinion, that no
place is so disagreeable and unimproving as a country town. I should
like to divide my time between the town and country; in a lone house,
with the business of farming and planting, where my mind would gain
strength by solitary musing; and in a metropolis to rub off the rust of
thought, and polish the taste which the contemplation of nature had
rendered just. Thus do we wish as we float down the stream of life,
whilst chance does more to gratify a desire of knowledge than our best-
laid plans. A degree of exertion, produced by some want, more or less
painful, is probably the price we must all pay for knowledge. How few
authors or artists have arrived at eminence who have not lived by their
employment?

LETTER XII

I left East Rusoer the day before yesterday. The weather was very
fine; but so calm that we loitered on the water near fourteen hours, only
to make about six and twenty miles.

It seemed to me a sort of emancipation when we landed at Hel-
geraac. The confinement which every where struck me whilst sojourn-
ing amongst the rocks, made me hail the earth as a land of promise; and
the situation shone with fresh lustre from the contrast—from appearing to be a free abode. Here it was possible to travel by land—I never
thought this a comfort before, and my eyes, fatigued by the sparkling of
the sun on the water, now contentedly reposed on the green expanse,
half persuaded that such verdant meads had never till then regaled
them.

I rose early to pursue my journey to Tonsberg. The country still
wore a face of joy—and my soul was alive to its charms. Leaving the
most lofty, and romantic of the cliffs behind us, we were almost continually descending to Tonsberg, through elysian scenes; for not only
the sea, but mountains, rivers, lakes, and groves, gave an almost endless
variety to the prospect. The cottagers were still leading home the hay;
and the cottages, on this road, looked very comfortable. Peace and plenty

—I mean not abundance, seemed to reign around—still I grew sad as I drew near my old abode. I was sorry to see the sun so high; it was broad noon. Tonsberg was something like a home—yet I was to enter without lighting-up pleasure in any eye—I dreaded the solitariness of my apartment, and wished for night to hide the starting tears, or to shed them on my pillow, and close my eyes on a world where I was destined to wander alone. Why has nature so many charms for me—calling forth and cherishing refined sentiments, only to wound the breast that fosters them? How illusive, perhaps the most so, are the plans of happiness founded on virtue and principle; what inlets of misery do they not open in a half civilized society? The satisfaction arising from conscious recti- tude, will not calm an injured heart, when tenderness is ever finding excuses; and self-applause is a cold solitary feeling, that cannot supply the place of disappointed affection, without throwing a gloom over every prospect, which, banishing pleasure, does not exclude pain. I reasoned and reasoned; but my heart was too* full to allow me to remain in the house, and I walked, till I was wearied out, to purchase rest—or rather forgetfulness.

Employment has beguiled this day, and tomorrow I set out for Moss, in my way to Stromstad. At Gothenburg I shall embrace my *Fannikin*; probably she will not know me again—and I shall be hurt if she do not. How childish is this! still it is a natural feeling. I would not permit my- self to indulge the "thick coming fears" of fondness, whilst I was de- tained by business.—Yet I never saw a calf bounding in a meadow, that did not remind me of my little frolicker. A calf, you say. Yes; but a *cap- ital* one, I own.

I cannot write composedly—I am every instant sinking into reveries —my heart flutters, I know not why. Fool! It is time thou wert at rest.

Friendship and domestic happiness are continually praised; yet how little is there of either in the world, because it requires more cultivation of mind to keep awake affection, even in our own hearts, than the com- mon run of people suppose. Besides, few like to be seen as they really are; and a degree of simplicity, and of undisguised confidence, which, to uninterested observers, would almost border on weakness, is the charm, nay the essence of love or friendship: all the bewitching graces of childhood again appearing. As objects merely to exercise my taste, I therefore like to see people together who have an affection for each other; every turn of their features touches me, and remains pictured on my imagination in indelible characters. The zest of novelty is, however, necessary to rouse the languid sympathies which have been hacknied

* "Two" in original text.—Editor.

in the world; as is the factitious behaviour, falsely termed good-breed-
ing, to amuse those, who, defective in taste, continually rely for pleasure
on their animal spirits, which not being maintained by the imagination,
are unavoidably sooner exhausted than the sentiments of the heart.
Friendship is in general sincere at the commencement, and lasts whilst
there is any thing to support it; but as a mixture of novelty and vanity
is the usual prop, no wonder if it fall with the slender stay. The fop in
the play, payed a greater compliment than he was aware of, when he
said to a person, whom he meant to flatter, "I like you almost as well as
a *new acquaintance.*"* Why am I talking of friendship, after which I
have had such a wild-goose chace.—I thought only of telling you that
the crows, as well as wild-geese, are here birds of passage.

from
LETTER XIX

Business having obliged me to go a few miles out of town this morning, I was surprised at meeting a crowd of people of every description;
and inquiring the cause, of a servant who spoke French, I was informed
that a man had been executed two hours before, and the body afterwards burnt. I could not help looking with horror around—the fields
lost their verdure—and I turned with disgust from the well-dressed
women, who were returning with their children from this sight. What
a spectacle for humanity! The seeing such a flock of idle gazers, plunged
me into a train of reflections, on the pernicious effects produced by false
notions of justice. And I am persuaded that till capital punishments be
entirely abolished, executions ought to have every appearance of horrour given to them; instead of being, as they are now, a scene of amusement for the gaping crowd, where sympathy is quickly effaced by
curiosity.

I have always been of opinion that the allowing actors to die, in the
presence of the audience, has an immoral tendency; but trifling when
compared with the ferocity acquired by viewing the reality as a show;
for it seems to me, that in all countries the common people go to executions to see how the poor wretch plays his part, rather than to com-
miserate his fate, much less to think of the breach of morality which has
brought him to such a deplorable end. Consequently executions, far
from being useful examples to the survivors, have, I am persuaded, a

* A reference to William Wycherley's play *The Country Wife*, where the fop,
Sparkish, says "For though I have known thee a great while, never go, if I do not love
thee as well as a new acquaintance."—Editor.

quite contrary effect, by hardening the heart they ought to terrify. Besides, the fear of an ignominious death, I believe, never deterred any one from the commission of a crime; because, in committing it, the mind is roused to activity about present circumstances. It is a game at hazard, at which all expect the turn of the die in their own favour; never reflecting on the chance of ruin, till it comes. In fact, from what I saw, in the fortresses of Norway, I am more and more convinced that the same energy of character, which renders a man a daring villain, would have rendered him useful to society, had that society been well organized. When a strong mind is not disciplined by cultivation, it is a sense of injustice that renders it unjust. . . .

Wealth does not appear to be sought for, amongst the Danes, to obtain the elegant luxuries of life; for a want of taste is very conspicuous at Copenhagen; so much so, that I am not surprised to hear that poor Matilda* offended the rigid Lutherans, by aiming to refine their pleasures. The elegance which she wished to introduce, was termed lasciviousness: yet I do not find that the absence of gallantry renders the wives more chaste, or the husbands more constant. Love here seems to corrupt the morals, without polishing the manners, by banishing confidence and truth, the charm as well as cement of domestic life. A gentleman, who has resided in this city some time, assures me that he could not find language to give me an idea of the gross debaucheries into which the lower order of people fall; and the promiscuous amours of the men of the middling class with their female servants, debases both beyond measure, weakening every species of family affection.

I have every where been struck by one characteristic difference in the conduct of the two sexes; women, in general, are seduced by their superiors, and men jilted by their inferiors; rank and manners awe the one, and cunning and wantonness subjugate the other; ambition creeping into the woman's passion, and tyranny giving force to the man's; for most men treat their mistresses as kings do their favourites: *ergo* is not man then the tyrant of the creation?

Still harping on the same subject, you will exclaim—How can I avoid it, when most of the struggles of an eventful life have been occasioned by the oppressed state of my sex: we reason deeply, when we forcibly feel.

* Caroline Matilda was the sister of the British King, George III. She was married while still in her teens to the cruel and unstable Danish King, Christian VII. Her affair with the court physician led to her imprisonment and his execution. Wollstonecraft admired Matilda for her advanced ideas in child-rearing and her efforts to refine the Danish court.—Editor.

from
LETTER XXII

Arriving at Sleswick, the residence of prince Charles of Hesse-Cassel, the sight of the soldiers recalled all the unpleasing ideas of German despotism, which imperceptibly vanished as I advanced into the country. I viewed, with a mixture of pity and horrour, these beings training to be sold to slaughter, or be slaughtered, and fell into reflections, on an old opinion of mine, that it is the preservation of the species, not of individuals, which appears to be the design of the Deity throughout the whole of nature. Blossoms come forth only to be blighted; fish lay their spawn where it will be devoured: and what a large portion of the human race are born merely to be swept prematurely away. Does not this waste of budding life emphatically assert, that it is not men, but man, whose preservation is so necessary to the completion of the grand plan of the universe? Children peep into existence, suffer, and die; men play like moths about a candle, and sink into the flame: war, and "the thousand ills which flesh is heir to," mow them down in shoals, whilst the more cruel prejudices of society palsies existence, introducing not less sure, though slower decay.

from
LETTER XXV

I left this letter unfinished, as I was hurried on board; and now I have only to tell you, that, at the sight of Dover cliffs, I wondered how any body could term them grand; they appear so insignificant to me, after those I had seen in Sweden and Norway.

Adieu! My spirit of observation seems to be fled—and I have been wandering round this dirty place, literally speaking, to kill time; though the thoughts, I would fain fly from, lie too close to my heart to be easily shook off, or even beguiled, by any employment, except that of preparing for my journey to London.—God bless you!

"On Poetry and Our Relish for the Beauties of Nature"

This essay appeared as a letter signed "W.Q." in the *Monthly Magazine* of April 1797; it was Wollstonecraft's first periodical contribution outside the *Analytical Review*. In 1798 the work was included by Godwin in *Posthumous Works*. Like *Letters Written . . . in Sweden* in its treatment of aesthetic appreciation and nature, the essay modifies the severe rationalism of the two *Vindications* and *The French Revolution*. In addition it reaffirms Wollstonecraft's belief in the significance and value of spontaneous emotions.

A TASTE for rural scenes, in the present state of society, appears to be very often an artificial sentiment, rather inspired by poetry and romances, than a real perception of the beauties of nature. But, as it is reckoned a proof of refined taste to praise the calm pleasures which the country affords, the theme is never exhausted. Yet it may be made a question, whether this romantic kind of declamation, has much effect on the conduct of those, who leave, for a season, the crowded cities in which they were bred.

I have been led to these reflections, by observing, when I have resided for any length of time in the country, how few people seem to contemplate nature with their own eyes. I have "brushed the dew away" in the morning; but, pacing over the printless grass, I have wondered that, in such delightful situations, the sun was allowed to rise in solitary majesty, whilst my eyes alone hailed its beautifying beams. The webs of the evening have still been spread across the hedged path, unless some labouring man, trudging to work, disturbed the fairy structure; yet, in spite of this supineness, when I joined the social circle, every tongue rang changes on the pleasures of the country.

Having frequently had occasion to make the same observation, I was led to endeavour, in one of my solitary rambles, to trace the cause, and likewise to enquire why the poetry written in the infancy of society, is most natural: which, strictly speaking (for *natural* is a very indefinite expression) is merely to say, that it is the transcript of immediate sensations, in all their native wildness and simplicity, when fancy, awakened by the sight of interesting objects, was most actively at work. At such moments, sensibility quickly furnishes smiles, and the sublimated spirits combine images, which rising spontaneously, it is not necessary coldly to ransack the understanding or memory, till the laborious efforts of judgment exclude present sensations, and damp the fire of enthusiasm.

The effusions of a vigorous mind, will ever tell us how far the understanding has been enlarged by thought, and stored with knowledge. The richness of the soil even appears on the surface; and the result of profound thinking, often mixing, with playful grace, in the reveries of the poet, smoothly incorporates with the ebullitions of animal spirits, when the finely fashioned nerve vibrates acutely with rapture, or when, relaxed by soft melancholy, a pleasing languor prompts the long-drawn sigh, and feeds the slowly falling tear.

The poet, the man of strong feelings, gives us only an image of his mind, when he was actually alone, conversing with himself, and marking the impression which nature had made on his own heart.— If, at this sacred moment, the idea of some departed friend, some tender recollection when the soul was most alive to tenderness, intruded unawares into his thoughts, the sorrow which it produced is artlessly, yet poetically expressed—and who can avoid sympathizing?

Love to man leads to devotion—grand and sublime images strike the imagination—God is seen in every floating cloud, and comes from the misty mountain to receive the noblest homage of an intelligent creature—praise. How solemn is the moment, when all affections and remembrances fade before the sublime admiration which the wisdom and goodness of God inspires, when he is worshipped in a *temple not made with hands*, and the world seems to contain only the mind that formed, and the mind that contemplates it! These are not the weak responses of ceremonial devotion; nor, to express them, would the poet need another poet's aid his heart burns within him, and he speaks the language of truth and nature with resistless energy.

Inequalities, of course, are observable in his effusions; and a less vigorous fancy, with more taste, would have produced more elegance and uniformity; but, as passages are softened or expunged during the cooler moments of reflection, the understanding is gratified at the expence of those involuntary sensations, which, like the beauteous tints of an evening sky, are so evanescent, that they melt into new forms before they can be analyzed. For however eloquently we may boast of our reason, man must often be delighted he cannot tell why, or his blunt feelings are not made to relish the beauties which nature, poetry, or any of the imitative arts, afford.

The imagery of the ancients seems naturally to have been borrowed from surrounding objects and their mythology. When a hero is to be transported from one place to another, across pathless wastes, is any vehicle so natural, as one of the fleecy clouds on which the poet has often gazed, scarcely conscious that he wished to make it his chariot? Again, when nature seems to present obstacles to his progress at almost every step, when the tangled forest and steep mountain stand as barriers, to pass over which the mind longs for supernatural aid; an interposing deity, who walks on the waves, and rules the storm, severely felt in the first attempts to cultivate a country, will receive from the impassioned fancy "a local habitation and a name."

It would be a philosophical enquiry, and throw some light on the history of the human mind, to trace, as far as our information will allow us to trace, the spontaneous feelings and ideas which have produced the images that now frequently appear unnatural, because they are remote; and disgusting, because they have been servilely copied by poets, whose habits of thinking, and views of nature must have been different; for, though the understanding seldom disturbs the current of our present feelings, without dissipating the gay clouds which fancy has been embracing, yet it silently gives the colour to the whole tenour of them, and the dream is over, when truth is grossly violated, or images introduced, selected from books, and not from local manners or popular prejudices.

In a more advanced state of civilization, a poet is rather the creature of art, than of nature. The books that he reads in his youth, become a hot-bed in which artificial fruits are produced, beautiful to the common eye, though they want the true hue and flavour. His images do not arise from sensations; they are copies; and, like the works of the painters who copy ancient statues when they draw men and women of their own times, we acknowledge that the features are fine, and the proportions just; yet they are men of stone; insipid figures, that never convey to the mind the idea of a portrait taken from life, where the soul gives spirit and homogeneity to the whole. The silken wings of fancy are shrivelled by rules; and a desire of attaining elegance of diction, occasions an attention to words, incompatible with sublime, impassioned thoughts.

A boy of abilities, who has been taught the structure of verse at school, and been roused by emulation to compose rhymes whilst he was reading works of genius, may, by practice, produce pretty verses, and even become what is often termed an elegant poet: yet his readers, without knowing what to find fault with, do not find themselves warmly interested. In the works of the poets who fasten on their affections, they see grosser faults, and the very images which shock their taste in the modern; still they do not appear as puerile or extrinsic in one as the other.—Why?—because they did not appear so to the author.

It may sound paradoxical, after observing that those productions want vigour, that are merely the work of imitation, in which the understanding has violently directed, if not extinguished, the blaze of fancy, to assert, that, though genius be only another word for exquisite sensibility, the first observers of nature, the true poets, exercised their understanding much more than their imitators. But they exercised it to discriminate things, whilst their followers were busy to borrow sentiments and arrange words.

Boys who have received a classical education, load their memory with words, and the correspondent ideas are perhaps never distinctly comprehended. As a proof of this assertion, I must observe, that I have known many young people who could write tolerably smooth verses, and string epithets prettily together, when their prose themes showed the barrenness of their minds, and how superficial the cultivation must have been, which their understanding had received.

Dr. Johnson, I know, has given a definition of genius, which would overturn my reasoning, if I were to admit it.—He imagines, that *a strong mind, accidentally led to some particular study* in which it excels, is a genius.*—Not to stop to investigate the causes which produced this happy *strength* of mind, experience seems to prove, that those minds have appeared most vigorous, that have pursued a study, after nature had discovered a bent; for it would be absurd to suppose, that a slight impression made on the weak faculties of a boy, is the fiat of fate, and not to be effaced by any succeeding impression, or unexpected difficulty. Dr. Johnson in fact, appears sometimes to be of the same opinion (how consistently I shall not now enquire), especially when he observes, "that Thomson looked on nature with the eye which she only gives to a poet."†

But, though it should be allowed that books may produce some

---

* In "Abraham Cowley," *Lives of the English Poets*, Samuel Johnson wrote, "The true genius is a mind of large general powers, accidentally determined to some particular direction."—Editor.

† A reference to Johnson's observation on James Thomson in *Lives of the English Poets*.—Editor.

poets, I fear they will never be the poets who charm our cares to sleep, or extort admiration. They may diffuse taste, and polish the language; but I am inclined to conclude that they will seldom rouse the passions, or amend the heart.

And, to return to the first subject of discussion, the reason why most people are more interested by a scene described by a poet, than by a view of nature, probably arises from the want of a lively imagination. The poet contracts the prospect, and, selecting the most picturesque part in his *camera,* the judgment is directed, and the whole force of the languid faculty turned towards the objects which excited the most forcible emotions in the poet's heart; the reader consequently feels the enlivened description, though he was not able to receive a first impression from the operations of his own mind.

Besides, it may be further observed, that gross minds are only to be moved by forcible representations. To rouse the thoughtless, objects must be presented, calculated to produce tumultuous emotions; the unsubstantial, picturesque forms which a contemplative man gazes on, and often follows with ardour till he is mocked by a glimpse of unattainable excellence, appear to them the light vapours of a dreaming enthusiast, who gives up the substance for the shadow. It is not within that they seek amusement; their eyes are seldom turned on themselves; consequently their emotions, though sometimes fervid, are always transient, and the nicer perceptions which distinguish the man of genuine taste, are not felt, or make such a slight impression as scarcely to excite any pleasurable sensations. Is it surprising then that they are often overlooked, even by those who are delighted by the same images concentrated by the poet?

But even this numerous class is exceeded, by witlings, who, anxious to appear to have wit and taste, do not allow their understandings or feelings any liberty; for, instead of cultivating their faculties and reflecting on their operations, they are busy collecting prejudices; and are predetermined to admire what the suffrage of time announces as excellent, not to store up a fund of amusement for themselves, but to enable them to talk.

These hints will assist the reader to trace some of the causes why the beauties of nature are not forcibly felt, when civilization, or rather luxury, has made considerable advances—those calm sensations are not sufficiently lively to serve as a relaxation to the voluptuary, or even to the moderate pursuer of artificial pleasures. In the present state of society, the understanding must bring back the feelings to nature, or the sensibility must have such native strength, as rather to be whetted than destroyed by the strong exercises of passion.

That the most valuable things are liable to the greatest perversion, is however as trite as true:—for the same sensibility, or quickness of senses, which makes a man relish the tranquil scenes of nature, when sensation, rather than reason, imparts delight, frequently makes a libertine of him, by leading him to prefer the sensual tumult of love a little refined by sentiment, to the calm pleasures of affectionate friendship, in whose sober satisfactions, reason, mixing her tranquillizing convictions, whispers, that content, not happiness, is the reward of virtue in this world.

"Hints. Chiefly designed to have been incorporated in the Second Part of the *Vindication of the Rights of Woman*"

The thirty-two discrete paragraphs which make up "Hints" first appeared in *Posthumous Works*. They were probably written by Wollstonecraft over a number of years. The first nine treat women and relate to the topics of *A Vindication of the Rights of Woman*. The remaining twenty-three have a variety of concerns, including education, poetry, religious belief, fancy, and taste. Several underline Wollstonecraft's trust in the imagination and are akin to passages in *Letters Written . . . in Sweden* and the essay "On Poetry."

22.

THE LOVER is ever most deeply enamoured, when it is with he knows not what—and the devotion of a mystic has a rude Gothic grandeur in it, which the respectful adoration of a philosopher will never reach. I may be thought fanciful; but it has continually occurred to me, that, though, I allow, reason in this world is the mother of wisdom—yet some flights of the imagination seem to reach what wisdom cannot teach—and, while they delude us here, afford a glorious hope, if not a foretaste, of what we may expect hereafter. He that created us, did not mean to mark us with ideal images of grandeur, the *baseless fabric of a vision*—No—that perfection we follow with hopeless ardour when the whisperings of reason are heard, may be found, when not incompatible with our state, in the round of eternity. Perfection indeed must, even then, be a comparative idea—but the wisdom, the happiness of a superior state, has been supposed to be intuitive, and the happiest effusions of human genius have seemed like inspiration—the deductions of reason destroy sublimity.

23.

I am more and more convinced, that poetry is the first effervescence of the imagination, and the forerunner of civilization.

24.

When the Arabs had no trace of literature or science, they composed beautiful verses on the subjects of love and war. The flights of the imagination, and the laboured deductions of reason, appear almost incompatible.

25.

Poetry certainly flourishes most in the first rude state of society. The passions speak most eloquently, when they are not shackled by reason. The sublime expression, which has been so often quoted, [Genesis, ch. 1, ver. 3.]* is perhaps a barbarous flight; or rather the grand conception of an uncultivated mind; for it is contrary to nature and experience, to suppose that this account is founded on facts—It is doubtless a sublime allegory. But a cultivated mind would not thus have described the creation—for, arguing from analogy, it appears that creation must have been a comprehensive plan, and that the Supreme Being always uses second causes, slowly and silently to fulfil his purpose. This is, in reality, a more sublime view of that power which wisdom supports: but it is not the sublimity that would strike the impassioned mind, in which the imagination took place of intellect. Tell a being, whose affections and passions have been more exercised than his reason, that God said, *Let there be light! and there was light*; and he would prostrate himself before the Being who could thus call things out of nothing, as if they were: but a man in whom reason had taken place of passion, would not adore, till wisdom was conspicuous as well as power, for his admiration must be founded on principle.

26.

Individuality is ever conspicuous in those enthusiastic flights of fancy, in which reason is left behind, without being lost sight of.

* "And God said, Let there be light: and there was light."—Editor.

28.

Mr. Kant has observed, that the understanding is sublime, the imagination beautiful*—yet it is evident, that poets, and men who undoubtedly possess the liveliest imagination, are most touched by the sublime, while men who have cold, enquiring minds, have not this exquisite feeling in any great degree, and indeed seem to lose it as they cultivate their reason.

* An idea suggested in Immanuel Kant's discussion of the sublime in the *Critique of Aesthetic Judgement* (1790).—Editor.

Part IV

Works of Fiction

This section consists of Wollstonecraft's fictional works and her comments on fiction. The first novel, *Mary, A Fiction*, was published in 1788 by Joseph Johnson. *The Wrongs of Woman: or, Maria* was left unfinished at her death in 1797; it was edited by Godwin and published in *Posthumous Works* in 1798. The reviews from the *Analytical Review* primarily date from the years 1788 to 1791, the period between Wollstonecraft's arrival in London as a reviewer for Joseph Johnson and her writing of *A Vindication of the Rights of Woman*.

In the late eighteenth century, women writers greatly favored novels and, as Wollstonecraft's reviews indicate, they produced a vast quantity of them for other women. Many people were concerned with the effect of this fictional deluge, among them Wollstonecraft, who feared that women would choose to live vicariously in the sensational world of fiction instead of in the duller world of reality. In her own novels she tried to avoid the wish fulfillment situations that would lead to such a choice and to present heroines of moral rather than physical beauty. In addition she followed others in the Johnson circle—authors such as William Godwin, Thomas Holcroft, and Mary Hays—in her use of the novel to direct attention to the social evils of inequality and poverty.

Mary, A Fiction

The novel was written while Wollstonecraft was governess to the Kingsborough children in Ireland. Through its autobiographical heroine, it reflects both her self-pity in this period and the confidence in her abilities that precipitated her shortly afterward into an independent life as a writer in London. The work is a good example of the novel of sensibility, which traces the development of the sensitive heroine; it is given distinction, however, by its "Advertisement," which presents a new aim for women's fiction—the delineation of "the mind of a woman, who has thinking powers"—and by the disturbing picture of the difficulties and denials inherent in a woman's achievement of autonomy.

The story concerns Mary, a young girl born into an unsympathetic family from which she flees into friendship with Ann, a character clearly modeled on Wollstonecraft's friend Fanny Blood. Different from her creator in wealth and social position, Mary is married off to a young man for the purpose of joining two estates. After the marriage the husband immediately goes abroad leaving Mary to support Ann in her last days. Accompanied by Mary and in search of health, Ann travels to Portugal, where, like Fanny Blood, she dies. Mary finds consolation from her grief in her love for the consumptive Henry, whom she is of course unable to marry. On Henry's death, she returns to her husband, taking comfort in good works and approaching death.

ADVERTISEMENT

IN DELINEATING the Heroine of this Fiction, the Author attempts to develop a character different from those generally portrayed. This woman is neither a Clarissa, a Lady G———, nor a Sophie.*—It would be vain to mention the various modifications of these models,

* Heroines of Samuel Richardson and Jean-Jacques Rousseau.—Editor.

as it would to remark, how widely artists wander from nature, when they copy the originals of great masters. They catch the gross parts; but the subtile spirit evaporates; and not having the just ties, affectation disgusts, when grace was expected to charm.

Those compositions only have power to delight, and carry us willing captives, where the soul of the author is exhibited, and animates the hidden springs. Lost in a pleasing enthusiasm, they live in the scenes they represent; and do not measure their steps in a beaten track, solicitous to gather expected flowers, and bind them in a wreath, according to the prescribed rules of art.

These chosen few, wish to speak for themselves, and not to be an echo—even of the sweetest sounds—or the reflector of the most sublime beams. The* paradise they ramble in, must be of their own creating—or the prospect soon grows insipid, and not varied by a vivifying principle, fades and dies.

In an artless tale, without episodes, the mind of a woman, who has thinking powers is displayed. The female organs have been thought too weak for this arduous employment; and experience seems to justify the assertion. Without arguing physically about *possibilities*—in a fiction, such a being may be allowed to exist; whose grandeur is derived from the operations of its own faculties, not subjugated to opinion; but drawn by the individual from the original source.

[*Mary's childhood*]
CHAPTER I

Mary, the heroine of this fiction, was the daughter of Edward, who married Eliza, a gentle, fashionable girl, with a kind of indolence in her temper, which might be termed negative good-nature: her virtues, indeed, were all of that stamp. She carefully attended to the *shews* of things, and her opinions, I should have said prejudices, were such as the generality approved of. She was educated with the expectation of a large fortune, of course became a mere machine: the homage of her attendants made a great part of her puerile amusements, and she never imagined there were any relative duties for her to fulfil: notions of her own consequence, by these means, were interwoven in her mind, and the years of youth spent in acquiring a few superficial accomplishments, without having any taste for them. When she was first introduced into the polite circle, she danced with an officer, whom she

---

* I here give the Reviewers an opportunity of being very witty about the Paradise of Fools, &c.—Wollstonecraft.

faintly wished to be united to; but her father soon after recommending another in a more distinguished rank of life, she readily submitted to his will, and promised to love, honour, and obey, (a vicious fool,) as in duty bound.

While they resided in London, they lived in the usual fashionable style, and seldom saw each other; nor were they much more sociable when they wooed rural felicity for more than half the year, in a delightful country, where Nature, with lavish hand, had scattered beauties around; for the master, with brute, unconscious gaze, passed them by unobserved, and sought amusement in country sports. He hunted in the morning, and after eating an immoderate dinner, generally fell asleep: this seasonable rest enabled him to digest the cumbrous load; he would then visit some of his pretty tenants; and when he compared their ruddy glow of health with his wife's countenance, which even rouge could not enliven, it is not necessary to say which a *gourmand* would give the preference to. Their vulgar dance of spirits were infinitely more agreeable to his fancy than her sickly, die-away languor. Her voice was but the shadow of a sound, and she had, to complete her delicacy, so relaxed her nerves, that she became a mere nothing.

Many such noughts are there in the female world! yet she had a good opinion of her own merit,—truly, she said long prayers,—and sometimes read her Week's Preparation:* she dreaded that horrid place vulgarly called *hell*, the regions below; but whether hers was a mounting spirit, I cannot pretend to determine; or what sort of a planet would have been proper for her, when she left her *material* part in this world, let metaphysicians settle; I have nothing to say to her unclothed spirit.

As she was sometimes obliged to be alone, or only with her French waiting-maid, she sent to the metropolis for all the new publications, and while she was dressing her hair, and she could turn her eyes from the glass, she ran over those most delightful substitutes for bodily dissipation, novels. I say bodily, or the animal soul, for a rational one can find no employment in polite circles. The glare of lights, the studied inelegancies of dress, and the compliments offered up at the shrine of false beauty, are all equally addressed to the senses.

When she could not any longer indulge the caprices of fancy one way, she tried another. The Platonic Marriage, Eliza Warwick, and some other interesting tales† were perused with eagerness. Nothing

---

* A work designed to help its readers become worthy of receiving Communion on a Sunday.—Editor.

† The type of silly love stories which Wollstonecraft so frequently attacked. Both were popular novels of the late eighteenth century. The incidents below occur in *The Platonic Marriage.*—Editor.

could be more natural than the developement of the passions, nor more striking than the views of the human heart. What delicate struggles! and uncommonly pretty turns of thought! The picture that was found on a bramblebush, the new sensitive-plant, or tree, which caught the swain by the upper-garment, and presented to his ravished eyes a portrait.—Fatal image!—It planted a thorn in a till then insensible heart, and sent a new kind of a knight-errant into the world. But even this was nothing to the catastrophe, and the circumstance on which it hung, the hornet settling on the sleeping lover's face. What a *heart-rending* accident! She planted, in imitation of those susceptible souls, a rose bush; but there was not a lover to weep in concert with her, when she watered it with her tears.—Alas! Alas!

If my readers would excuse the sportiveness of fancy, and give me credit for genius, I would go on and tell them such tales as would force the sweet tears of sensibility to flow in copious showers down beautiful cheeks, to the discomposure of rouge, &c. &c. Nay, I would make it so interesting, that the fair peruser should beg the hair-dresser to settle the curls himself, and not interrupt her.

She had besides another resource, two most beautiful dogs, who shared her bed, and reclined on cushions near her all the day. These she watched with the most assiduous care, and bestowed on them the warmest caresses. This fondness for animals was not that kind of *attendrissement** which makes a person take pleasure in providing for the subsistence and comfort of a living creature; but it proceeded from vanity, it gave her an opportunity of lisping out the prettiest French expressions of ecstatic fondness, in accents that had never been attuned by tenderness.

She was chaste, according to the vulgar acceptation of the word, that is, she did not make any actual *faux pas*;† she feared the world, and was indolent; but then, to make amends for this seeming self-denial, she read all the sentimental novels, dwelt on the love-scenes, and, had she thought while she read, her mind would have been contaminated; as she accompanied the lovers to the lonely arbors, and would walk with them by the clear light of the moon. She wondered her husband did not stay at home. She was jealous—why did he not love her, sit by her side, squeeze her hand, and look unutterable things? Gentle reader, I will tell thee; they neither of them felt what they could not utter. I will not pretend to say that they always annexed an idea to a word; but they had none of those feelings which are not easily analyzed.

---

* Compassion or sensibility.—Editor.

† An act compromising to a woman's reputation.—Editor.

CHAPTER II

In due time she brought forth a son, a feeble babe; and the following year a daughter. After the mother's throes she felt very few sentiments of maternal tenderness: the children were given to nurses, and
she played with her dogs. Want of exercise prevented the least chance
of her recovering strength; and two or three milk-fevers brought on a
consumption, to which her constitution tended. Her children all died
in their infancy, except the two first, and she began to grow fond of
the son, as he was remarkably handsome. For years she divided her
time between the sofa, and the card-table. She thought not of death,
though on the borders of the grave; nor did any of the duties of her
station occur to her as necessary. Her children were left in the nursery;
and when Mary, the little blushing girl, appeared, she would send the
awkward thing away. To own the truth, she was awkward enough, in
a house without any play-mates; for her brother had been sent to
school, and she scarcely knew how to employ herself; she would ramble about the garden, admire the flowers, and play with the dogs. An
old house-keeper told her stories, read to her, and, at last, taught her
to read. Her mother talked of enquiring for a governess when her
health would permit; and, in the interim desired her own maid to
teach her French. As she had learned to read, she perused with avidity
every book that came in her way. Neglected in every respect, and left
to the operations of her own mind, she considered every thing that came
under her inspection, and learned to think. She had heard of a separate
state, and that angels sometimes visited this earth. She would sit in a
thick wood in the park, and talk to them; make little songs addressed
to them, and sing them to tunes of her own composing; and her native
wood notes wild were sweet and touching.

Her father always exclaimed against female acquirements, and was
glad that his wife's indolence and ill health made her not trouble herself about them. She had besides another reason, she did not wish to
have a fine tall girl brought forward into notice as her daughter; she
still expected to recover, and figure away in the gay world. Her husband was very tyrannical and passionate; indeed so very easily irritated
when inebriated, that Mary was continually in dread lest he should
frighten her mother to death; her sickness called forth all Mary's tenderness, and exercised her compassion so continually, that it became
more than a match for self-love, and was the governing propensity of
her heart through life. She was violent in her temper; but she saw her
father's faults, and would weep when obliged to compare his temper

with her own.—She did more; artless prayers rose to Heaven for pardon, when she was conscious of having erred; and her contrition was so exceedingly painful, that she watched diligently the first movements of anger and impatience, to save herself this cruel remorse.

Sublime ideas filled her young mind—always connected with devotional sentiments; extemporary effusions of gratitude, and rhapsodies of praise would burst often from her, when she listened to the birds, or pursued the deer. She would gaze on the moon, and ramble through the gloomy path, observing the various shapes the clouds assumed, and listen to the sea that was not far distant. The wandering spirits, which she imagined inhabited every part of nature, were her constant friends and confidants. She began to consider the Great First Cause, formed just notions of his attributes, and, in particular, dwelt on his wisdom and goodness. Could she have loved her father or mother, had they returned her affection, she would not so soon, perhaps, have sought out a new world.

Her sensibility prompted her to search for an object to love; on earth it was not to be found: her mother had often disappointed her, and the apparent partiality she shewed to her brother gave her exquisite pain—produced a kind of habitual melancholy, led her into a fondness for reading tales of woe, and made her almost realize the fictitious distress.

She had not any notion of death till a little chicken expired at her feet; and her father had a dog hung in a passion. She then concluded animals had souls, or they would not have been subjected to the caprice of man; but what was the soul of man or beast? In this style year after year rolled on, her mother still vegetating.

A little girl who attended in the nursery fell sick. Mary paid her great attention; contrary to her wish, she was sent out of the house to her mother, a poor woman, whom necessity obliged to leave her sick child while she earned her daily bread. The poor wretch, in a fit of delirium stabbed herself, and Mary saw her dead body, and heard the dismal account; and so strongly did it impress her imagination, that every night of her life the bleeding corpse presented itself to her when she first began to slumber. Tortured by it, she at last made a vow, that if she was ever mistress of a family she would herself watch over every part of it. The impression that this accident made was indelible.

As her mother grew imperceptibly worse and worse, her father, who did not understand such a lingering complaint, imagined his wife was only grown still more whimsical, and that if she could be prevailed on to exert herself, her health would soon be re-established. In general he treated her with indifference; but when her illness at all interfered with his pleasures, he expostulated in the most cruel manner, and visibly harassed the invalid. Mary would then assiduously try to turn his attention to something else; and when sent out of the room, would watch at the door, until the storm was over, for unless it was, she could not rest. Other causes also contributed to disturb her repose: her mother's lukewarm manner of performing her religious duties, filled her with anguish; and when she observed her father's vices, the unbidden tears would flow. She was miserable when beggars were driven from the gate without being relieved; if she could do it unperceived, she would give them her own breakfast, and feel gratified, when, in consequence of it, she was pinched by hunger.

She had once, or twice, told her little secrets to her mother; they were laughed at, and she determined never to do it again. In this manner was she left to reflect on her own feelings; and so strengthened were they by being meditated on, that her character early became singular and permanent. Her understanding was strong and clear, when not clouded by her feelings; but she was too much the creature of impulse, and the slave of compassion.

CHAPTER III

Near her father's house lived a poor widow, who had been brought up in affluence, but reduced to great distress by the extravagance of her husband; he had destroyed his constitution while he spent his fortune; and dying, left his wife, and five small children, to live on a very scanty pittance. The eldest daughter was for some years educated by a distant relation, a Clergyman. While she was with him a young gentleman, son to a man of property in the neighbourhood, took particular notice of her. It is true, he never talked of love; but then they played and sung in concert; drew landscapes together, and while she worked he read to her, cultivated her taste, and stole imperceptibly her heart. Just at this juncture, when smiling, unanalyzed hope made every prospect bright, and gay expectation danced in her eyes, her benefactor died. She returned to her mother—the companion of her youth forgot her, they took no more sweet counsel together. This disappointment spread a sadness over her countenance, and made it interesting. She grew fond of solitude, and her character appeared similar to Mary's, though her natural disposition was very different.

She was several years older than Mary, yet her refinement, her taste, caught her eye, and she eagerly sought her friendship: before her return she had assisted the family, which was almost reduced to the last ebb; and now she had another motive to actuate her.

As she had often occasion to send messages to Ann, her new friend, mistakes were frequently made; Ann proposed that in future they should be written ones, to obviate this difficulty, and render their intercourse more agreeable. Young people are mostly fond of scribbling; Mary had had very little instruction; but by copying her friend's letters, whose hand she admired, she soon became a proficient; a little practice made her write with tolerable correctness, and her genius gave force to it. In conversation, and in writing, when she felt, she was pathetic, tender and persuasive; and she expressed contempt with such energy, that few could stand the flash of her eyes.

As she grew more intimate with Ann, her manners were softened, and she acquired a degree of equality in her behaviour: yet still her spirits were fluctuating, and her movements rapid. She felt less pain on account of her mother's partiality to her brother, as she hoped now to experience the pleasure of being beloved; but this hope led her into new sorrows, and, as usual, paved the way for disappointment. Ann only felt gratitude; her heart was entirely engrossed by one object, and friendship could not serve as a substitute; memory officiously retraced past scenes, and unavailing wishes made time loiter.

Mary was often hurt by the involuntary indifference which these consequences produced. When her friend was all the world to her, she found she was not as necessary to her happiness; and her delicate mind could not bear to obtrude her affection, or receive love as an alms, the offspring of pity. Very frequently has she ran to her with delight, and not perceiving any thing of the same kind in Ann's countenance, she has shrunk back; and, falling from one extreme into the other, instead of a warm greeting that was just slipping from her tongue, her expressions seemed to be dictated by the most chilling insensibility.

She would then imagine that she looked sickly or unhappy, and then all her tenderness would return like a torrent, and bear away all reflection. In this manner was her sensibility called forth, and exercised, by her mother's illness, her friend's misfortunes, and her own unsettled mind.

from
CHAPTER IV

Near to her father's house was a range of mountains; some of them were, literally speaking, cloud-capt, for on them clouds continually rested, and gave grandeur to the prospect; and down many of their sides the little bubbling cascades ran till they swelled a beautiful river. Through the straggling trees and bushes the wind whistled, and on them the birds sung, particularly the robins; they also found shelter in the ivy of an old castle, a haunted one, as the story went; it was situated on the brow of one of the mountains, and commanded a view of the sea. This castle had been inhabited by some of her ancestors; and many tales had the old house-keeper told her of the worthies who had resided there.

When her mother frowned, and her friend looked cool, she would steal to this retirement, where human foot seldom trod—gaze on the sea, observe the grey clouds, or listen to the wind which struggled to free itself from the only thing that impeded its course. When more cheerful, she admired the various dispositions of light and shade, the beautiful tints the gleams of sunshine gave to the distant hills; then she rejoiced in existence, and darted into futurity.

One way home was through the cavity of a rock covered with a thin layer of earth, just sufficient to afford nourishment to a few stunted shrubs, and wild plants, which grew on its sides, and nodded over the summit. A clear stream broke out of it, and ran amongst the pieces of rocks fallen into it. Here twilight always reigned—it seemed the Temple of Solitude; yet, paradoxical as the assertion may appear, when the foot sounded on the rock, it terrified the intruder, and inspired a strange feeling, as if the rightful sovereign was dislodged. In this retreat she read Thomson's *Seasons*, Young's *Night-Thoughts*,* and *Paradise Lost*.

At a little distance from it were the huts of a few poor fishermen, who supported their numerous children by their precarious labour. In these little huts she frequently rested, and denied herself every childish gratification, in order to relieve the necessities of the inhabitants. Her heart yearned for them, and would dance with joy when she had relieved their wants, or afforded them pleasure.

In these pursuits she learned the luxury of doing good; and the sweet tears of benevolence frequently moistened her eyes, and gave them a sparkle which, exclusive of that, they had not; on the contrary, they were rather fixed, and would never have been observed if her soul had not animated them. They were not at all like those brilliant ones which look like polished diamonds, and dart from every superfice, giving more light to the beholders than they receive themselves.

Her benevolence, indeed, knew no bounds; the distress of others

* James Thompson's *Seasons* (1726–30) and Edward Young's *Night Thoughts* (1742–45) were long poems describing God's presence in nature and reflecting on the purpose of life and death; they were immensely popular in the late eighteenth century. —Editor.

carried her out of herself; and she rested not till she had relieved or comforted them. The warmth of her compassion often made her so diligent, that many things occurred to her, which might have escaped a less interested observer.

In like manner, she entered with such spirit into whatever she read, and the emotions thereby raised were so strong, that it soon became a part of her mind.

Enthusiastic sentiments of devotion at this period actuated her; her Creator was almost apparent to her senses in his works; but they were mostly the grand or solemn features of Nature which she delighted to contemplate. She would stand and behold the waves rolling, and think of the voice that could still the tumultuous deep.

These propensities gave the colour to her mind, before the passions began to exercise their tyrannic sway, and particularly pointed out those which the soil would have a tendency to nurse.

Years after, when wandering through the same scenes, her imagination has strayed back, to trace the first placid sentiments they inspired, and she would earnestly desire to regain the same peaceful tranquillity.

[*Social awakening*]
from
CHAPTER XXII

In England then landed the forlorn wanderer.* She looked round for some few moments—her affections were not attracted to any particular part of the Island. She knew none of the inhabitants of the vast city to which she was going: the mass of buildings appeared to her a huge body without an informing soul. As she passed through the streets in an hackney-coach, disgust and horror alternately filled her mind. She met some women drunk; and the manners of those who attacked the sailors, made her shrink into herself, and exclaim, are these my fellow creatures!

Detained by a number of carts near the water-side, for she came up the river in the vessel, not having reason to hasten on shore, she saw vulgarity, dirt, and vice—her soul sickened; this was the first time such complicated misery obtruded itself on her sight.—Forgetting her own griefs, she gave the world a much indebted tear; mourned for a world in ruins. . . .

* Mary had just arrived from Portugal.—Editor.

from
CHAPTER XXIII

Unhappy, she wandered about the village, and relieved the poor; it was the only employment that eased her aching heart; she became more intimate with misery—the misery that rises from poverty and the want of education. She was in the vicinity of a great city; the vicious poor in and about it must ever grieve a benevolent contemplative mind.

One evening a man who stood weeping in a little lane, near the house she resided in, caught her eye. She accosted him; in a confused manner, he informed her, that his wife was dying, and his children crying for the bread he could not earn. Mary desired to be conducted to his habitation; it was not very distant, and was the upper room in an old mansion-house, which had been once the abode of luxury. Some tattered shreds of rich hangings still remained, covered with cobwebs and filth; round the ceiling, through which the rain drop'd, was a beautiful cornice mouldering; and a spacious gallery was rendered dark by the broken windows being blocked up; through the apertures the wind forced its way in hollow sounds, and reverberated along the former scene of festivity.

It was crowded with inhabitants: som[e] were scolding, others swearing, or singing indecent songs. What a sight for Mary! Her blood ran cold; yet she had sufficient resolution to mount to the top of the house. On the floor, in one corner of a very small room, lay an emaciated figure of a woman; a window over her head scarcely admitted any light, for the broken panes were stuffed with dirty rags. Near her were five children, all young, and covered with dirt; their sallow cheeks, and languid eyes, exhibited none of the charms of childhood. Some were fighting, and others crying for food; their yells were mixed with their mother's groans, and the wind which rushed through the passage. Mary was petrified; but soon assuming more courage, approached the bed, and, regardless of the surrounding nastiness, knelt down by the poor wretch, and breathed the most poisonous air; for the unfortunate creature was dying of a putrid fever, the consequence of dirt and want.

[*Marriage*]
from
CHAPTER XXX

. . . at last [Mary] conquered her disgust, and wrote her *husband* an account of what had passed since she had dropped his correspondence.

He came in person to answer the letter. Mary fainted when he approached her unexpectedly. Her disgust returned with additional force, in spite of previous reasonings, whenever he appeared; yet she was prevailed on to promise to live with him, if he would permit her to pass one year, travelling from place to place; he was not to accompany her.

The time too quickly elapsed, and she gave him her hand—the struggle was almost more than she could endure. She tried to appear calm; time mellowed her grief, and mitigated her torments; but when her husband would take her hand, or mention any thing like love, she would instantly feel a sickness, a faintness at her heart, and wish, involuntarily, that the earth would open and swallow her.

CHAPTER XXXI

Mary visited the continent, and sought health in different climates; but her nerves were not to be restored to their former state. She then retired to her house in the country, established manufactories, threw the estate into small farms; and continually employed herself this way to dissipate care, and banish unavailing regret. She visited the sick, supported the old, and educated the young.

These occupations engrossed her mind; but there were hours when all her former woes would return and haunt her.—Whenever she did, or said, any thing she thought Henry* would have approved of—she could not avoid thinking with anguish, of the rapture his approbation ever conveyed to her heart—a heart in which there was a void, that even benevolence and religion could not fill. The latter taught her to struggle for resignation; and the former rendered life supportable.

Her delicate state of health did not promise long life. In moments of solitary sadness, a gleam of joy would dart across her mind—She thought she was hastening to that world *where there is neither marrying*, nor giving in marriage.

---

* The man whom Mary had met and loved in Portugal. He died shortly after their meeting.—Editor.

The Wrongs of Woman: or, Maria

Wollstonecraft's unfinished novel, *The Wrongs of Woman*, is in many ways a sequel to *A Vindication of the Rights of Woman*. It gives dramatic form to the earlier descriptions of women's oppression and weakness. In addition it shows Wollstonecraft's concern—primarily directed to the middle class in *The Rights of Woman*—extended now to the very lowest class of women.

The novel opens with the heroine, Maria, imprisoned in an asylum sorrowing over the loss of her child. Her imprisonment is due to her husband, Mr. Venables, who wishes to possess her fortune. In the asylum Maria meets Jemima, the attendant, a woman who has earlier been a thief and prostitute, and Darnford, a man with many of the traits of Gilbert Imlay. Maria and Darnford are attracted to each other and Jemima arranges their meetings. At these, Maria, Darnford, and Jemima each narrate their life stories. Maria describes the influence on her of defective parents and of a kind and sensitive uncle; Darnford gives an account of his self-indulgent life in Europe and America, while Jemima speaks of her miserable experience in the streets and pauper institutions of London. The fragment of the novel ends with the escape of all three characters from the asylum. Maria goes to live with Darnford, who is subsequently charged with adultery. In his defense Maria writes a paper which becomes also her protest against unjust marriage laws. What the conclusion of the book was to be remains unclear, but there is a strong suggestion that Darnford would prove false and that Jemima would rescue Maria from suicide.

The Wrongs of Woman seems to have been fairly widely read in its time, and Charlotte Smith in her novel *The Young Philosopher* was at pains to defend herself from a charge of plagiarism from the work. In addition it was reviewed extensively, usually in a hostile manner. The *Anti-Jacobin Review* of 1798, for example, criticized Wollstonecraft for failing to prove that her heroine's miseries arose from the unequal position of women and for showing that they were in fact due to her poor choice of husband. The *British Critic* of the same year was harsher: it considered the system of morality in the work offensive to the purity of female virtue and the precepts of religion. Because she

· supported women's right to passion and marital happiness, the author
was judged a sensualist without refinement.

AUTHOR'S PREFACE

THE WRONGS OF WOMAN, like the wrongs of the oppressed part of
mankind, may be deemed necessary by their oppressors: but surely
there are a few, who will dare to advance before the improvement of
the age, and grant that my sketches are not the abortion of a distem-
pered fancy, or the strong delineations of a wounded heart.

In writing this novel, I have rather endeavoured to pourtray passions than manners.

In many instances I could have made the incidents more dramatic,
would I have sacrificed my main object, the desire of exhibiting the
misery and oppression, peculiar to women, that arise out of the partial
laws and customs of society.

In the invention of the story, this view restrained my fancy; and
the history ought rather to be considered, as of woman, than of an
individual.

The sentiments I have embodied.

In many works of this species, the hero is allowed to be mortal, and
to become wise and virtuous as well as happy, by a train of events and
circumstances. The heroines, on the contrary, are to be born immaculate, and to act like goddesses of wisdom, just come forth highly finished
Minervas from the head of Jove.

[The following is an extract of a letter from the author to a friend,
to whom she communicated her manuscript.]

For my part, I cannot suppose any situation more distressing, than
for a woman of sensibility, with an improving mind, to be bound to
such a man as I have described for life; obliged to renounce all the
humanizing affections, and to avoid cultivating her taste, lest her perception of grace and refinement of sentiment, should sharpen to agony
the pangs of disappointment. Love, in which the imagination mingles
its bewitching colouring, must be fostered by delicacy. I should despise,
or rather call her an ordinary woman, who could endure such a husband as I have sketched.

These appear to me (matrimonial despotism of heart and conduct) to be the peculiar Wrongs of Woman, because they degrade the mind. What are termed great misfortunes, may more forcibly impress the mind of common readers; they have more of what may justly be termed *stage-effect*; but it is the delineation of finer sensations, which, in my opinion, constitutes the merit of our best novels. This is what I have in view; and to shew the wrongs of different classes of women, equally oppressive, though, from the difference of education, necessarily various.

[The Narrative of Jemima]
from
CHAPTER 5

"My father," said Jemima, "seduced my mother, a pretty girl, with whom he lived fellow-servant; and she no sooner perceived the natural, the dreaded consequence, than the terrible conviction flashed on her— that she was ruined. Honesty, and a regard for her reputation, had been the only principles inculcated by her mother; and they had been so forcibly impressed, that she feared shame, more than the poverty to which it would lead. Her incessant importunities to prevail upon my father to screen her from reproach by marrying her, as he had promised in the fervour of seduction, estranged him from her so completely, that her very person became distasteful to him; and he began to hate, as well as despise me, before I was born.

"My mother, grieved to the soul by his neglect, and unkind treatment, actually resolved to famish herself; and injured her health by the attempt; though she had not sufficient resolution to adhere to her project, or renounce it entirely. Death came not at her call; yet sorrow, and the methods she adopted to conceal her condition, still doing the work of a house-maid, had such an effect on her constitution, that she died in the wretched garret, where her virtuous mistress had forced her to take refuge in the very pangs of labour, though my father, after a slight reproof, was allowed to remain in his place—allowed by the mother of six children, who, scarcely permitting a footstep to be heard, during her month's indulgence, felt no sympathy for the poor wretch, denied every comfort required by her situation.

"The day my mother died, the ninth after my birth, I was consigned to the care of the cheapest nurse my father could find; who suckled her own child at the same time, and lodged as many more as she could get, in two cellar-like apartments.

"Poverty, and the habit of seeing children die off her hands, had

so hardened her heart, that the office of a mother did not awaken the
tenderness of a woman; nor were the feminine caresses which seem a
part of the rearing of a child, ever bestowed on me. The chicken has a
wing to shelter under; but I had no bosom to nestle in, no kindred
warmth to foster me. Left in dirt, to cry with cold and hunger till I
was weary, and sleep without ever being prepared by exercise, or lulled
by kindness to rest; could I be expected to become any thing but a
weak and rickety babe? Still, in spite of neglect, I continued to exist,
to learn to curse existence, [her countenance grew ferocious as she
spoke,] and the treatment that rendered me miserable, seemed to
sharpen my wits. Confined then in a damp hovel, to rock the cradle
of the succeeding tribe, I looked like a little old woman, or a hag
shrivelling into nothing. The furrows of reflection and care contracted
the youthful cheek, and gave a sort of supernatural wildness to the
ever watchful eye. During this period, my father had married another
fellow-servant, who loved him less, and knew better how to manage
his passion, than my mother. She likewise proving with child, they
agreed to keep a shop: my step-mother, if, being an illegitimate offspring, I may venture thus to characterize her, having obtained a sum
of a rich relation, for that purpose.

"Soon after her lying-in, she prevailed on my father to take me
home, to save the expence of maintaining me, and of hiring a girl to
assist her in the care of the child. I was young, it was true, but appeared a knowing little thing, and might be made handy. Accordingly
I was brought to her house; but not to a home—for a home I never
knew. Of this child, a daughter, she was extravagantly fond; and it
was a part of my employment, to assist to spoil her, by humouring all
her whims, and bearing all her caprices. Feeling her own consequence,
before she could speak, she had learned the art of tormenting me, and
if I ever dared to resist, I received blows, laid on with no compunctious
hand, or was sent to bed dinnerless, as well as supperless. I said that it
was a part of my daily labour to attend this child, with the servility of
a slave; still it was but a part. I was sent out in all seasons, and from
place to place, to carry burdens far above my strength, without being
allowed to draw near the fire, or ever being cheered by encouragement
or kindness. No wonder then, treated like a creature of another species,
that I began to envy, and at length to hate, the darling of the house.
Yet, I perfectly remember, that it was the caresses, and kind expressions of my step-mother, which first excited my jealous discontent.
Once, I cannot forget it, when she was calling in vain her wayward
child to kiss her, I ran to her, saying, 'I will kiss you, ma'am!' and how
did my heart, which was in my mouth, sink, what was my debasement

of soul, when pushed away with—'I do not want you, pert thing!' Another day, when a new gown had excited the highest good humour,
and she uttered the appropriate *dear*, addressed unexpectedly to me,
I thought I could never do enough to please her; I was all alacrity, and
rose proportionably in my own estimation.

"As her daughter grew up, she was pampered with cakes and fruit,
while I was, literally speaking, fed with the refuse of the table, with
her leavings. A liquorish tooth is, I believe, common to children, and
I used to steal any thing sweet, that I could catch up with a chance of
concealment. When detected, she was not content to chastize me herself at the moment, but, on my father's return in the evening (he was
a shopman), the principal discourse was to recount my faults, and
attribute them to the wicked disposition which I had brought into the
world with me, inherited from my mother. He did not fail to leave
the marks of his resentment on my body, and then solaced himself by
playing with my sister.—I could have murdered her at those moments.
To save myself from these unmerciful corrections, I resorted to falshood, and the untruths which I sturdily maintained, were brought in
judgment against me, to support my tyrant's inhuman charge of my
natural propensity to vice. Seeing me treated with contempt, and always being fed and dressed better, my sister conceived a contemptuous
opinion of me, that proved an obstacle to all affection; and my father,
hearing continually of my faults, began to consider me as a curse en-
tailed on him for his sins: he was therefore easily prevailed on to bind
me apprentice to one of my step-mother's friends, who kept a slop-shop
in Wapping.* I was represented (as it was said) in my true colours;
but she, 'warranted,' snapping her fingers, 'that she should break my
spirit or heart.'

"My mother replied, with a whine, 'that if any body could make
me better, it was such a clever woman as herself; though, for her own
part, she had tried in vain; but good-nature was her fault.'

"I shudder with horror, when I recollect the treatment I had now
to endure. Not only under the lash of my task-mistress, but the drudge
of the maid, apprentices and children, I never had a taste of human
kindness to soften the rigour of perpetual labour. I had been introduced as an object of abhorrence into the family; as a creature of whom
my step-mother, though she had been kind enough to let me live in
the house with her own child, could make nothing. I was described as
a wretch, whose nose must be kept to the grinding stone—and it was

---

* A slop-shop sold ready-made clothes; Wapping is a district in the docks area of
London.—Editor.

held there with an iron grasp. It seemed indeed the privilege of their superior nature to kick me about, like the dog or cat. If I were attentive, I was called fawning, if refractory, an obstinate mule, and like a mule I received their censure on my loaded back. Often has my mistress, for some instance of forgetfulness, thrown me from one side of the kitchen to the other, knocked my head against the wall, spit in my face, with various refinements on barbarity that I forbear to enumerate, though they were all acted over again by the servant, with additional insults, to which the appellation of *bastard*, was commonly added, with taunts or sneers. But I will not attempt to give you an adequate idea of my situation, lest you, who probably have never been drenched with the dregs of human misery, should think I exaggerate.

"I stole now, from absolute necessity,—bread; yet whatever else was taken, which I had it not in my power to take, was ascribed to me. I was the filching cat, the ravenous dog, the dumb brute, who must bear all; for if I endeavoured to exculpate myself, I was silenced, without any enquiries being made, with 'Hold your tongue, you never tell truth.' Even the very air I breathed was tainted with scorn; for I was sent to the neighbouring shops with Glutton, Liar, or Thief, written on my forehead. This was, at first, the most bitter punishment; but sullen pride, or a kind of stupid desperation, made me, at length, almost regardless of the contempt, which had wrung from me so many solitary tears at the only moments when I was allowed to rest.

"Thus was I the mark of cruelty till my sixteenth year; and then I have only to point out a change of misery; for a period I never knew. Allow me first to make one observation. Now I look back, I cannot help attributing the greater part of my misery, to the misfortune of having been thrown into the world without the grand support of life—a mother's affection. I had no one to love me; or to make me respected, to enable me to acquire respect. I was an egg dropped on the sand; a pauper by nature, hunted from family to family, who belonged to nobody—and nobody cared for me. I was despised from my birth, and denied the chance of obtaining a footing for myself in society. Yes; I had not even the chance of being considered as a fellow-creature— yet all the people with whom I lived, brutalized as they were by the low cunning of trade, and the despicable shifts of poverty, were not without bowels, though they never yearned for me. I was, in fact, born a slave, and chained by infamy to slavery during the whole of existence, without having any companions to alleviate it by sympathy, or teach me how to rise above it by their example. But, to resume the thread of my tale—

"At sixteen, I suddenly grew tall, and something like comeliness appeared on a Sunday, when I had time to wash my face, and put on clean clothes. My master had once or twice caught hold of me in the passage; but I instinctively avoided his disgusting caresses. One day however, when the family were at a methodist meeting,* he contrived to be alone in the house with me, and by blows—yes; blows and menaces, compelled me to submit to his ferocious desire; and, to avoid my mistress's fury, I was obliged in future to comply, and skulk to my loft at his command, in spite of increasing loathing.

"The anguish which was now pent up in my bosom, seemed to open a new world to me: I began to extend my thoughts beyond myself, and grieve for human misery, till I discovered, with horror—ah! what horror!—that I was with child. I know not why I felt a mixed sensation of despair and tenderness, excepting that, ever called a bastard, a bastard appeared to me an object of the greatest compassion in creation.

"I communicated this dreadful circumstance to my master, who was almost equally alarmed at the intelligence; for he feared his wife, and public censure at the meeting. After some weeks of deliberation had elapsed, I in continual fear that my altered shape would be noticed, my master gave me a medicine in a phial, which he desired me to take, telling me, without any circumlocution, for what purpose it was designed. I burst into tears, I thought it was killing myself—yet was such a self as I worth preserving? He cursed me for a fool, and left me to my own reflections. I could not resolve to take this infernal potion; but I wrapped it up in an old gown, and hid it in a corner of my box.

"Nobody yet suspected me, because they had been accustomed to view me as a creature of another species. But the threatening storm at last broke over my devoted head—never shall I forget it! One Sunday evening when I was left, as usual, to take care of the house, my master came home intoxicated, and I became the prey of his brutal appetite. His extreme intoxication made him forget his customary caution, and my mistress entered and found us in a situation that could not have been more hateful to her than me. Her husband was 'pot-valiant,' he feared her not at the moment, nor had he then much reason, for she instantly turned the whole force of her anger another way. She tore off my cap, scratched, kicked, and buffetted me, till she had exhausted her strength, declaring, as she rested her arm, 'that I had wheedled her husband from her.—But, could any thing better be expected from a wretch, whom she had taken into her house out of pure charity?' What a torrent of abuse rushed out? till, almost breathless, she con-

* Wollstonecraft considered Methodism fanatical and intolerant.—Editor.

cluded with saying, 'that I was born a strumpet; it ran in my blood, and nothing good could come to those who harboured me.'

"My situation was, of course, discovered, and she declared that I should not stay another night under the same roof with an honest family. I was therefore pushed out of doors, and my trumpery thrown after me, when it had been contemptuously examined in the passage, lest I should have stolen any thing.

"Behold me then in the street, utterly destitute! Whither could I creep for shelter? To my father's roof I had no claim, when not pursued by shame—now I shrunk back as from death, from my mother's cruel reproaches, my father's execrations. I could not endure to hear him curse the day I was born, though life had been a curse to me. Of death I thought, but with a confused emotion of terror, as I stood leaning my head on a post, and starting at every footstep, lest it should be my mistress coming to tear my heart out. One of the boys of the shop passing by, heard my tale, and immediately repaired to his master, to give him a description of my situation; and he touched the right key—the scandal it would give rise to, if I were left to repeat my tale to every enquirer. This plea came home to his reason, who had been sobered by his wife's rage, the fury of which fell on him when I was out of her reach, and he sent the boy to me with half-a-guinea, desiring him to conduct me to a house, where beggars, and other wretches, the refuse of society, nightly lodged.

"This night was spent in a state of stupefaction, or desperation. I detested mankind, and abhorred myself.

"In the morning I ventured out, to throw myself in my master's way, at his usual hour of going abroad. I approached him, he 'damned me for a b———, declared I had disturbed the peace of the family, and that he had sworn to his wife, never to take any more notice of me.' He left me; but, instantly returning, he told me that he should speak to his friend, a parish-officer,* to get a nurse for the brat I laid to him; and advised me, if I wished to keep out of the house of correction, not to make free with his name.

"I hurried back to my hole, and, rage giving place to despair, sought for the potion that was to procure abortion, and swallowed it, with a wish that it might destroy me, at the same time that it stopped the sensations of new-born life, which I felt with indescribable emotion. My head turned round, my heart grew sick, and in the horrors of approaching dissolution, mental anguish was swallowed up. The effect

---

* The parish officer was responsible for the destitute and helpless in a parish, including illegitimate and abandoned children.—Editor.

of the medicine was violent, and I was confined to my bed several days; but, youth and a strong constitution prevailing, I once more crawled out, to ask myself the cruel question, 'Whither I should go?' I had but two shillings left in my pocket, the rest had been expended, by a poor woman who slept in the same room, to pay for my lodging, and purchase the necessaries of which she partook.

"With this wretch I went into the neighbouring streets to beg, and my disconsolate appearance drew a few pence from the idle, enabling me still to command a bed; till, recovering from my illness, and taught to put on my rags to the best advantage, I was accosted from different motives, and yielded to the desire of the brutes I met, with the same detestation that I had felt for my still more brutal master. I have since read in novels of the blandishments of seduction, but I had not even the pleasure of being enticed into vice.

"I shall not," interrupted Jemima, "lead your imagination into all the scenes of wretchedness and depravity, which I was condemned to view; or mark the different stages of my debasing misery. Fate dragged me through the very kennels of society: I was still a slave, a bastard, a common property. Become familiar with vice, for I wish to conceal nothing from you, I picked the pockets of the drunkards who abused me; and proved by my conduct, that I deserved the epithets, with which they loaded me at moments when distrust ought to cease.

"Detesting my nightly occupation, though valuing, if I may so use the word, my independence, which only consisted in choosing the street in which I should wander, or the roof, when I had money, in which I should hide my head, I was some time before I could prevail on myself to accept of a place in a house of ill fame, to which a girl, with whom I had accidentally conversed in the street, had recommended me. I had been hunted almost into a fever, by the watchmen of the quarter of the town I frequented; one, whom I had unwittingly offended, giving the word to the whole pack. You can scarcely conceive the tyranny exercised by these wretches: considering themselves as the instruments of the very laws they violate, the pretext which steels their conscience, hardens their heart. Not content with receiving from us, outlaws of society (let other women talk of favours) a brutal gratification gratuitously as a privilege of office, they extort a tithe of prostitution, and harrass with threats the poor creatures whose occupation affords not the means to silence the growl of avarice.* To escape from this persecution, I once more entered into servitude.

* The eighteenth-century watchmen were notorious for their eagerness to take bribes. Street-walkers had to bribe first the watch, then the constable, and finally the magistrate if they appeared before him.—Editor.

"A life of comparative regularity restored my health; and—do not start—my manners were improved, in a situation where vice sought to render itself alluring, and taste was cultivated to fashion the person, if not to refine the mind. Besides, the common civility of speech, contrasted with the gross vulgarity to which I had been accustomed, was something like the polish of civilization. I was not shut out from all intercourse of humanity. Still I was galled by the yoke of service, and my mistress often flying into violent fits of passion, made me dread a sudden dismission, which I understood was always the case. I was therefore prevailed on, though I felt a horror of men, to accept the offer of a gentleman, rather in the decline of years, to keep his house, pleasantly situated in a little village near Hampstead.

"He was a man of great talents, and of brilliant wit; but, a worn-out votary of voluptuousness, his desires became fastidious in proportion as they grew weak, and the native tenderness of his heart was undermined by a vitiated imagination. A thoughtless carreer of libertinism and social enjoyment, had injured his health to such a degree, that, whatever pleasure his conversation afforded me (and my esteem was ensured by proofs of the generous humanity of his disposition), the being his mistress was purchasing it at a very dear rate. With such a keen perception of the delicacies of sentiment, with an imagination invigorated by the exercise of genius, how could he sink into the grossness of sensuality!

"But, to pass over a subject which I recollect with pain, I must remark to you, as an answer to your often-repeated question, 'Why my sentiments and language were superior to my station?' that I now began to read, to beguile the tediousness of solitude, and to gratify an inquisitive, active mind. I had often, in my childhood, followed a ballad-singer, to hear the sequel of a dismal story, though sure of being severely punished for delaying to return with whatever I was sent to purchase. I could just spell and put a sentence together, and I listened to the various arguments, though often mingled with obscenity, which occurred at the table where I was allowed to preside: for a literary friend or two frequently came home with my master, to dine and pass the night. Having lost the privileged respect of my sex, my presence, instead of restraining, perhaps gave the reins to their tongues; still I had the advantage of hearing discussions, from which, in the common course of life, women are excluded.

"You may easily imagine, that it was only by degrees that I could comprehend some of the subjects they investigated, or acquire from their reasoning what might be termed a moral sense. But my fondness of reading increasing, and my master occasionally shutting himself up in this retreat, for weeks together, to write, I had many opportunities of improvement. At first, considering money (I was right!" exclaimed Jemima, altering her tone of voice) "as the only means, after my loss of reputation, of obtaining respect, or even the toleration of humanity, I had not the least scruple to secrete a part of the sums intrusted to me, and to screen myself from detection by a system of falshood. But, acquiring new principles, I began to have the ambition of returning to the respectable part of society, and was weak enough to suppose it possible. The attention of my unassuming instructor, who, without being ignorant of his own powers, possessed great simplicity of manners, strengthened the illusion. Having sometimes caught up hints for thought, from my untutored remarks, he often led me to discuss the subjects he was treating, and would read to me his productions, previous to their publication, wishing to profit by the criticism of unsophisticated feeling. The aim of his writings was to touch the simple springs of the heart; for he despised the would-be oracles, the self-elected philosophers, who fright away fancy, while sifting each grain of thought to prove that slowness of comprehension is wisdom.

"I should have distinguished this as a moment of sunshine, a happy period in my life, had not the repugnance the disgusting libertinism of my protector inspired, daily become more painful.—And, indeed, I soon did recollect it as such with agony, when his sudden death (for he had recourse to the most exhilarating cordials to keep up the convivial tone of his spirits) again threw me into the desert of human society. Had he had any time for reflection, I am certain he would have left the little property in his power to me: but, attacked by the fatal apoplexy in town, his heir, a man of rigid morals, brought his wife with him to take possession of the house and effects, before I was even informed of his death,—'to prevent,' as she took care indirectly to tell me, 'such a creature as she supposed me to be, from purloining any of them, had I been apprized of the event in time.'

"The grief I felt at the sudden shock the information gave me, which at first had nothing selfish in it, was treated with contempt, and I was ordered to pack up my clothes; and a few trinkets and books, given me by the generous deceased, were contested, while they piously hoped, with a reprobating shake of the head, 'that God would have mercy on his sinful soul!' With some difficulty, I obtained my arrears of wages; but asking—such is the spirit-grinding consequence of poverty and infamy—for a character for honesty and economy, which God knows I merited, I was told by this—why must I call her woman?— 'that it would go against her conscience to recommend a kept mistress.' Tears started in my eyes, burning tears; for there are situations in which a wretch is humbled by the contempt they are conscious they do not deserve.

"I returned to the metropolis; but the solitude of a poor lodging was inconceivably dreary, after the society I had enjoyed. To be cut off from human converse, now I had been taught to relish it, was to wander a ghost among the living. Besides, I foresaw, to aggravate the severity of my fate, that my little pittance would soon melt away. I endeavoured to obtain needlework; but, not having been taught early, and my hands being rendered clumsy by hard work, I did not sufficiently excel to be employed by the ready-made linen shops, when so many women, better qualified, were suing for it. The want of a character prevented my getting a place; for, irksome as servitude would have been to me, I should have made another trial, had it been feasible. Not that I disliked employment, but the inequality of condition to which I must have submitted. I had acquired a taste for literature, during the five years I had lived with a literary man, occasionally conversing with men of the first abilities of the age; and now to descend to the lowest vulgarity, was a degree of wretchedness not to be imagined unfelt. I had not, it is true, tasted the charms of affection, but I had been familiar with the graces of humanity.

"One of the gentlemen, whom I had frequently dined in company with, while I was treated like a companion, met me in the street, and enquired after my health. I seized the occasion, and began to describe my situation; but he was in haste to join, at dinner, a select party of choice spirits; therefore, without waiting to hear me, he impatiently put a guinea into my hand, saying, 'It was a pity such a sensible woman should be in distress—he wished me well from his soul.'

"To another I wrote, stating my case, and requesting advice. He was an advocate for unequivocal sincerity; and had often, in my presence, descanted on the evils which arise in society from the despotism of rank and riches.

"In reply, I received a long essay on the energy of the human mind, with continual allusions to his own force of character. He added, 'That the woman who could write such a letter as I had sent him, could never be in want of resources, were she to look into herself, and exert her powers; misery was the consequence of indolence, and, as to my being shut out from society, it was the lot of man to submit to certain privations.'

"How often have I heard," said Jemima, interrupting her narrative, "in conversation, and read in books, that every person willing to work may find employment? It is the vague assertion, I believe, of insensible indolence, when it relates to men; but, with respect to women, I am sure of its fallacy, unless they will submit to the most menial bodily labour; and even to be employed at hard labour is out of the reach of many, whose reputation misfortune or folly has tainted.

"How writers, professing to be friends to freedom, and the improvement of morals, can assert that poverty is no evil, I cannot imagine."

"No more can I," interrupted Maria, "yet they even expatiate on the peculiar happiness of indigence, though in what it can consist, excepting in brutal rest, when a man can barely earn a subsistence, I cannot imagine. The mind is necessarily imprisoned in its own little tenement; and, fully occupied by keeping it in repair, has not time to rove abroad for improvement. The book of knowledge is closely clasped, against those who must fulfil their daily task of severe manual labour or die; and curiosity, rarely excited by thought or information, seldom moves on the stagnate lake of ignorance."

"As far as I have been able to observe," replied Jemima, "prejudices, caught up by chance, are obstinately maintained by the poor, to the exclusion of improvement; they have not time to reason or reflect to any extent, or minds sufficiently exercised to adopt the principles of action, which form perhaps the only basis of contentment in every station."*

"And independence," said Darnford, "they are necessarily strangers to, even the independence of despising their persecutors. If the poor are happy, or can be happy, *things are very well as they are*. And I cannot conceive on what principle those writers contend for a change of system, who support this opinion. The authors on the other side of the question are much more consistent, who grant the fact; yet, insisting that it is the lot of the majority to be oppressed in this life, kindly turn them over to another, to rectify the false weights and measures of this, as the only way to justify the dispensations of Providence. I have not," continued Darnford, "an opinion more firmly fixed by observation in my mind, than that, though riches may fail to produce proportionate happiness, poverty most commonly excludes it, by shutting up all the avenues to improvement."

"And as for the affections," added Maria, with a sigh, "how gross, and even tormenting do they become, unless regulated by an improving mind! The culture of the heart ever, I believe, keeps pace with that of the mind. But pray go on," addressing Jemima, "though your narrative gives rise to the most painful reflections on the present state of society."

* The copy which appears to have received the author's last corrections, ends at this place.—Godwin.

"Not to trouble you," continued she, "with a detailed description of all the painful feelings of unavailing exertion, I have only to tell you, that at last I got recommended to wash in a few families, who did me the favour to admit me into their houses, without the most strict enquiry, to wash from one in the morning till eight at night, for eighteen or twenty-pence a day. On the happiness to be enjoyed over a washing-tub I need not comment; yet you will allow me to observe, that this was a wretchedness of situation peculiar to my sex. A man with half my industry, and, I may say, abilities, could have procured a decent livelihood, and discharged some of the duties which knit mankind together; whilst I, who had acquired a taste for the rational, nay, in honest pride let me assert it, the virtuous enjoyments of life, was cast aside as the filth of society. Condemned to labour, like a machine, only to earn bread, and scarcely that, I became melancholy and desperate.

"I have now to mention a circumstance which fills me with remorse, and fear it will entirely deprive me of your esteem. A tradesman became attached to me, and visited me frequently,—and I at last obtained such a power over him, that he offered to take me home to his house.—Consider, dear madam, I was famishing: wonder not that I became a wolf!—The only reason for not taking me home immediately, was the having a girl in the house, with child by him—and this girl—I advised him—yes, I did! would I could forget it!—to turn out of doors: and one night he determined to follow my advice. Poor wretch! She fell upon her knees, reminded him that he had promised to marry her, that her parents were honest!—What did it avail?—She was turned out.

"She approached her father's door, in the skirts of London,—listened at the shutters,—but could not knock. A watchman had observed her go and return several times—Poor wretch!—[The remorse Jemima spoke of, seemed to be stinging her to the soul, as she proceeded.]

"She left it, and, approaching a tub where horses were watered, she sat down in it, and, with desperate resolution, remained in that attitude—till resolution was no longer necessary!

"I happened that morning to be going out to wash, anticipating the moment when I should escape from such hard labour. I passed by, just as some men, going to work, drew out the stiff, cold corpse—Let me not recal the horrid moment —I recognized her pale visage; I listened to the tale told by the spectators, and my heart did not burst. I thought of my own state, and wondered how I could be such a monster!—I worked hard; and, returning home, I was attacked by a fever. I suffered both in body and mind. I determined not to live with the wretch. But he did not try me; he left the neighbourhood. I once more returned to the wash-tub.

"Still this state, miserable as it was, admitted of aggravation. Lifting one day a heavy load, a tub fell against my shin, and gave me great pain. I did not pay much attention to the hurt, till it became a serious wound; being obliged to work as usual, or starve. But, finding myself at length unable to stand for any time, I thought of getting into an hospital. Hospitals, it should seem (for they are comfortless abodes for the sick) were expressly endowed for the reception of the friendless; yet I, who had on that plea a right to assistance, wanted the recommendation of the rich and respectable, and was several weeks languishing for admittance;* fees were demanded on entering; and, what was still more unreasonable, security for burying me, that expence not coming into the letter of the charity. A guinea was the stipulated sum—I could as soon have raised a million; and I was afraid to apply to the parish for an order, lest they should have passed me, I knew not whither. The poor woman at whose house I lodged, compassionating my state, got me into the hospital; and the family where I received the hurt, sent me five shillings, three and six-pence of which I gave at my admittance—I know not for what.

"My leg grew quickly better; but I was dismissed before my cure was completed, because I could not afford to have my linen washed to appear decently, as the virago of a nurse said, when the gentlemen (the surgeons) came. I cannot give you an adequate idea of the wretchedness of an hospital; every thing is left to the care of people intent on gain. The attendants seem to have lost all feeling of compassion in the bustling discharge of their offices; death is so familiar to them, that they are not anxious to ward it off. Every thing appeared to be conducted for the accommodation of the medical men and their pupils, who came to make experiments on the poor, for the benefit of the rich. One of the physicians, I must not forget to mention, gave me half-a-crown, and ordered me some wine, when I was at the lowest ebb. I thought of making my case known to the lady-like matron; but her forbidding countenance prevented me. She condescended to look on the patients, and make general enquiries, two or three times a week; but the nurses knew the hour when the visit of ceremony would commence, and every thing was as it should be.

"After my dismission, I was more at a loss than ever for a subsistence, and, not to weary you with a repetition of the same unavailing

---

* Poor patients were accepted in hospitals only after a recommendation. Although in many ways brutal and unhygienic, the London hospitals in the eighteenth century cured and patched up a remarkably high proportion of their patients.—Editor.

attempts, unable to stand at the washing-tub, I began to consider the rich and poor as natural enemies, and became a thief from principle. I could not now cease to reason, but I hated mankind. I despised myself, yet I justified my conduct. I was taken, tried, and condemned to six months' imprisonment in a house of correction. My soul recoils with horror from the remembrance of the insults I had to endure, till, branded with shame, I was turned loose in the street, pennyless. I wandered from street to street, till, exhausted by hunger and fatigue, I sunk down sense-less at a door, where I had vainly demanded a morsel of bread. I was sent by the inhabitant to the work-house, to which he had surlily bid me go, saying, he 'paid enough in conscience to the poor,' when, with parched tongue, I implored his charity.* If those well-meaning people who ex-claim against beggars, were acquainted with the treatment the poor re-ceive in many of these wretched asylums, they would not stifle so easily involuntary sympathy, by saying that they have all parishes to go to, or wonder that the poor dread to enter the gloomy walls. What are the common run of workhouses, but prisons, in which many respectable old people, worn out by immoderate labour, sink into the grave in sorrow, to which they are carried like dogs!"

Alarmed by some indistinct noise, Jemima rose hastily to listen, and Maria, turning to Darnford, said, "I have indeed been shocked beyond expression when I have met a pauper's funeral. A coffin carried on the shoulders of three or four ill-looking wretches, whom the imagination might easily convert into a band of assassins, hastening to conceal the corpse, and quarrelling about the prey on their way. I know it is of little consequence how we are consigned to the earth; but I am led by this brutal insensibility, to what even the animal creation appears forcibly to feel, to advert to the wretched, deserted manner in which they died."

"True," rejoined Darnford, "and, till the rich will give more than a part of their wealth, till they will give time and attention to the wants of the distressed, never let them boast of charity. Let them open their hearts, and not their purses, and employ their minds in the service, if they are really actuated by humanity; or charitable institutions will al-ways be the prey of the lowest order of knaves."

Jemima returning, seemed in haste to finish her tale. "The overseer farmed the poor of different parishes, and out of the bowels of poverty was wrung the money with which he purchased this dwelling, as a pri-

---

* Workhouses, originally intended to provide work for the able-bodied, quickly be-came dumps for the old, destitute, and unemployable. They were notoriously over-crowded and fever-ridden. Maintained by the parishes, they were paid for by poor rates levied on local householders, a system which broke down in some of the densely popu-lated areas of London where the poor greatly outnumbered the householders.—Editor.

vate receptacle for madness. He had been a keeper at a house of the same description, and conceived that he could make money much more readily in his old occupation. He is a shrewd—shall I say it?—villain. He observed something resolute in my manner, and offered to take me with him, and instruct me how to treat the disturbed minds he meant to intrust to my care. The offer of forty pounds a year, and to quit a workhouse, was not to be despised, though the condition of shutting my eyes and hardening my heart was annexed to it.

"I agreed to accompany him; and four years have I been attendant on many wretches, and"—she lowered her voice,—"the witness of many enormities. In solitude my mind seemed to recover its force, and many of the sentiments which I imbibed in the only tolerable period of my life, returned with their full force. Still what should induce me to be the champion for suffering humanity?—Who ever risked any thing for me?—Who ever acknowledged me to be a fellow-creature?"—

[*Love and Marriage*]
from
CHAPTER 10

"Those who support a system of what I term false refinement, and will not allow great part of love in the female, as well as male breast, to spring in some respects involuntarily, may not admit that charms are as necessary to feed the passion, as virtues to convert the mellowing spirit into friendship. To such observers I have nothing to say, any more than to the moralists, who insist that women ought to, and can love their husbands, because it is their duty. To you, my child,* I may add, with a heart tremblingly alive to your future conduct, some observations, dictated by my present feelings, on calmly reviewing this period of my life. When novelists or moralists praise as a virtue, a woman's coldness of constitution, and want of passion; and make her yield to the ardour of her lover out of sheer compassion, or to promote a frigid plan of future comfort, I am disgusted. They may be good women, in the ordinary acceptation of the phrase, and do no harm; but they appear to me not to have those 'finely fashioned nerves,' which render the senses exquisite. They may possess tenderness; but they want that fire of the imagination, which produces *active* sensibility, and *positive* virtue. How does the woman deserve to be characterized, who marries one man, with a heart and imagination devoted to another? Is she not an object of pity or contempt, when thus sacrilegiously violating the purity of her own

---

* Maria is addressing her narrative to the daughter she has lost.—Editor.

feelings? Nay, it is as indelicate, when she is indifferent, unless she be constitutionally insensible; then indeed it is a mere affair of barter; and I have nothing to do with the secrets of trade. Yes; eagerly as I wish you to possess true rectitude of mind, and purity of affection, I must insist that a heartless conduct is the contrary of virtuous. Truth is the only basis of virtue; and we cannot, without depraving our minds, endeavour to please a lover or husband, but in proportion as he pleases us. Men, more effectually to enslave us, may inculcate this partial morality, and lose sight of virtue in subdividing it into the duties of particular stations; but let us not blush for nature without a cause! . . ."

" 'The marriage state is certainly that in which women, generally speaking, can be most useful;* but I am far from thinking that a woman, once married, ought to consider the engagement as indissoluble (especially if there be no children to reward her for sacrificing her feelings) in case her husband merits neither her love, nor esteem.† Esteem will often supply the place of love; and prevent a woman from being wretched, though it may not make her happy. The magnitude of a sacrifice ought always to bear some proportion to the utility in view; and for a woman to live with a man, for whom she can cherish neither affection nor esteem, or even be of any use to him, excepting in the light of a house-keeper, is an abjectness of condition, the enduring of which no concurrence of circumstances can ever make a duty in the sight of God or just men. If indeed she submits to it merely to be maintained in idleness, she has no right to complain bitterly of her fate; or to act, as a person of independent character might, as if she had a title to disregard general rules.

"But the misfortune is, that many women only submit in appearance, and forfeit their own respect to secure their reputation in the world. The situation of a woman separated from her husband, is undoubtedly very different from that of a man who has left his wife. He, with lordly dignity, has shaken of a clog; and the allowing her food and raiment, is thought sufficient to secure his reputation from taint. And, should she have been inconsiderate, he will be celebrated for his generosity and forbearance. Such is the respect paid to the master-key of property! A woman, on the contrary, resigning what is termed her natural protector (though he never was so, but in name) is despised

* Maria's kindly uncle is speaking.—Editor.

† In eighteenth-century England it was extremely difficult for a woman to obtain a divorce. Even at the end of the next century it required conspicuous cruelty in the husband.—Editor.

and shunned, for asserting the independence of mind distinctive of a rational being, and spurning at slavery.'

[*Women and the Law*]
from
CHAPTER 11

"The tender mother* cannot *lawfully* snatch from the gripe of the gambling spendthrift, or beastly drunkard, unmindful of his offspring, the fortune which falls to her by chance; or (so flagrant is the injustice) what she earns by her own exertions. No; he can rob her with impunity, even to waste publicly on a courtezan; and the laws of her country—if women have a country—afford her no protection or redress from the oppressor, unless she have the plea of bodily fear; yet how many ways are there of goading the soul almost to madness, equally unmanly, though not so mean? When such laws were framed, should not impartial lawgivers have first decreed, in the style of a great assembly, who recognized the existence of an *être suprême*,† to fix the national belief, that the husband should always be wiser and more virtuous than his wife, in order to entitle him, with a show of justice, to keep this idiot, or perpetual minor, for ever in bondage."

from
CHAPTER 13

"She‡ began by telling me, 'That she had saved a little money in service; and was over-persuaded (we must all be in love once in our lives) to marry a likely man, a footman in the family, not worth a groat. My plan,' she continued, 'was to take a house, and let out lodgings; and all went on well, till my husband got acquainted with an impudent slut, who chose to live on other people's means—and then all went to rack and ruin. He ran in debt to buy her fine clothes, such clothes as I never thought of wearing myself, and—would you believe it?—he signed an execution on my very goods, bought with the money I worked so hard to get; and they came and took my bed from under me, before I heard a word of the matter.§ Aye, madam, these are mis-

---

* Maria is speaking.—Editor.
† Supreme being.—Editor.
‡ The landlady is speaking to Maria.—Editor.
§ Not until the Married Women's Property Act of 1870 did women gain a measure of control over their own property and earnings.—Editor.

fortunes that you gentlefolks know nothing of,—but sorrow is sorrow, let it come which way it will.

" 'I sought for a service again—very hard, after having a house of my own!—but he used to follow me, and kick up such a riot when he was drunk, that I could not keep a place; nay, he even stole my clothes, and pawned them; and when I went to the pawnbroker's, and offered to take my oath that they were not bought with a farthing of his money, they said, "It was all as one, my husband had a right to whatever I had."

" 'At last he listed for a soldier, and I took a house, making an agreement to pay for the furniture by degrees; and I almost starved myself, till I once more got before-hand in the world.

" 'After an absence of six years (God forgive me! I thought he was dead) my husband returned; found me out, and came with such a penitent face, I forgave him, and clothed him from head to foot. But he had not been a week in the house, before some of his creditors arrested him; and, he selling my goods, I found myself once more reduced to beggary; for I was not as well able to work, go to bed late, and rise early, as when I quitted service; and then I thought it hard enough. He was soon tired of me, when there was nothing more to be had, and left me again.

" 'I will not tell you how I was buffeted about, till, hearing for certain that he had died in an hospital abroad, I once more returned to my old occupation; but have not yet been able to get my head above water: so, madam, you must not be angry if I am afraid to run any risk, when I know so well, that women have always the worst of it, when law is to decide.' "

from
CHAPTER 17

Convinced that the subterfuges of the law were disgraceful, [Maria] wrote a paper, which she expressly desired might be read in court:

"Married when scarcely able to distinguish the nature of the engagement, I yet submitted to the rigid laws which enslave women, and obeyed the man whom I could no longer love. Whether the duties of the state are reciprocal, I mean not to discuss; but I can prove repeated infidelities which I overlooked or pardoned. Witnesses are not wanting to establish these facts. I at present maintain the child of a maid servant, sworn to him, and born after our marriage. I am ready to allow, that education and circumstances lead men to think and act with less delicacy, than the preservation of order in society demands from women; but surely I may without assumption declare, that, though I could ex-

cuse the birth, I could not the desertion of this unfortunate babe:—
and, while I despised the man, it was not easy to venerate the husband.
With proper restrictions however, I revere the institution which frater-
nizes the world. I exclaim against the laws which throw the whole
weight of the yoke on the weaker shoulders, and force women, when
they claim protectorship as mothers, to sign a contract, which renders
them dependent on the caprice of the tyrant, whom choice or necessity
has appointed to reign over them. Various are the cases, in which a
woman ought to separate herself from her husband; and mine, I may
be allowed emphatically to insist, comes under the description of the
most aggravated.

"I will not enlarge on those provocations which only the individual
can estimate; but will bring forward such charges only, the truth of
which is an insult upon humanity. In order to promote certain destructive speculations, Mr. Venables prevailed on me to borrow certain sums
of a wealthy relation; and, when I refused further compliance, he
thought of bartering my person; and not only allowed opportunities to,
but urged, a friend from whom he borrowed money, to seduce me.
On the discovery of this act of atrocity, I determined to leave him, and
in the most decided manner, for ever. I consider all obligations as made
void by his conduct; and hold, that schisms which proceed from want
of principles, can never be healed.

"He received a fortune with me to the amount of five thousand
pounds. On the death of my uncle, convinced that I could provide for
my child, I destroyed the settlement of that fortune. I required none
of my property to be returned to me, nor shall enumerate the sums
extorted from me during six years that we lived together.

"After leaving, what the law considers as my home, I was hunted
like a criminal from place to place, though I contracted no debts, and
demanded no maintenance—yet, as the laws sanction such proceeding, and make women the property of their husbands, I forbear to
animadvert. After the birth of my daughter, and the death of my uncle,
who left a very considerable property to myself and child, I was exposed
to new persecution; and, because I had, before arriving at what is
termed years of discretion, pledged my faith, I was treated by the world,
as bound for ever to a man whose vices were notorious. Yet what are
the vices generally known, to the various miseries that a woman may
be subject to, which, though deeply felt, eating into the soul, elude
description, and may be glossed over! A false morality is even established, which makes all the virtue of women consist in chastity, submission, and the forgiveness of injuries.

"I pardon my oppressor—bitterly as I lament the loss of my child,
torn from me in the most violent manner. But nature revolts, and my

soul sickens at the bare supposition, that it could ever be a duty to pretend affection, when a separation is necessary to prevent my feeling hourly aversion.

"To force me to give my fortune, I was imprisoned—yes; in a private mad-house.*—There, in the heart of misery, I met the man charged with seducing me. We became attached—I deemed, and ever shall deem, myself free. The death of my babe dissolved the only tie which subsisted between me and my, what is termed, lawful husband.

"To this person, thus encountered, I voluntarily gave myself, never considering myself as any more bound to transgress the laws of moral purity, because the will of my husband might be pleaded in my excuse, than to transgress those laws to which [the policy of artificial society has] annexed [positive] punishments.—While no command of a husband can prevent a woman from suffering for certain crimes, she must be allowed to consult her conscience, and regulate her conduct, in some degree, by her own sense of right. The respect I owe to myself, demanded my strict adherence to my determination of never viewing Mr. Venables in the light of a husband, nor could it forbid me from encouraging another. If I am unfortunately united to an unprincipled man, am I for ever to be shut out from fulfilling the duties of a wife and mother?—I wish my country to approve of my conduct; but, if laws exist, made by the strong to oppress the weak, I appeal to my own sense of justice, and declare that I will not live with the individual, who has violated every moral obligation which binds man to man.

"I protest equally against any charge being brought to criminate the man, whom I consider as my husband. I was six-and-twenty when I left Mr. Venables' roof; if ever I am to be supposed to arrive at an age to direct my own actions, I must by that time have arrived at it.—I acted with deliberation.—Mr. Darnford found me a forlorn and oppressed woman, and promised the protection women in the present state of society want.—But the man who now claims me—was he deprived of my society by this conduct? The question is an insult to common sense, considering where Mr. Darnford met me.—Mr. Venables' door was indeed open to me—nay, threats and intreaties were used to induce me to return; but why? Was affection or honour the motive?— I cannot, it is true, dive into the recesses of the human heart—yet I presume to assert, [borne out as I am by a variety of circumstances,] that he was merely influenced by the most rapacious avarice.

"I claim then a divorce, and the liberty of enjoying, free from

---

* As late as 1840 the British courts upheld a husband's right to imprison a wife who had tried to escape.—Editor.

molestation, the fortune left to me by a relation, who was well aware of the character of the man with whom I had to contend.—I appeal to the justice and humanity of the jury—a body of men, whose private judgment must be allowed to modify laws, that must be unjust, because definite rules can never apply to indefinite circumstances—and I deprecate punishment upon the man of my choice, freeing him, as I solemnly do, from the charge of seduction.

"I did not put myself into a situation to justify a charge of adultery, till I had, from conviction, shaken off the fetters which bound me to Mr. Venables.—While I lived with him, I defy the voice of calumny to sully what is termed the fair fame of woman.—Neglected by my husband, I never encouraged a lover; and preserved with scrupulous care, what is termed my honour, at the expence of my peace, till he, who should have been its guardian, laid traps to ensnare me. From that moment I believed myself, in the sight of heaven, free—and no power on earth shall force me to renounce my resolution."

The judge, in summing up the evidence, alluded to "the fallacy of letting women plead their feelings, as an excuse for the violation of the marriage-vow. For his part, he had always determined to oppose all innovation, and the new-fangled notions which incroached on the good old rules of conduct. We did not want French principles* in public or private life—and, if women were allowed to plead their feelings, as an excuse or palliation of infidelity, it was opening a flood-gate for immorality. What virtuous woman thought of her feelings?—It was her duty to love and obey the man chosen by her parents and relations, who were qualified by their experience to judge better for her, than she could for herself. As to the charges brought against the husband, they were vague, supported by no witnesses, excepting that of imprisonment in a private madhouse. The proofs of an insanity in the family, might render that however a prudent measure; and indeed the conduct of the lady did not appear that of a person of sane mind. Still such a mode of proceeding could not be justified, and might perhaps entitle the lady [in another court] to a sentence of separation from bed and board, during the joint lives of the parties; but he hoped that no Englishman would legalize adultery, by enabling the adulteress to enrich her seducer. Too many restrictions could not be thrown in the way of divorces, if we wished to maintain the sanctity of marriage; and, though they might bear a little hard on a few, very few individuals, it was evidently for the good of the whole."

* A common phrase of the time used to brand liberal or unconventional ideas as foreign, revolutionary, and un-British.—Editor.

Reviews of Novels

Wollstonecraft was a reviewer for the *Analytical Review* from 1787 until her visit to France in 1792 and from 1796 until her death. She contributed many reviews during these years, all of them anonymous, as was the custom of the journal. The following reviews have been ascribed to Wollstonecraft on the basis of style, subject matter, and the use of an initial—M or W. The vast majority of the reviews deal with fiction, a matter about which she was deeply concerned—as her other works testify. Other frequent subjects were educational books and travel accounts, especially those dealing with countries familiar to her such as Portugal and France. All of Wollstonecraft's reviews, whatever the subject matter, are united by a warm dislike of affectation and pomposity and a clear concern for writing as a serious and moral art.

FROM *Emmeline, the Orphan of the Castle.* By Charlotte Smith. [I, May–August, 1788] Initialled M.

Few of the numerous productions termed novels, claim any attention; and while we distinguish this one, we cannot help lamenting that it has the same tendency as the generality, whose preposterous sentiments our young females imbibe with such avidity. Vanity thus fostered, takes deep root in the forming mind, and affectation banishes natural graces, or at least obscures them. We do not mean to confound affectation and vice, or allude to those pernicious writings that obviously vitiate the heart, while they lead the understanding astray. But we must observe, that the false expectations these wild scenes excite, tend to debauch the mind, and throw an insipid kind of uniformity over the moderate and rational prospects of life, consequently *adventures* are sought for and created, when duties are neglected, and content despised.

From *The School for Fathers; or the Victim of a Curse. A Novel.* [II, September–December, 1788] Initialled W.

We imagine it is a female production, and taking this for granted, think the lady deserves praise for preserving the feminine character by strictly attending to modesty and even delicacy, and not suffering her imagination to revel in scenes which her young readers ought not to peruse. One circumstance however, as an exception, we must allude to: it appears strange that the heroine should so often dwell on the *beauty* of her lover, it is inconsistent with her character; for certainly a woman may love a man who has not white teeth or fine eyes; and to tell him of them is 'passing strange,' or rather a breach of that decorum which is not artificial but instinctive.

From *Arundel.* [III, January–April, 1789] Initialled W.

From the number of novels that daily appear, and the few good, or even tolerable, which are to be found amongst them, it seems obvious that to write a good novel requires uncommon abilities. Shakespeare created monsters; but he gave such *reality* to his characters, that we do not hesitate a moment to deliver our imaginations, and even reason, into his hands; we follow their wild yet not fantastic foot-steps through wood and bog, nothing loath—thinking them new, though not unnatural.

Richardson too, availing himself of the happy prerogative of genius, peopled his scenes with beings who scarcely resemble human creatures. When we contemplate his finished pictures adorned with the most graceful drapery, we are nevertheless interested in the detail and opening of the characters; we find them made up of mortal passions, and are affected by those delicate shades and tints which suddenly give a glimpse of the heart, and tie the whole family on earth together.

We apprehend that the author of Arundel has not only o'er-stepped, but lost sight of the modesty of nature, and introduced characters and scenes which cannot interest a person of discernment or taste, yet may injure young minds by exhibiting life through a false medium; and undermining, under the disguise of refinement, the out-works and safe-guards of virtue. . . .

The mother and daughter both loving the same man produce in the mind an emotion of disgust, rather than pity—pity must be supported by respect, to leave a lasting impression. Throughout, sensation is termed sensibility; and vice, or rather sensuality, varnished over with a gloss, which the author seems to think virtue. He rambled into the country of chimeras for phantoms, whose like never were clothed with flesh, though all its infirmities are ascribed to them. Surely a novel of this kind must inspire the young women who eagerly peruse it, with false notions and hopes, teach them affectation, and shake their principles by representing love as irresistible, love at first sight.

The Child of Woe. A Novel. By Mrs. Elizabeth Norman. [III, January–April, 1789] Initialled W.

The Child of Woe having no marked features to characterize it, we can only term it a truly feminine novel. Indeed, the generality of them, in which improper descriptions are not introduced, are so near akin to each other, that with a few very trifling alterations, the same review would serve for almost all of them. More or less emphasis might be laid on the particular ingredients which compose the following receipt for a novel. Unnatural characters, improbable incidents, sad tales of woe rehearsed in an affected, half-prose, half-poetical style, exquisite double-refined sensibility, dazzling beauty, and *elegant* drapery, to adorn the celestial body, (these descriptions cannot be too minute) should never be forgotten in a book intended to amuse the fair.

This account will be a just one of ninety-nine novels out of a hundred; our readers must, then, excuse us, if we use the same words when we speak of productions in which we find so little variety; immoral ones we shall censure, and praise the *good*; the intermediate tribe which only infuse vanity and affectation into the minds of young readers, we shall not attempt so nicely to discriminate, as to point out the different shades of merit. Let not the female novelist be offended, who rises a tint above her contemporaries, if her darling is confounded with performances of the same complexion; for *scrupulous* exactness is never expected in any kind of classing.

Mount Pelham. A Novel. [III, January–April, 1789] Initialled W.

Much ado about nothing. We place this novel without any reservation, at the bottom of the second class. The language is affected; and it has all the faults we have before enumerated. The morality is rather lax; for the author, a female, says, 'so gentle, so forgiving, is the nature of a virtuous female; and so prone are we to love the offender, yet detest the offense.' This is the varnish of sentiment to hide sensuality.

The Ill Effects of a rash Vow. A Novel. [III, January–April, 1789] Initialled W.

The style of this novel is tolerable; and some characters and incidents rather interesting: but the catastrophe, which turns on the absurd rash vow, is so *ridiculously* dreadful, that we smiled at the numbers death swept away; and quietly place this sad tale in the numerous class of middling performances, except the conclusion, which deviating so widely from nature, sinks below mediocrity.

Juliet: or, The Cottager. A Novel. By a Lady. [III, January–April, 1789] Uninitialled.

It has been judiciously observed by one of our brother Reviewers, that the publication of Miss Burney's novels formed a new era in this flimsy kind of writing.* A varied combination of the same events has been adopted, and like timid sheep, the lady authors jump over the hedge one after the other, and do not dream of deviating either to the right or left. Richardson destroyed the giants and dwarfs that figured away in romances, and substituted old ugly women to keep the beauteous damsel in durance vile; however she had still to protect her chastity with vigilant care against violent assaults, and after having passed unsullied through the ordeal trial, a *demi*-hero freed her, and matrimony wound up the plot, &c. &c.†

Now the method is altered; the fortress is not stormed, but undermined, and the belles must guard their hearts from the soft contagion, and not listen to the insidious sigh, when the hand is gently pressed, nor trust the equivocal protestations of love—and then they obtain a husband, &c. &c.

The author of this novel has tripped back; the *sentimental* heroine is twice carried off, but no harm ensues, except that she is hurried by sorrow to the very brink of the grave, when her true love opportunely appears to bid her revive, and the drooping flower raises its head, to lean on the offered support.

More minute criticism on this novel would be absurd, as it sinks before discriminate censure.

Beatrice, or the Inconstant, A Tragic Novel. [IV, May–August, 1789] Uninitialled.

This insignificant knot of adventures, written in a series of letters, has not a shadow of interest to make the reader for a moment forget the absence of common sense.

* Fanny Burney (1752–1840) published many novels; the first and most important was *Evelina* (1778), which made popular the theme of the entry into society of a young, inexperienced, but virtuous girl.—Editor.

† A reference to Samuel Richardson's *Pamela* (1740), in which the heroine astutely defends her virtue and is rewarded with marriage to the hero.—Editor.

The Ramble of Philo, and his Man Sturdy. [IV, May–August, 1789] Uninitialled.

A narrative equally uninteresting and absurd; the author attempts to introduce some humorous scenes; but the caricature blocks cannot by their antic tricks, extort even a smile from a reader who is not tickled by a straw.

The Vicar of Lansdowne; or, Country Quarters. A Tale. By Maria Regina Dalton. [IV, May–August, 1789] Uninitialled.

As we imagine the author must be a *very* young lady, and deeply read in poetry and novels, we forbear to censure in a sarcastic style; yet we cannot agree with her that this work is *unstudied*; nay, we think that labouring to *ornament* it, she has rendered many passages unintelligible. If she will listen to the warning voice of experience, we advise her to throw aside her pen, and not attempt to enter *the road of glory*, as she fancifully calls publishing a novel. There is certainly nothing immoral to be found in the volumes, though exquisite sensibility is as usual the cardinal virtue.

Zelia in the Desart. From the French. [IV, May–August, 1789] Uninitialled.

The beginning of this story is certainly entertaining; but Zelia's delicate scruples, and the conversations and letters they produce, would have prejudiced us against it as we advanced, if the prolix account of Ninette's unnatural passion, equally ridiculous and indelicate, had not occurred. We cannot recommend this book, on the whole, to the perusal of those who would otherwise have found it very amusing, as we do not wish our fair countrywomen to imbibe such overstrained notions of love; the two extremes too frequently meet, and the grossest sensuality often lies concealed under double refined sentiments.

The style is unaffected, and many of the reflections just, though strongly tinctured with French romance.

The Exiles; or Memoirs of the Count de Cronstadt. By Clara Reeve. [IV, May–August, 1789] Uninitialled.

This improbable tale is tolerably well told, and comparatively speaking, has a little merit; but it is spun out to a tedious length, and raises curiosity rather than interest.

The ladies are very fond of a dismal catastrophe, and dying for love is the favourite theme. A weakness too often is exalted into an excellence, and the passion that should exercise the understanding, and ever

be made, at least in books intended for the perusal of the rising generation, subordinate to reason, on the contrary is brought forward as the
grand spring of action, the main business of life, and the director of the
darts of death.

From *Louis and Nina, or an Excursion to Yverdun.* [IV, May–August,
1789] Uninitialled.

In these most *dismal* tales, sentimental to the very marrow, the tender feelings are torn to tatters, and the shreds vaingloriously displayed.
Sudden death, everlasting love, methodical madness, bad weather, a
breaking heart, putrid body, worn out night cap, &c. &c. Nothing but
sentiment! the finely fashioned nerves vibrate to every touch—Alas
poor Yorick!* If an earthly wight could punish thee for having, in
the mere wantonness of unbridled vanity, scattered unseemly weeds
amongst the sweet flowers genius had culled, thou wouldst be condemned to review all the sentimental wire-drawn imitations of thy
original interesting pages—not a dash shouldst thou be allowed to pass
over, without measuring it with thine eyes. In *sober* sadness lost, we
might then listen in vain for the magic transitions which bid us weep,
and smile amidst our tears.

From *The Bastile: or History of Charles Townly. A Man of the World.*
[IV, May–August, 1789] Uninitialled.

It may sound like high treason to our fair readers, yet truth compels
us to declare that we open a novel with a degree of pleasure, when
written by a lady, is not inserted in the title page; it is almost needless
to premise, that we allude to the flock of novelists, who by painting in
gaudy colours the idle reveries of their imaginations, neither cultivated
by experience nor curbed by fixed principles, mislead the ignorant
whom they have not abilities to improve, and catch the wandering eye
that is seldom employed; nay, scarcely able to discriminate.

Honoria Sommerville: a Novel. [V, September–December, 1789] Uninitialled.

The adventures of a young amiable woman, who, instead of sinking
under her misfortunes, behaves with dignity and propriety in various
trying situations, will afford young female readers many striking and
useful examples of conduct brought on a level with their understand-

* Wollstonecraft is referring to the character in Laurence Sterne's *Sentimental
Journey* (1768), who moves through France, encountering sentimental adventures at
every turn. The book was extremely popular and widely imitated in the late eighteenth
century.—Editor.

ings, and carried home to their hearts. A hackneyed story has a turn of novelty given to it, and some humour and individuality of character render the whole amusing.—We should now proceed to point out its faults, if we did not recollect that we have determined to avoid the fastidious spirit of criticism when we review a tolerable novel.

The Mental Triumph: a sentimental Novel. By a Lady. [V, September–December, 1789] Uninitialled.

The tendency of this novel, which the author whimsically addresses to herself, is unexceptionable; an artless well-educated female, destitute of beauty, attracts the attention of a worthy man.—So far, so good; but why is virtue to be always rewarded with a coach and six? or how could a writer, who seems to respect religion and virtue, insert the following sentence,

> 'Parental love, though heightened by every possible attachment, is as much inferior to that state of unutterable bliss—which the union of two *congenial souls* affords—as *eternal happiness* is superior to *temporal felicity.*'

The Parson's Wife: a Novel. Written by a Lady. [V, September–December, 1789] Uninitialled.

Such a number of insipid trifling incidents, such mere *nothings,* are here strung together, that in the language of the vulgar, we wonder what the author would be at; however, the whole had a harmless lulling effect on us; but those whom it can keep awake, may read to the end, and begin again, though we should scruple to call such reading amusing pastime.

The Cottage of Friendship: a legendary Pastoral. By Silviana Pastorella. [V, September–December, 1789] Initialled M.

The romantic unnatural fabrication of a *very* young lady, we suppose, from the little knowledge of life which appears, and as her playmates will find neither instruction nor amusement in this ridiculous pastoral, as it is called, we advise her to throw aside her pen and pursue a more useful employment.

Albertina. A Novel. [V, September–December, 1789] Uninitialled.

The author of this novel has endeavoured to imitate Sterne, but only his pathetic tales; for he has steered clear of his indecencies and impiety, the faults which our witlings have in general copied when they laboured to write like him: if he could not catch that humourist's in-

teresting beauties, he has not given us a rough draught of his gross defects. We agree with the writer, that his story is strictly moral; and the
sentiments, though frequently trite, are seldom absurd. There is a kind
of feudal dignity in the characters, and tragic, heroical turns in the tale,
which carry us back to the days of chivalry; and we should have termed
this a romance, if it had not been called a Novel in the title page.

It is an insipid, harmless production, which, resembling that numerous class, termed *good sort of people*, deserves neither praise nor
censure;—the comparison may be stretched still further:—we bear with
these good sort of people, when forced into their company by accident
or business; leave them without pain, and never recollect that they exist,
till we see them again.

The Fair Hibernian. [V, September–December, 1789] Uninitialled.

It has been sarcastically said, by a snarling poet, that most women
have no character at all:* we shall apply it to their productions—Novels.
The one before us, evidently written by a lady, is so like many other
flimsy novels we have reviewed, that we scarcely know how to charac-
terise it. The story is short, and has neither probability nor novelty to
render it interesting. Mountains are laboriously raised, to be levelled
with a magic touch, when the author is disposed to make the imaginary
personages she has drawn forth happy—perfectly happy! Without a
knowledge of life, or the human heart, why will young misses presume to write? They would not attempt to play in company on an instrument whose principles they know nothing of:—how then can they
have the assurance to publish their foolish fancies? Nay, after talking
of the soul of sentiment—double-refined delicacy—how can they, without blushing, own that they have allowed their imaginations to revel
in *sensual* love scenes?—for we cannot help calling them so, though
the gauze veil of artificial sentiments is drawn over them. The composing of these letters must have been a pleasing dream to the writer:
she describes the beings she has conversed with in other novels; and
the happiness—(we suppose she has never changed her name)—the
superlative, the celestial happiness of the marriage state, when congenial souls meet, and the whitest hand in the world receives the most
impassioned kisses from the handsomest *male* mouth in the world—a
baronet, lord, or duke—nothing less! Yet we must do justice to the
author, and say, that there are fewer embraces brought forward to
notice than usual; and the handsome Sir Edward is only once dying for

* Alexander Pope, *Moral Essays,* II.—Editor.

love:—our strictures, then, apply to the genus; we do not mean to single out this gay flower.

There is an air of sprightliness running through these letters, and some good sense, which leads us to think the author will employ her time better when she is married.

Almeria Belmore. A Novel, in a Series of Letters. Written by a Lady. [V, September–December, 1789] Initialled M.

Miss O'Connor complains, in her address to the public, of a celebrated clergyman, who approved of her novel when *she* read it to him, and afterwards was a little inclined to recant, and not repeat the praise the eyes of a young, fair *authoress*—for we will, to heighten the scene, suppose her fair—extorted from him: but we wish the gentleman had not been under undue influence, he would then have spoken out, and spared us some trouble. Yet, on further consideration, we must add, that we do not think that he would have had power, with all his eloquence, to prevail on her to throw her bantling into the fire. She has not sufficient judgment—we had·almost said modesty—to follow such sound advice, or she could never have written, and afterwards read (to a *man*) the unnatural tragi-comic tale we have just been laughing at; in which there is no discrimination of character, no acquaintance with life, nor—do not start, fair lady!—any passion: but, perhaps, we are not able to discover such an elegant sensation. This kind of trash, these whipped syllabubs, overload young, weak stomachs, and render them squeamish, unable to relish the simple food nature prepares.

From *Julia*. By Helen Maria Williams. [VII, May–August, 1790] Uninitialled.

Miss W[illiams] is, probably, a warm admirer of Mrs. Smith's novels;* but if, in descriptions of nature, and lively characteristic conversations, she falls far short of her model, the reader of taste will never be disgusted with theatrical attitudes, artificial feelings, or a display of studied unimpassioned false grace. This lady seems to be an exception to Pope's rule, 'that every woman is at heart a rake'—and that two passions divide the sex—love of pleasure and sway; for no scenes of dissipation are here sketched by the dancing spirits of an intoxicated imagination; nor dresses described with the earnest minuteness of vanity. In short, her mind does not seem to be *debauched,* if we may

---

* Charlotte Smith (1749–1806), author of many popular novels. See the first review in this section.—Editor.

be allowed the expression, by reading novels; but every sentiment is uttered in an original way, which proves that it comes directly from her heart with the artless energy of feeling, that rather wishes to be understood than admired. Without any acquaintance with Miss W[illiams] only from the perusal of this production, we should venture to affirm, that sound principles animate her conduct, and that the sentiments they dictate are the pillars instead of being the fanciful ornaments of her character.

There is such feminine sweetness in her style and observations— such modesty and indulgence in her satire—such genuine unaffected piety in her effusions and remarks, that we warmly recommend her novel to our young female readers, who will here meet with refinement of sentiment, without a very great alloy of romantic notions:—if the conclusion, that love is not to be conquered by reason, had been omitted, this would be an unexceptionable book for young people. . . .

'The purpose of these pages,' says Miss W[illiams] in the advertisement, 'is to trace the danger arising from the uncontrouled indulgence of strong affections; not in those instances where they lead to the guilty excesses of passion in a corrupted mind—but, when disapproved by reason, and uncircumscribed by prudence, they involve even the virtuous in calamity.'

This plan gives the author an opportunity to display the most exemplary degree of rectitude in the conduct of her heroine. But a reader, with the least discernment, must soon perceive that Julia's principles are so fixed that nothing can tempt her to act wrong; and as she appears like a rock, against which the waves vainly beat, no anxiety will be felt for her safety:—she is viewed with respect, and left very tranquilly to quiet her feelings, because it cannot be called a contest. A good tragedy or novel, if the criterion be the effect which it has on the reader, is not always the most moral work, for it is not the reveries of sentiment, but the struggles of passion—of those *human passions*, that too frequently cloud the reason, and lead *mortals* into dangerous errors, if not into absolute guilt, which raise the most lively emotions, and leave the most lasting impression on the memory; an impression rather made by the heart than the understanding; for our affections are not quite so voluntary as the suffrage of reason.

From *A Simple Story*. By Mrs. Inchbald. [X, May–August, 1791] Uninitialled.

Mrs. I[nchbald] had evidently a very useful moral in view, namely to show the advantage of a good education; but it is to be lamented that she did not, for the benefit of her young readers, inforce it by contrasting the characters of the mother and daughter, whose history must warmly interest them. It were to be wished, in fact, in order to insinuate a useful moral into thoughtless unprincipled minds, that the faults of the vain, giddy Miss Milner had not been softened, or rather gracefully withdrawn from notice by the glare of such splendid, yet fallacious virtues, as flow from sensibility. And to have rendered the contrast more useful still, her daughter should have possessed greater dignity of mind. Educated in adversity she should have learned (to prove that a cultivated mind is a real advantage) how to bear, nay, rise above her misfortunes, instead of suffering her health to be undermined by the trials of her patience, which ought to have strengthened her understanding. Why do all female writers, even when they display their abilities, always give a sanction to the libertine reveries of men? Why do they poison the minds of their own sex, by strengthening a male prejudice that makes women systematically weak? We alluded to the absurd fashion that prevails of making the heroine of a novel boast of a delicate constitution; and the still more ridiculous and deleterious custom of spinning the most picturesque scenes out of fevers, swoons, and tears.

Clarentine. A Novel. [XXIV, July–December, 1796] Initialled M.

The good sense and humour scattered through these volumes made us lament their prolixity; yet we recommend them to the perusal of our young female readers, whose patience is not as often put to the proof, in this way, as that of poor reviewers, condemned to read though dulness, perched on their eye-lids, invites to sleep or forgetfulness.

The character of Clarentine is amiable, and her conduct exactly proper, according to established rules. The story is made up of perplexities, and will afford harmless amusement, conveyed in an easy style. It seems, indeed, to be an imitation of Evelina* in watercolours.

* Fanny Burney's popular novel of 1778.—Editor.

Part V

Letters

Wollstonecraft was a prolific writer of letters. She wrote to her sisters, to a variety of friends, and to her lovers, Gilbert Imlay and William Godwin. Many of the letters are powerful and moving documents, expressing the quick surge of happiness as well as the slow undercurrent of misery. They well reveal the movement of Wollstonecraft's mind and suggest the experiential basis of much of her theory.

The two series of letters from which the extracts have been taken were written between 1793 and 1797, the last years of Wollstonecraft's life. As examples of her style and thought, they should be placed in their literary context: the raw, emotional letters to Imlay require the more restrained *Letters Written . . . in Sweden*, with which they are contemporary, while the primarily joyful and domestic letters to Godwin can be balanced by the bleak novel of female isolation, *The Wrongs of Woman*, on which Wollstonecraft was working just before her death.

The letters are private. In the case of the letters to Imlay, a justification for their inclusion among public works is their early publication; from 1798 onward they have been a part of the published corpus, and reaction to Wollstonecraft has to some extent been based on them. A more important justification for inclusion of both Imlay and Godwin letters is their high literary merit and appeal.

Letters to Imlay

The work consists of a series of seventy-seven letters written by Wollstonecraft to Gilbert Imlay and edited and published by Godwin in *Posthumous Works* in 1798. The letters were written from France, England, and Scandinavia between 1793 and 1796, and they record the growth and disintegration of Wollstonecraft's relationship with Imlay. The printing of the letters caused some furore in England, although the use of private love letters in a public way was certainly not without precedent. Two years earlier, Wollstonecraft's London friend Mary Hays had worked her love letters to William Frend into a novel of unrequited passion entitled *The Memoirs of Emma Courtney*.

Most immediate criticism of the letters to Imlay concentrated on the picture of Wollstonecraft derived both from the letters themselves and from Godwin's *Memoirs of the Author of A Vindication of the Rights of Woman*. Reaction to this picture was extremely hostile: by the *European Magazine* of 1798 Wollstonecraft was described as an unhappy woman whose frailties should have been buried in oblivion, while for the *Anti-Jacobin Review* she became an illustration of Jacobin immorality and a warning to other women against throwing off the proper modesty of their sex. A few critics, like those of the *Analytical Review*, the *Critical Review*, and the *Monthly Mirror*, concentrated on the style and sensibility of the letters, both of which were commended. The highest praise was, however, given by Godwin, who described the letters as "offspring of a glowing imagination, and a heart penetrated with the passion it essays to describe."

from
LETTER II

[Neuilly, August, 1793]

You CAN SCARCELY imagine with what pleasure I anticipate the day, when we are to begin almost to live together;* and you would smile to hear how many plans of employment I have in my head, now that I am confident my heart has found peace in your bosom.—Cherish me with that dignified tenderness, which I have only found in you; and your own dear girl will try to keep under a quickness of feeling, that has sometimes given you pain—Yes, I will be *good*, that I may deserve to be happy; and whilst you love me, I cannot again fall into the miserable state, which rendered life a burthen almost too heavy to be borne.

But, good-night!—God bless you! Sterne says, that is equal to a kiss†—yet I would rather give you the kiss into the bargain, glowing with gratitude to Heaven, and affection to you. I like the word affection, because it signifies something habitual; and we are soon to meet, to try whether we have mind enough to keep our hearts warm.

MARY.

I will be at the barrier a little after ten o'clock to-morrow.‡

from
LETTER IV

[Paris, September, 1793]§

With ninety-nine men out of a hundred, a very sufficient dash of folly is necessary to render a woman *piquante*, a soft word for desirable; and, beyond these casual ebullitions of sympathy, few look for enjoyment by fostering a passion in their hearts. One reason, in short, why I wish my whole sex to become wiser, is, that the foolish ones may not, by their pretty folly, rob those whose sensibility keeps down their van-

* Wollstonecraft and Imlay later lived together in Paris and Le Havre.—Editor.
† The reference is to "La Fille de Chambre" in Laurence Sterne's *Sentimental Journey*. Wollstonecraft later used the same phrase to Godwin.—Editor.
‡ The child is in a subsequent letter called the "barrier girl," probably from a supposition that she owed her existence to this interview.—Godwin. The barrier was the toll-gate in the city wall of Paris where Wollstonecraft and Imlay used to meet during the summer of 1793.—Editor.
§ This and the thirteen following letters appear to have been written during a separation of several months; the date, Paris.—Godwin.

ity, of the few roses that afford them some solace in the thorny road of life.

I do not know how I fell into these reflections, excepting one thought produced it—that these continual separations were necessary to warm your affection.—Of late, we are always separating.—Crack!—crack!—and away you go.—This joke wears the sallow cast of thought; for, though I began to write cheerfully, some melancholy tears have found their way into my eyes, that linger there, whilst a glow of tenderness at my heart whispers that you are one of the best creatures in the world.—Pardon then the vagaries of a mind, that has been almost "crazed by care," as well as "crossed in hapless love,"* and bear with me a *little* longer!—When we are settled in the country together, more duties will open before me, and my heart, which now, trembling into peace, is agitated by every emotion that awakens the remembrance of old griefs, will learn to rest on yours, with that dignity your character, not to talk of my own, demands.

Take care of yourself—and write soon to your own girl (you may add dear, if you please) who sincerely loves you, and will try to convince you of it, by becoming happier.

from
LETTER V

[Paris, November, 1793]

Ever since you last saw me inclined to faint, I have felt some gentle twitches, which make me begin to think, that I am nourishing a creature who will soon be sensible of my care.—This thought has not only produced an overflowing of tenderness to you, but made me very attentive to calm my mind and take exercise, lest I should destroy an object, in whom we are to have a mutual interest, you know.·Yesterday—do not smile!—finding that I had hurt myself by lifting precipitately a large log of wood, I sat down in an agony, till I felt those said twitches again.

from
LETTER VI

[Paris, December, 1793]

I am not angry with thee, my love, for I think that it is a proof of stupidity, and likewise of a milk-and-water affection, which comes to

* A reference to Thomas Gray's "Elegy Written in a Country Churchyard": "craz'd with care, or cross'd in hopeless love."—Editor.

the same thing, when the temper is governed by a square and compass.—There is nothing picturesque in this straight-lined equality, and the passions always give grace to the actions.

Recollection now makes my heart bound to thee; but, it is not to thy money-getting face, though I cannot be seriously displeased with the exertion which increases my esteem, or rather is what I should have expected from thy character.—No; I have thy honest countenance before me—Pop—relaxed by tenderness; a little—little wounded by my whims; and thy eyes glistening with sympathy.—Thy lips then feel softer than soft—and I rest my cheek on thine, forgetting all the world. —I have not left the hue of love out of the picture—the rosy glow; and fancy has spread it over my own cheeks, I believe, for I feel them burning, whilst a delicious tear trembles in my eye, that would be all your own, if a grateful emotion directed to the Father of nature, who has made me thus alive to happiness, did not give more warmth to the sentiment it divides—I must pause a moment.

Need I tell you that I am tranquil after writing thus?—I do not know why, but I have more confidence in your affection, when absent, than present; nay, I think that you must love me, for, in the sincerity of my heart let me say it, I believe I deserve your tenderness, because I am true, and have a degree of sensibility that you can see and relish.

from
LETTER VII

[Paris, December 29, 1793]

Well! but, my love, to the old story—am I to see you this week, or this month?—I do not know what you are about—for, as you did not tell me, I would not ask Mr. ———, who is generally pretty communicative.

I long to see Mrs. ———; not to hear from you, so do not give yourself airs, but to get a letter from Mr. ———. And I am half angry with you for not informing me whether she had brought one with her or not. —On this score I will cork up some of the kind things that were ready to drop from my pen, which has never been dipt in gall when addressing you; or, will only suffer an exclamation—"The creature!" or a kind look, to escape me when I pass the slippers which I could not remove from my *salle* door, though they are not the handsomest of their kind.

Be not too anxious to get money!—for nothing worth having is to be purchased. God bless you.

from
LETTER X

[Paris, January 1, 1794]

I hate commerce. How differently must ————'s head and heart be organized from mine! You will tell me, that exertions are necessary: I am weary of them! The face of things, public and private, vexes me. The "peace" and clemency which seemed to be dawning a few days ago, disappear again. "I am fallen," as Milton said, "on evil days;" for I really believe that Europe will be in a state of convulsion, during half a century at least. Life is but a labour of patience: it is always rolling a great stone up a hill; for, before a person can find a resting-place, imagining it is lodged, down it comes again, and all the work is to be done over anew!

Should I attempt to write any more, I could not change the strain. My head aches, and my heart is heavy. The world appears an "unweeded garden" where "things rank and vile" flourish best.*

If you do not return soon—or, which is no such mighty matter, talk of it—I will throw your slippers out at window, and be off—nobody knows where. . . .

Considering the care and anxiety a woman must have about a child before it comes into the world, it seems to me, by a *natural right*, to belong to her. When men get immersed in the world, they seem to lose all sensations, excepting those necessary to continue or produce life!— Are these the privileges of reason? Amongst the feathered race, whilst the hen keeps the young warm, her mate stays by to cheer her; but it is sufficient for man to condescend to get a child, in order to claim it.—A man is a tyrant!

You may now tell me, that, if it were not for me, you would be laughing away with some honest fellows in L[ondo]n. The casual exercise of social sympathy would not be sufficient for me—I should not think such an heartless life worth preserving.—It is necessary to be in good-humour with you, to be pleased with the world.

* A reference to *Hamlet*, Act I: " 'Tis an unweeded garden,/That grows to seed; things rank and gross in nature/Possess it merely."—Editor.

from
LETTER XI

[Paris, January 6, 1794]

I have just received your kind and rational letter, and would fain hide my face, glowing with shame for my folly.—I would hide it in your bosom, if you would again open it to me, and nestle closely till you bade my fluttering heart be still, by saying that you forgave me. With eyes overflowing with tears, and in the humblest attitude, I entreat you. —Do not turn from me, for indeed I love you fondly, and have been very wretched, since the night I was so cruelly hurt by thinking that you had no confidence in me—

It is time for me to grow more reasonable, a few more of these caprices of sensibility would destroy me. I have, in fact, been very much indisposed for a few days past, and the notion that I was tormenting, or perhaps killing, a poor little animal, about whom I am grown anxious and tender, now I feel it alive, made me worse. My bowels have been dreadfully disordered, and every thing I ate or drank disagreed with my stomach; still I feel intimations of its existence, though they have been fainter.

Do you think that the creature goes regularly to sleep? I am ready to ask as many questions as Voltaire's Man of Forty Crowns.* Ah! do not continue to be angry with me! You perceive that I am already smiling through my tears—You have lightened my heart, and my frozen spirits are melting into playfulness.

LETTER XII

[Paris, January, 1794]

I will never, if I am not entirely cured of quarrelling, begin to encourage "quick-coming fancies," when we are separated. Yesterday, my love, I could not open your letter for some time; and, though it was not half as severe as I merited, it threw me into such a fit of trembling, as seriously alarmed me. I did not, as you may suppose, care for a little pain on my own account; but all the fears which I have had for a few days past, returned with fresh force. This morning I am better; will you not be glad to hear it? You perceive that sorrow has almost made a child of me, and that I want to be soothed to peace.

---

* A reference to Voltaire's satire on French fiscal legislation (1768), a work written mainly in the form of questions and answers.—Editor.

One thing you mistake in my character, and imagine that to be coldness which is just the contrary. For, when I am hurt by the person most dear to me, I must let out a whole torrent of emotions, in which tenderness would be uppermost, or stifle them altogether; and it appears to me almost a duty to stifle them, when I imagine *that I am treated with coldness.*

I am afraid that I have vexed you, my own [Imlay]. I know the quickness of your feelings—and let me, in the sincerity of my heart, assure you, there is nothing I would not suffer to make you happy. My own happiness wholly depends on you—and, knowing you, when my reason is not clouded, I look forward to a rational prospect of as much felicity as the earth affords—with a little dash of rapture into the bargain, if you will look at me, when we meet again, as you have sometimes greeted, your humbled, yet most affectionate

[Mary]

from
LETTER XV

[Paris, January 12, 1794]
I cannot boast of being quite recovered, yet I am (I must use my Yorkshire phrase; for, when my heart is warm, pop come the expressions of childhood into my head) so *lightsome*, that I think it will not *go badly with me.*—And nothing shall be wanting on my part, I assure you; for I am urged on, not only by an enlivened affection for you, but by a new-born tenderness that plays cheerly round my dilating heart.

I was, therefore, in defiance of cold and dirt, out in the air the greater part of yesterday; and, if I get over this evening without a return of the fever that has tormented me, I shall talk no more of illness. I have promised the little creature, that its mother, who ought to cherish it, will not again plague it, and begged it to pardon me; and, since I could not hug either it or you to my breast, I have to my heart.

LETTER XVIII

[Le Havre, March, 1794]*
We are such creatures of habit, my love, that, though I cannot say I was sorry, childishly so, for your going, when I knew that you were to stay such a short time, and I had a plan of employment; yet I could not

* Wollstonecraft moved to Le Havre to be with Imlay in January 1794. On March 11, Imlay went to Paris for a short period.—Editor.

sleep.—I turned to your side of the bed, and tried to make the most of the comfort of the pillow, which you used to tell me I was churlish about; but all would not do.—I took nevertheless my walk before breakfast, though the weather was not very inviting—and here I am, wishing you a finer day, and seeing you peep over my shoulder, as I write, with one of your kindest looks—when your eyes glisten, and a suffusion creeps over your relaxing features.

But I do not mean to dally with you this morning—So God bless you! Take care of yourself—and sometimes fold to your heart your affectionate

[Mary]

from
LETTER XXI

[Le Havre, August 19, 1794]*

I have only to tell you, what is sufficiently obvious, that the earnest desire I have shown to keep my place, or gain more ground in your heart, is a sure proof how necessary your affection is to my happiness.— Still I do not think it false delicacy, or foolish pride, to wish that your attention to my happiness should arise *as much* from love, which is always rather a selfish passion, as reason—that is, I want you to promote my felicity, by seeking your own.—For, whatever pleasure it may give me to discover your generosity of soul, I would not be dependent for your affection on the very quality I most admire. No; there are qualities in your heart, which demand my affection; but, unless the attachment appears to me clearly mutual, I shall labour only to esteem your character, instead of cherishing a tenderness for your person.

I write in a hurry, because the little one, who has been sleeping a long time, begins to call for me. Poor thing! when I am sad, I lament that all my affections grow on me, till they become too strong for my peace, though they all afford me snatches of exquisite enjoyment—This for our little girl was at first very reasonable—more the effect of reason, a sense of duty, than feeling—now, she has got into my heart and imagination, and when I walk out without her, her little figure is ever dancing before me.

You too have somehow clung round my heart—I found I could not eat my dinner in the great room—and, when I took up the large knife to carve for myself, tears rushed into my eyes.—Do not however sup-

---

* Imlay went again to Paris in August. Wollstonecraft and their child, Fanny, born in May 1794, remained in Le Havre.—Editor.

pose that I am melancholy—for, when you are from me, I not only wonder how I can find fault with you—but how I can doubt your affection.

LETTER XXIII

[Paris, September 22, 1794]*

I have just written two letters, that are going by other conveyances, and which I reckon on your receiving long before this. I therefore merely write, because I know I should be disappointed at seeing any one who had left you, if you did not send a letter, were it ever so short, to tell me why you did not write a longer—and you will want to be told, over and over again, that our little Hercules is quite recovered.

Besides looking at me, there are three other things, which delight her—to ride in a coach, to look at a scarlet waistcoat, and hear loud music—yesterday, at the *fête*,† she enjoyed the two latter; but, to honour J. J. Rousseau, I intend to give her a sash, the first she has ever had round her—and why not?—for I have always been half in love with him.

Well, this you will say is trifling—shall I talk about alum or soap?‡ There is nothing picturesque in your present pursuits; my imagination then rather chuses to ramble back to the barrier with you, or to see you coming to meet me, and my basket of grapes.—With what pleasure do I recollect your looks and words, when I have been sitting on the window, regarding the waving corn!

Believe me, sage sir, you have not sufficient respect for the imagination—I could prove to you in a trice that it is the mother of sentiment, the great distinction of our nature, the only purifier of the passions—animals have a portion of reason, and equal, if not more exquisite, senses; but no trace of imagination, or her offspring taste, appears in any of their actions. The impulse of the senses, passions, if you will, and the conclusions of reason, draw men together; but the imagination is the true fire, stolen from heaven, to animate this cold creature of clay, producing all those fine sympathies that lead to rapture, rendering men

* This is the first of a series of letters written during a separation of many months, to which no cordial meeting ever succeeded. They were sent from Paris, and bear the address of London.—Godwin. Wollstonecraft had followed Imlay to Paris from Le Havre.—Editor.

† September 21, 1794 was celebrated by a fête in Paris to mark the removal of Marat's body to the Panthéon; it replaced that of Mirabeau, a moderate revolutionary out of favor with the Jacobins.—Editor.

‡ The articles in which Imlay was supposed to be trading. Wollstonecraft always blamed Imlay for his obsession with money and commerce.—Editor.

social by expanding their hearts, instead of leaving them leisure to calculate how many comforts society affords.

If you call these observations romantic, a phrase in this place which
would be tantamount to nonsensical, I shall be apt to retort, that you
are embruted by trade, and the vulgar enjoyments of life—Bring me
then back your barrier-face, or you shall have nothing to say to my
barrier-girl; and I shall fly from you, to cherish the remembrances that
will ever be dear to me; for I am yours truly,

[Mary]

from
LETTER XXIV

[Paris, September 23, 1794]
I have been playing and laughing with the little girl so long, that I
cannot take up my pen to address you without emotion. Pressing her to
my bosom, she looked so like you (*entre nous*, your best looks, for I do
not admire your commercial face) every nerve seemed to vibrate to the
touch, and I began to think that there was something in the assertion
of man and wife being one—for you seemed to pervade my whole
frame, quickening the beat of my heart, and lending me the sympathetic tears you excited.

from
LETTER XXXI

[Paris, December 30, 1794]
I do not like this life of continual inquietude—and, *entre nous*, I
am determined to try to earn some money here myself, in order to convince you that, if you chuse to run about the world to get a fortune, it
is for yourself—for the little girl and I will live without your assistance,
unless you are with us. I may be termed proud—Be it so—but I will
never abandon certain principles of action.

The common run of men have such an ignoble way of thinking,
that, if they debauch their hearts, and prostitute their persons, following perhaps a gust of inebriation, they suppose the wife, slave rather,
whom they maintain, has no right to complain, and ought to receive the
sultan, whenever he deigns to return, with open arms, though his have
been polluted by half an hundred promiscuous amours during his
absence.

I consider fidelity and constancy as two distinct things; yet the for-

mer is necessary, to give life to the other—and such a degree of respect
do I think due to myself, that, if only probity, which is a good thing in
its place, brings you back, never return!—for, if a wandering of the
heart, or even a caprice of the imagination detains you—there is an end
of all my hopes of happiness—I could not forgive it, if I would.

I have gotten into a melancholy mood, you perceive. You know my
opinion of men in general; you know that I think them systematic tyrants, and that it is the rarest thing in the world, to meet with a man
with sufficient delicacy of feeling to govern desire. When I am thus sad,
I lament that my little darling, fondly as I doat on her, is a girl.—I am
sorry to have a tie to a world that for me is ever sown with thorns.

from
LETTER XXXII

[Paris, January 9, 1795]

I just now received one of your hasty *notes*; for business so entirely
occupies you, that you have not time, or sufficient command of thought,
to write letters. Beware! you seem to be got into a whirl of projects and
schemes, which are drawing you into a gulph, that, if it do not absorb
your happiness, will infallibly destroy mine.

Fatigued during my youth by the most arduous struggles, not only
to obtain independence, but to render myself useful, not merely pleasure, for which I had the most lively taste, I mean the simple pleasures
that flow from passion and affection, escaped me, but the most melancholy views of life were impressed by a disappointed heart on my mind.
Since I knew you, I have been endeavouring to go back to my former
nature, and have allowed some time to glide away, winged with the delight which only spontaneous enjoyment can give.—Why have you so
soon dissolved the charm?

from
LETTER XXXV

[Paris, February 9, 1795]

The melancholy presentiment has for some time hung on my spirits,
that we were parted for ever; and the letters I received this day, by Mr.
———, convince me that it was not without foundation.* You allude

---

* Imlay had written of his decision to stay in London for a longer period.—Editor.

to some other letters, which I suppose have miscarried; for most of those I have got, were only a few hasty lines, calculated to wound the tenderness the sight of the superscriptions excited.

I mean not however to complain; yet so many feelings are struggling for utterance, and agitating a heart almost bursting with anguish, that I find it very difficult to write with any degree of coherence.

You left me indisposed, though you have taken no notice of it; and the most fatiguing journey I ever had, contributed to continue it. However, I recovered my health; but a neglected cold, and continual inquietude during the last two months, have reduced me to a state of weakness I never before experienced. Those who did not know that the canker-worm was at work at the core, cautioned me about suckling my child too long.—God preserve this poor child, and render her happier than her mother!

But I am wandering from my subject: indeed my head turns giddy, when I think that all the confidence I have had in the affection of others is come to this.

I did not expect this blow from you. I have done my duty to you and my child; and if I am not to have any return of affection to reward me, I have the sad consolation of knowing that I deserved a better fate. My soul is weary—I am sick at heart; and, but for this little darling, I would cease to care about a life, which is now stripped of every charm.

You see how stupid I am, uttering declamation, when I meant simply to tell you, that I consider your requesting me to come to you, as merely dictated by honour.—Indeed, I scarcely understand you.—You request me to come, and then tell me, that you have not given up all thoughts of returning to this place.

When I determined to live with you, I was only governed by affection.—I would share poverty with you, but I turn with affright from the sea of trouble on which you are entering.—I have certain principles of action: I know what I look for to found my happiness on.—It is not money.—With you I wished for sufficient to procure the comforts of life—as it is, less will do —I can still exert myself to obtain the necessaries of life for my child, and she does not want more at present.—I have two or three plans in my head to earn our subsistence; for do not suppose that, neglected by you, I will lie under obligations of a pecuniary kind to you!—No; I would sooner submit to menial service.—I wanted the support of your affection—that gone, all is over!—I did not think, when I complained of ———'s contemptible avidity to accumulate money, that he would have dragged you into his schemes.

from
LETTER XXXVI

[Paris, February 10, 1795]

This has been such a period of barbarity and misery, I ought not to complain of having my share. I wish one moment that I had never heard of the cruelties that have been practised here, and the next envy the mothers who have been killed with their children. Surely I had suffered enough in life, not to be cursed with a fondness, that burns up the vital stream I am imparting. You will think me mad: I would I were so, that I could forget my misery—so that my head or heart would be still.—

from
LETTER XXXVIII

[Le Havre, April 7, 1795]

I sit, lost in thought, looking at the sea*—and tears rush into my eyes, when I find that I am cherishing any fond expectations.—I have indeed been so unhappy this winter, I find it as difficult to acquire fresh hopes, as to regain tranquillity.—Enough of this—lie still, foolish heart!—But for the little girl, I could almost wish that it should cease to beat, to be no more alive to the anguish of disappointment.

Sweet little creature! I deprived myself of my only pleasure, when I weaned her, about ten days ago.—I am however glad I conquered my repugnance.—It was necessary it should be done soon, and I did not wish to embitter the renewal of your acquaintance with her, by putting it off till we met.—It was a painful exertion to me, and I thought it best to throw this inquietude with the rest, into the sack that I would fain throw over my shoulder.—I wished to endure it alone, in short—Yet, after sending her to sleep in the next room for three or four nights, you cannot think with what joy I took her back again to sleep in my bosom!

* Wollstonecraft and Fanny were at Le Havre on their way to join Imlay in England.—Editor.

from
LETTER XL

[London, May 22, 1795]

I have laboured to calm my mind since you left me*—Still I find that tranquillity is not to be obtained by exertion; it is a feeling so different from the resignation of despair!—I am however no longer angry with you—nor will I ever utter another complaint—there are arguments which convince the reason, whilst they carry death to the heart. —We have had too many cruel explanations, that not only cloud every future prospect; but embitter the remembrances which alone give life to affection.—Let the subject never be revived!

It seems to me that I have not only lost the hope, but the power of being happy.—Every emotion is now sharpened by anguish.—My soul has been shook, and my tone of feelings destroyed.—I have gone out— and sought for dissipation, if not amusement, merely to fatigue still more, I find, my irritable nerves—

My friend—my dear friend—examine yourself well—I am out of the question; for, alas! I am nothing—and discover what you wish to do—what will render you most comfortable—or, to be more explicit— whether you desire to live with me, or part for ever? When you can once ascertain it, tell me frankly, I conjure you!—for, believe me, I have very involuntarily interrupted your peace.

from
LETTER XLII

[Hull, June 10, 1795]†

We arrived here about an hour ago. I am extremely fatigued with the child, who would not rest quiet with any body but me, during the night—and now we are here in a comfortless, damp room, in a sort of a tomb-like house. This however I shall quickly remedy, for, when I

---

* The meeting with Imlay was unsuccessful and was followed by Wollstonecraft's first suicide attempt.—Editor

† Wollstonecraft, with Fanny, was about to journey to Scandinavia as Imlay's business representative. He had in May signed a document empowering "Mary Imlay my best friend and wife" to act in his behalf and, before she left, he had promised to meet her in Basel when her Scandinavian business should be completed. See note 11, Chapter VIII of Ralph Wardle's biography for the dispute concerning the dating of this letter.—Editor.

have finished this letter, (which I must do immediately, because the post goes out early), I shall sally forth, and enquire about a vessel and an inn.

I will not distress you by talking of the depression of my spirits, or the struggle I had to keep alive my dying heart.—It is even now too full to allow me to write with composure.—I[mlay],—dear I[mlay],—am I always to be tossed about thus?—shall I never find an asylum to rest *contented* in? How can you love to fly about continually—dropping down, as it were, in a new world—cold and strange!—every other day? Why do you not attach those tender emotions round the idea of home, which even now dim my eyes?—This alone is affection—every thing else is only humanity, electrified by sympathy.

from
LETTER XLIV

[Hull, June 12, 1795]*

The general observations which apply to the state of your own mind, appear to me just, as far as they go; and I shall always consider it as one of the most serious misfortunes of my life, that I did not meet you, before satiety had rendered your senses so fastidious, as almost to close up every tender avenue of sentiment and affection that leads to your sympathetic heart. You have a heart, my friend, yet, hurried away by the impetuosity of inferior feelings, you have sought in vulgar excesses, for that gratification which only the heart can bestow.

The common run of men, I know, with strong health and gross appetites, must have variety to banish *ennui*, because the imagination never lends its magic wand, to convert appetite into love, cemented by according reason.—Ah! my friend, you know not the ineffable delight, the exquisite pleasure, which arises from a unison of affection and desire, when the whole soul and senses are abandoned to a lively imagination, that renders every emotion delicate and rapturous. Yes; these are emotions, over which satiety has no power, and the recollection of which, even disappointment cannot disenchant; but they do not exist without self-denial. These emotions, more or less strong, appear to me to be the distinctive characteristic of genius, the foundation of taste, and of that exquisite relish for the beauties of nature, of which the common herd of eaters and drinkers and *child-begeters*, certainly have no idea. You will smile at an observation that has just occurred to me:

* Written during the many days Wollstonecraft spent waiting for a boat to Scandinavia.—Editor.

—I consider those minds as the most strong and original, whose imagination acts as the stimulus to their senses.

Well! you will ask, what is the result of all this reasoning? Why I cannot help thinking that it is possible for you, having great strength of mind, to return to nature, and regain a sanity of constitution, and purity of feeling—which would open your heart to me.—I would fain rest there!

Yet, convinced more than ever of the sincerity and tenderness of my attachment to you, the involuntary hopes, which a determination to live has revived, are not sufficiently strong to dissipate the cloud, that despair has spread over futurity. I have looked at the sea, and at my child, hardly daring to own to myself the secret wish, that it might become our tomb; and that the heart, still so alive to anguish, might there be quieted by death. At this moment ten thousand complicated sentiments press for utterance, weigh on my heart, and obscure my sight.

from
LETTER XLVIII

[Hull, June 17, 1795]

What are you about? How are your affairs going on? It may be a long time before you answer these questions. My dear friend, my heart sinks within me!—Why am I forced thus to struggle continually with my affections and feelings?—Ah! why are those affections and feelings the source of so much misery, when they seem to have been given to vivify my heart, and extend my usefulness! But I must not dwell on this subject.—Will you not endeavour to cherish all the affection you can for me? What am I saying?—Rather forget me, if you can—if other gratifications are dearer to you.—How is every remembrance of mine embittered by disappointment? What a world is this!—They only seem happy, who never look beyond sensual or artificial enjoyments.—Adieu!

from
LETTER L

[June 20, 1795]

How am I altered by disappointment!—When going to [Lisbon], ten years ago, the elasticity of my mind was sufficient to ward off weariness—and the imagination still could dip her brush in the rainbow of fancy, and sketch futurity in smiling colours. Now I am going towards the North in search of sunbeams!—Will any ever warm this desolated heart? All nature seems to frown—or rather mourn with me.—Every thing is cold—cold as my expectations! Before I left the shore, tormented, as I now am, by these North east *chillers*, I could not help exclaiming—Give me, gracious Heaven! at least, genial weather, if I am never to meet the genial affection that still warms this agitated bosom —compelling life to linger there.

I am now going on shore with the captain, though the weather be rough, to seek for milk, &c. at a little village, and to take a walk—after which I hope to sleep—for. confined here, surrounded by disagreeable smells, I have lost the little appetite I had; and I lie awake, till thinking almost drives me to the brink of madness—only to the brink, for I never forget, even in the feverish slumbers I sometimes fall into, the misery I am labouring to blunt the sense of, by every exertion in my power.

from
LETTER LV

[Göteborg, Sweden, July 3, 1795]
I grow more and more attached to my little girl—and I cherish this affection without fear, because it must be a long time before it can become bitterness of soul.—She is an interesting creature.—On shipboard, how often as I gazed at the sea, have I longed to bury my troubled bosom in the less troubled deep; asserting with Brutus, "that the virtue I had followed too far, was merely an empty name!" and nothing but the sight of her—her playful smiles, which seemed to cling and twine round my heart—could have stopped me.

What peculiar misery has fallen to my share! To act up to my principles, I have laid the strictest restraint on my very thoughts—yes; not to sully the delicacy of my feelings, I have reined in my imagination; and started with affright from every sensation, (I allude to ———) that stealing with balmy sweetness into my soul, led me to scent from afar the fragance of reviving nature.

My friend, I have dearly paid for one conviction.—Love, in some minds, is an affair of sentiment, arising from the same delicacy of perception (or taste) as renders them alive to the beauties of nature, poetry, &c., alive to the charms of those evanescent graces that are, as it were, impalpable—they must be felt, they cannot be described.

Love is a want of my heart. I have examined myself lately with more care than formerly, and find, that to deaden is not to calm the mind—Aiming at tranquillity, I have almost destroyed all the energy of my soul—almost rooted out what renders it estimable—Yes, I have damped that enthusiasm of character, which converts the grossest materials into a fuel, that imperceptibly feeds hopes, which aspire above common enjoyment. Despair, since the birth of my child, has rendered me stupid—soul and body seemed to be fading away before the withering touch of disappointment.

from
LETTER LVIII

[Larvik, Norway, July 14, 1795]
I am now on my journey to [Tönsberg]. I felt more at leaving my child than I thought I should*—and, whilst at night I imagined every instant that I heard the half-formed sounds of her voice,—I asked myself how I could think of parting with her for ever, of leaving her thus helpless?

Poor lamb! It may run very well in a tale, that "God will temper the winds to the shorn lamb!"† but how can I expect that she will be shielded, when my naked bosom has had to brave continually the pitiless storm? Yes; I could add, with poor Lear—What is the war of elements to the pangs of disappointed affection, and the horror arising from a discovery of a breach of confidence, that snaps every social tie!

All is not right somewhere!—When you first knew me, I was not thus lost. I could still confide—for I opened my heart to you—of this only comfort you have deprived me, whilst my happiness, you tell me, was your first object. Strange want of judgment!

I will not complain; but, from the soundness of your understanding, I am convinced, if you give yourself leave to reflect, you will also feel, that your conduct to me, so far from being generous, has not been just. —I mean not to allude to factitious principles of morality; but to the simple basis of all rectitude.—However I did not intend to argue— Your not writing is cruel—and my reason is perhaps disturbed by constant wretchedness.

from
LETTER LXIV

[Göteborg, August 26, 1795]
I arrived here last night, and with the most exquisite delight, once more pressed my babe to my heart. We shall part no more. You perhaps

* Fearing the rigors of the journey, Wollstonecraft left Fanny behind in Göteborg.—Editor.

† A reference to "Maria" in Laurence Sterne's *Sentimental Journey*: "God tempers the wind, said Maria, to the shorn lamb."—Editor.

cannot conceive the pleasure it gave me, to see her run about, and play alone. Her increasing intelligence attaches me more and more to her. I have promised her that I will fulfil my duty to her; and nothing in future shall make me forget it. I will also exert myself to obtain an independence for her; but I will not be too anxious on this head.

I have already told you, that I have recovered my health. Vigour, and even vivacity of mind, have returned with a renovated constitution. As for peace, we will not talk of it. I was not made, perhaps, to enjoy the calm contentment so termed.—

Certainly you are right; our minds are not congenial. I have lived in an ideal world, and fostered sentiments that you do not comprehend —or you would not treat me thus. I am not, I will not be, merely an object of compassion—a clog, however light, to tease* you. Forget that I exist: I will never remind you. Something emphatical whispers me to put an end to these struggles. Be free—I will not torment, when I cannot please.

from
LETTER LXV

[Copenhagen, September 6, 1795]
Gracious God! It is impossible for me to stifle something like resentment, when I receive fresh proofs of your indifference. What I have suffered this last year, is not to be forgotten! I have not that happy substitute for wisdom, insensibility—and the lively sympathies which bind me to my fellow-creatures, are all of a painful kind.—They are the agonies of a broken heart—pleasure and I have shaken hands.

I see here nothing but heaps of ruins, and only converse with people immersed in trade and sensuality.

I am weary of travelling—yet seem to have no home—no resting place to look to.—I am strangely cast off.—How often, passing through the rocks, I have thought, "But for this child, I would lay my head on one of them, and never open my eyes again!" With a heart feelingly alive to all the affections of my nature—I have never met with one, softer than the stone that I would fain take for my last pillow. I once thought I had, but it was all a delusion. I meet with families continually, who are bound together by affection or principle—and, when I am conscious that I have fulfilled the duties of my station, almost to a

---

* "Teize" in Godwin's text.—Editor.

forgetfulness of myself, I am ready to demand, in a murmuring tone, of Heaven, "Why am I thus abandoned?"

from
LETTER LXVII

[Hamburg, September 27, 1795]

The tremendous power who formed this heart, must have foreseen that, in a world in which self-interest, in various shapes, is the principal mobile, I had little chance of escaping misery.—To the fiat of fate I submit.—I am content to be wretched; but I will not be contemptible. —Of me you have no cause to complain, but for having had too much regard for you—for having expected a degree of permanent happiness, when you only sought for a momentary gratification.

I am strangely deficient in sagacity.—Uniting myself to you, your tenderness seemed to make me amends for all my former misfortunes. —On this tenderness and affection with what confidence did I rest!— but I leaned on a spear, that has pierced me to the heart.—You have thrown off a faithful friend, to pursue the caprices of the moment.— We certainly are differently organized; for even now, when conviction has been stamped on my soul by sorrow, I can scarcely believe it possible. It depends at present on you, whether you will see me or not.—I shall take no step, till I see or hear from you.

Preparing myself for the worst—I have determined, if your next letter be like the last, to write to Mr. ——— to procure me an obscure lodging, and not to inform any body of my arrival.—There I will endeavour in a few months to obtain the sum necessary to take me to France—from you I will not receive any more.—I am not yet sufficiently humbled to depend on your beneficence.

Some people, whom my unhappiness has interested, though they know not the extent of it, will assist me to attain the object I have in view, the independence of my child. Should a peace take place, ready money will go a great way in France—and I will borrow a sum, which my industry *shall* enable me to pay at my leisure, to purchase a small estate for my girl.—The assistance I shall find necessary to complete her education, I can get at an easy rate at Paris—I can introduce her to such society as she will like—and thus, securing for her all the chance for happiness, which depends on me, I shall die in peace, persuaded that the felicity which has hitherto cheated my expectation, will not always elude my grasp.

from
LETTER LXXIV*

[London, November 27, 1795]
It seems to me, that my conduct has always been governed by the strictest principles of justice and truth.—Yet, how wretched have my social feelings and delicacy of sentiment rendered me!—I have loved with my whole soul, only to discover that I had no chance of a return—and that existence is a burthen without it. . . .

I have been treated ungenerously—if I understand what is generosity.—You seem to me only to have been anxious to shake me off—regardless whether you dashed me to atoms by the fall.—In truth, I have been rudely handled. *Do you judge coolly*, and I trust you will not continue to call those capricious feelings "the most refined," which would undermine not only the most sacred principles, but the affections which unite mankind.—You would render mothers unnatural—and there would be no such thing as a father!—If your theory of morals is the most "exalted," it is certainly the most easy.—It does not require much magnanimity, to determine to please ourselves for the moment, let others suffer what they will!

LETTER LXXVI†

[London, December, 1795]‡
As the parting from you for ever is the most serious event of my life, I will once expostulate with you, and call not the language of truth and feeling ingenuity!
I know the soundness of your understanding—and know that it is impossible for you always to confound the caprices of every wayward inclination with the manly dictates of principle.
You tell me "that I torment you."—Why do I?—Because you cannot estrange your heart entirely from me—and you feel that justice is on my side. You urge, "that your conduct was unequivocal."—It was not.—When your coolness has hurt me, with what tenderness have you endeavoured to remove the impression!—and even before I returned to

* Godwin erroneously numbered this letter LXXV in *Posthumous Works*.—Editor.
† Letter LXXVII in *Posthumous Works*.—Editor.
‡ Wollstonecraft returned to London to learn of new infidelities by Imlay. She attempted suicide for the second time in November, 1795.—Editor.

England, you took great pains to convince me, that all my uneasiness was occasioned by the effect of a worn-out constitution—and you concluded your letter with these words, "Business alone has kept me from you.—Come to any port, and I will fly down to my two dear girls with a heart all their own."

With these assurances, is it extraordinary that I should believe what I wished? I might—and did think that you had a struggle with old propensities; but I still thought that I and virtue should at last prevail. I still thought that you had a magnanimity of character, which would enable you to conquer yourself.

[Imlay], believe me, it is not romance, you have acknowledged to me feelings of this kind.—You could restore me to life and hope, and the satisfaction you would feel, would amply repay you.

In tearing myself from you, it is my own heart I pierce—and the time will come, when you will lament that you have thrown away a heart, that, even in the moment of passion, you cannot despise.—I would owe every thing to your generosity—but, for God's sake, keep me no longer in suspense!—Let me see you once more!—

LETTER LXXVII*

[London, Spring, 1796]†
You must do as you please with respect to the child.—I could wish that it might be done soon, that my name may be no more mentioned to you. It is now finished.—Convinced that you have neither regard nor friendship, I disdain to utter a reproach, though I have had reason to think, that the "forbearance" talked of, has not been very delicate.— It is however of no consequence.—I am glad you are satisfied with your own conduct.

I now solemnly assure you, that this is an eternal farewel.—Yet I flinch not from the duties which tie me to life.

That there is "sophistry" on one side or other, is certain; but now it matters not on which. On my part it has not been a question of words. Yet your understanding or mine must be strangely warped—for what you term "delicacy," appears to me to be exactly the contrary. I have no criterion for morality, and have thought in vain, if the sensations which lead you to follow an ancle or step, be the sacred foundation of principle and affection. Mine has been of a very different nature, or it would not have stood the brunt of your sarcasms.

* Letter LXXVIII in *Posthumous Works*.—Editor.
† Some editors have dated this letter December 1795, but Godwin in his *Memoirs* states that the last letter to Imlay was written in February or March of 1796.—Editor.

The sentiment in me is still sacred. If there be any part of me that will survive the sense of my misfortunes, it is the purity of my affections. The impetuosity of your senses, may have led you to term mere animal desire, the source of principle; and it may give zest to some years to come.—Whether you will always think so, I shall never know.

It is strange that, in spite of all you do, something like conviction forces me to believe, that you are not what you appear to be.

I part with you in peace.

Letters to Godwin

Wollstonecraft had met William Godwin in 1791 in her early days with Joseph Johnson, but neither had been impressed with the other. In January 1796 they met again at the house of their common acquaintance, Mary Hays, and a friendship quickly developed. Some time in August 1796 they appear to have become lovers. By March 1797 Wollstonecraft realized that she was pregnant, and she and Godwin were quietly married. After their marriage, they lived partially together, but continued to work and visit alone. Their relationship was affectionate and only occasionally strained—notably in June 1797 when Wollstonecraft blamed Godwin for his friendship with another woman.

The letters to Godwin were not published by Godwin but, after his wife's death, he did arrange them chronologically and supply them with dates.

LETTER 12

[August 17, 1796]*

I HAVE NOT LATELY passed so painful a night as the last. I feel that I cannot speak clearly on the subject to you, let me then briefly explain myself now I am alone. Yet, struggling as I have been a long time to attain peace of mind (or apathy) I am afraid to trace emotions to their source, which border on agony.

Is it not sufficient to tell you that I am thoroughly out of humour with myself? Mortified and humbled, I scarcely know why—still, despising false delicacy I almost fear that I have lost sight of the true. Could a wish have transported me to France or Italy, last night, I should

* The letter seems to have arisen from Wollstonecraft's fears after she and Godwin became lovers.—Editor.

William Godwin by J. Northcote.

have caught up my Fanny and been off in a twinkle, though convinced that it is my mind, not the place, which requires changing. My imagination is for ever betraying me into fresh misery, and I perceive that I shall be a child to the end of the chapter. You talk of the roses which grow profusely in every path of life—I catch at them; but only encounter the thorns.—

I would not be unjust for the world—I can only say that you appear to me to have acted injudiciously; and that full of your own feelings, little as I comprehend them, you forgot mine—or do not understand my character. It is my turn to have a fever to day—I am not well—I am hurt—But I mean not to hurt you. Consider what has passed as a fever of your imagination; one of the slight mortal shakes to which you are liable—and I—will become again a *Solitary Walker*. Adieu! I was going to add God bless you!—

LETTER 14

[August 17, 1796]

I like your last—may I call it *love* letter?* better than the first—and can I give you a higher proof of my esteem than to tell you, the style of my letter will whether I will or no, that it has calmed my mind—a mind that had been painfully active all the morning, haunted by old sorrows that seemed to come forward with new force to sharpen the present anguish—Well! well—it is almost gone—I mean all my unreasonable fears—and a whole train of tormentors, which you have routed—I can scarcely describe to you their ugly shapes so quickly do they vanish—and let them go, we will not bring them back by talking of them. You may see me when you please. I shall take this letter, just before dinner time, to ask you to come and dine with me, and Fanny, whom I have shut out to day. Should you be engaged come in the evening. Miss H— seldom stays late, never to supper—or to morrow—as you wish—I shall be content—You say you want soothing—will it sooth you to tell you the truth? I cannot hate you—I do not think you deserve it. Nay, more I cannot withhold my friendship from you, and will try to merit yours, that *necessity* may bind you to me.

* Godwin had replied reassuringly to Wollstonecraft's previous letter: "You do not know how honest I am. I swear to you that I told you nothing but the strict & literal truth, when I described to you the manner in which you set my imagination on fire. . . . It is best that we should be friends in every sense of the word. . . ." *Godwin & Mary*, ed. Ralph Wardle (Lawrence: University of Kansas Press, 1966), pp. 16–17. —Editor.

One word of my ONLY fault*—our imaginations have been rather differently employed—I am more of a painter than you—I like to tell the truth, my taste for the picturesque has been more cultivated—I delight to view the grand scenes of nature and the various changes of the human countenance—Beautiful as they are animated by intelligence or sympathy—My affections have been more exercised than yours, I believe, and my senses are quick, without the aid of fancy—yet tenderness always prevails, which inclines me to be angry with myself, when I do not animate and please those I [love?].

Now will you not be a good boy, and smile upon me, I dine at half past four—you ought to come and give me an appetite for my dinner, as you deprived me of one for my breakfast.

LETTER 31

[September 4, 1796]

Labouring all the morning, in vain, to overcome an oppression of spirits, which some things you uttered yesterday, produced; I will try if I can shake it off by describing to you the nature of the feelings you excited.

I allude to what you remarked, relative to my manner of writing— that there was a radical defect in it—a worm in the bud—&c What is to be done, I must either disregard your opinion, think it unjust, or throw down my pen in despair; and that would be tantamount to resigning existence; for at fifteen I resolved never to marry for interested motives, or to endure a life of dependence. You know not how painfully my sensibility, call it false if you will, has been wounded by some of the steps I have been obliged to take for others. I have even now plans at heart, which depend on my exertions; and my entire confidence in Mr. Imlay plunged me into some difficulties, since we parted, that I could scarcely away with. I know that many of my cares have been the natural consequence of what, nine out of ten would [have] termed folly—yet I cannot coincide in the opinion, without feeling a contempt for mankind. In short, I must reckon on doing some good, and getting the money I want, by my writings, or go to sleep for ever. I shall not be content merely to keep body and soul together—By what I have already written Johnson,† I am sure, has been a gainer. And, for I would wish

---

* Godwin had written "Upon consideration I find in you one fault, & but one. You have the feelings of nature, & you have the honesty to avow them. . . . But do not let them tyrannise over you," *Godwin & Mary*, p. 17.—Editor.

† Joseph Johnson, her publisher.—Editor.

you to see my heart and mind just as it appears to myself, without drawing any veil of affected humility over it, though this whole letter is a proof of painful diffidence, I am compelled to think that there is some thing in my writings more valuable, than in the productions of some people on whom you bestow warm elogiums—I mean more mind—denominate it as you will—more of the observations of my own senses, more of the combining of my own imagination—the effusions of my own feelings and passions than the cold workings of the brain on the materials procured by the senses and imagination of other writers—

I am more out of patience with myself than you can form any idea of, when I tell you that I have scarcely written a line to please myself (and very little with respect to quantity) since you saw my M.S. I have been endeavouring all this morning; and with such dissatisfied sensations I am almost afraid to go into company—But these are idle complaints to which I ought not to give utterance, even to you*—I must then have done—

from
LETTER 34

[September 10, 1796]
Fanny was so importunate with her "go this way Mama, me wants to see Man," this morning that you would have seen us had I not had a glimpse of a blue coat at your door, when we turned down the Street— I have always a great deal to say to you, which I say to myself so kindly that 'tis pity you do not hear me—

I wanted to tell you that I felt as if I had not done justice to your essay, for it interested me extremely—and has been running in my head while other recollections were all alive in my heart—You are a tender considerate creature; but, entre nous, do not make too many philosophical experiments, for when a philosopher is put on his metal, to use your own phrase, there is no knowing where he will stop—and I have not reckoned on having a wild-goose chace after a—wise man—You will ask me what I am writing about—Why, as if you had been listening to my thoughts—

I am almost afraid on reflection that an indistinct intuition on our affection produced the effect on Miss H[ays] that distresses me—She has owned to me that she cannot endure to see others enjoy the mutual affection from which she is debarred—I will write a kind note to her

---

* Wollstonecraft soon overcame her annoyance at Godwin's criticism of her style; a few days later she was accepting his lessons in grammar.—Editor.

to day to ease my conscience, for when I am happy myself, I am made up of milk and honey, I would fain make every body else so—

I shall come to you to night, probably before nine—May I ask you to be at home—I may be tired and not like to ramble further—Shou[l]d I be later—you will forgive me—It will not be my heart that will loiter —By the bye—I do not tell *any* body*—especially yourself—it is alway on my lips at your door—

The return of the fine weather has led me to form a vague wish that we might *vagabondize* one day in the country—before the summer is clear gone. I love the country and like to leave certain associations in my memory, which seem, as it were, the land marks of affection—Am I very obscure?

Now I will go and write—I am in a humour to write—at least to you—Send me one line—if it be but—Bo! to a goose—

from
LETTER 36

[September 13, 1796]

Now by these presents let me assure you that you are not only in my heart, but my veins, this morning. I turn from you half abashed— yet you haunt me, and some look, word or touch thrills through my whole frame—yes, at the very moment when I am labouring to think of something, if not somebody, else. Get ye gone Intruder! though I am forced to add dear—which is a call back—

When the heart and reason accord there is no flying from volup- tuous sensations, I find, do what a woman can—Can a philosopher do more?

from
LETTER 52

[September 30, 1796]

If you go out, at two, you will, perhaps call and tell me that you thought as kindly of me last night, as I did of you; for I am glad to dis- cover great powers of mind in you, even at my own expence. One rea- son, I believe, why I wish you to have a good opinion of me is a convic- tion that the strongest affection is the most involuntary—yet I should not like you to love, you could not tell what, though it be a french com-

---

* Wollstonecraft and Godwin tried to keep secret their relationship until after their marriage.—Editor.

pliment of the first class, without my explanation of it: the being enamoured of some fugitive charm, that seeking somewhere, you find
every where: yes; I would fain live in your heart and employ your
imagination—Am I not very reasonable?

You do not know how much I admired your self-government, last
night, when your voice betrayed the struggle it cost you—I am glad
that you force me to love you more and more, in spite of my fear of being pierced to the heart by every one on whom I rest my mighty stock
of affection.—Your tenderness was considerate, as well as kind,—Miss
Hays entering, in the midst of the last sentence, I hastily laid my letter
aside, without finishing, and have lost the remain—Is it sunk in the
quicksand of Love?

LETTER 63

[November 10, 1796]

I send you your household linen—I am not sure that I did not feel
a sensation of pleasure at thus acting the part of a wife, though you
have so little respect for the character. There is such a magic in affection that I have been more gratified by your clasping your hands round
my arm, in company, than I could have been by all the admiration in
the world, tho' I am a woman—and to mount a step higher in the scale
of vanity, an author.

I shall call toward one o'clock not to deprive the world of your bright
thoughts, this exhilarating day.

LETTER 91

[January 12, 1797]

I am better this morning. But it snows, so incessantly, that I do not
know how I shall be able to keep my appointment this evening. What
say you? But you have no petticoats to dangle in the snow. Poor Women
how they are beset with plagues—within—and without.

from
LETTER 123

[May 21, 1797]

I am sorry we entered on an altercation this morning, which probably has led us both to justify ourselves at the expence of the other.
Perfect confidence, and sincerity of action is, I am persuaded, incompatible with the present state of reason. I am sorry for the bitterness of

Mary Wollstonecraft by John Opie, painted shortly before her
death in 1797.

your expressions when you denominated, what I think a just contempt of a false principle of action, *savage resentment, and the worst of vices,* not because I winced under the lash, but as it led me to infer that the coquetish candour of vanity was a much less generous motive. I know that respect is the shadow of wealth, and commonly obtained, when that is wanted, by a criminal compliance with the prejudice of society. Those who comply can alone tell whether they do it from benevolence or a desire to secure their own ease.* There is certainly an original defect in my mind—for the cruelest experience will not eradicate the foolish tendency I have to cherish, and expect to meet with, romantic tenderness.

from
LETTER 128

[June 6, 1797]

I was not quite well the day after you left me; but it is past, and I am well and tranquil, excepting the disturbance produced by Master William's joy, who took it into his head to frisk a little at being informed of your remembrance.† I begin to love this little creature, and to anticipate his birth as a fresh twist to a knot, which I do not wish to untie. Men are spoilt by frankness, I believe, yet I must tell you that I love you better than I supposed I did, when I promised to love you for ever —and I will add what will gratify your benevolence, if not your heart, that on the whole I may be termed happy. You are a tender, affectionate creature; and I feel it thrilling through my frame giving and promising pleasure.

Fanny wanted to know "what you are gone for," and endeavours to pronounce Etruria. Poor papa is her word of kindness—She has been turning your letter on all sides, and has promised to play with Bobby till I have finished my answer.

I find you can write the kind of letter a friend ought to write,‡ and

* Wollstonecraft wrote "easy."—Editor.

† Wollstonecraft and Godwin had determined that the child she was carrying would be a boy.—Editor.

‡ Godwin had begun "I write at this moment from Hampton Lucy in sight of the house and park of Sir Thomas Lucy, the great benefactor of mankind, who prosecuted William Shakespeare for deer stealing, & obliged him to take refuge in the metropolis. Montagu has just had a vomit, to carry off a certain quantity of punch with the drinking of which he concluded the Sunday evening.
"Is that the right style for a letter?"
See *Godwin & Mary*, pp. 78–79.—Editor.

give an account of your movements. I hailed the sunshine, and moon-light and travelled with you scenting the fragrant gale—Enable me still to be your company, and I will allow you to peep over my shoulder, and see me under the shade of my green blind, thinking of you, and all I am to hear, and feel when you return—you may read my heart—if you will. . . .

I am not fatigued with solitude—yet I have not relished my solitary dinner. A husband is a convenient part of the furniture of a house, un-less he be a clumsy fixture. I wish you, from my soul, to be rivetted in my heart; but I do not desire to have you always at my elbow—though at this moment I did not care if you were.

from
LETTER 140

[July 4, 1797]

To be frank with you, your behaviour yesterday brought on my troublesome pain.* But I lay no great stress on that circumstance, be-cause, were not my health in a more delicate state than usual, it could not be so easily affected. I am absurd to look for the affection which I have only found in my own tormented heart; and how can you blame me for taking† refuge in the idea of a God, when I despair of finding sincerity on earth?

I think you *wrong*—yes; with the most decided conviction I dare to say it, having still in my mind the *unswervable* principles of justice and humanity. You judge not in your own case as in that of another. You give a softer name to folly and immorality when it flatters—yes, I must say it—your vanity, than to mistaken passion when it was extended to another—you termed Miss Hay's conduct‡ insanity when only her own happiness was involved—I cannot forget the strength of your ex-pressions.—and you treat with a mildness calculated to foster it, a ro-mantic, selfishness, and pamper conceit, which will even lead the object to—I was going to say misery—but I believe her incapable of feeling it. Her want of sensibility with respect to her family first disgusted me —Then to obtrude herself on me, to see affection, and instead of feel-

---

* The letter was occasioned by a quarrel over Godwin's friendship with a Miss Pinkerton. The friendship was discontinued a few weeks later; by early August Woll-stonecraft could write "I do not now feel the least resentment."—Editor.

† Wollstonecraft wrote "taken."—Editor.

‡ Mary Hays publicly admitted her love for a man who was indifferent to her. —Editor.

ing sympathy, to endeavour to undermine* it, certainly resembles the conduct of the fictitious being, to whose dignity she aspires. Yet you, at the very moment, commenced a correspondence with her whom you had previously almost neglected—you brought me a letter without a conclusion—and you changed countenance at the reply—My old wounds bleed afresh—What did not blind confidence, and unsuspecting truth, lead me to—my very soul trembles sooner than endure the hundred[th] part of what I have suffer[ed], I could wish my poor Fanny and self asleep at the bottom of the sea.

One word more—I never blamed the woman for whom I was abandoned. I offered to see, nay, even to live with her, and I should have tried to improve her. But even she was deceived with respect to my character, and had her scruples when she heard the truth—But enough of the effusions of a sick heart—I only intend[ed] to write a line or two—†

LETTER 158

[August 30, 1797]‡

I have no doubt of seeing the animal to day; but must wait for Mrs Blenkinsop§ to guess at the hour—I have sent for her—Pray send me the news paper—I wish I had a novel, or some book of sheer amusement, to excite curiosity, and while away the time—Have you any thing of the kind?

LETTER 160

[August 30, 1797]

Mrs. Blenkinsop tells me that I am in the most natural state, and can promise me a safe delivery—But that I must have a little patience||

* Wollstonecraft wrote "undermined."—Editor.

† Godwin immediately replied that he was "much hurt" by this letter. See *Godwin & Mary*, p. 112.—Editor.

‡ Mary Wollstonecraft Godwin was born later in the day. Wollstonecraft's death occurred on September 10.—Editor.

§ The midwife.—Editor.

|| Probably the last words Wollstonecraft wrote. Godwin reported that her mother's dying words were "A little patience, and all will be over!"—Editor.

Letter to a Friend

Shortly after Wollstonecraft died in 1797, her friend Mary Hays wrote a biographical sketch of her in *Annual Necrology for 1797–8*. Hays quoted copiously from the letters to Imlay, recently published by Godwin, and toward the end included a section from a letter to a friend. In it Wollstonecraft offered her view of the significance of her life and achievement.

THOSE WHO are bold enough to advance before the age they live in, and to throw off, by the force of their own minds, the prejudices which the maturing reason of the world will in time disavow, must learn to brave censure. We ought not to be too anxious respecting the opinion of others.—I am not fond of vindications.—Those who know me will suppose that I acted from principle.—Nay, as we in general give others credit for worth, in proportion as we possess it—I am easy with regard to the opinions of the *best* part of mankind—I *rest* on my own.

BIBLIOGRAPHY

I. *Original Works of Mary Wollstonecraft*

Thoughts on the Education of Daughters: with Reflections on Female Conduct, in the more Important Duties of Life. London: Joseph Johnson, 1787. Facsimile by Garland Publishing Inc., 1974.

Mary, A Fiction. London: Joseph Johnson, 1788. Facsimile by Garland Publishing Inc., 1974. Reprinted by Oxford University Press, 1976, and by Schocken Books, Inc. 1977.

Original Stories from Real Life: with Conversations Calculated To Regulate the Affections and Form the Mind to Truth and Goodness. London: Joseph Johnson, 1788.

The Female Reader; or Miscellaneous Pieces, in Prose and Verse; Selected from the Best Writers, and Disposed under Proper Heads; for the Improvement of Young Women. London: Joseph Johnson, 1789.

A Vindication of the Rights of Men, in a Letter to the Right Honourable Edmund Burke. London: Joseph Johnson, 1790. Facsimile by Scholars' Facsimiles & Reprints, 1960.

A Vindication of the Rights of Woman with Strictures on Political and Moral Subjects. London: Joseph Johnson, 1792. Reprinted by W. W. Norton & Company, 1967 and 1975, and by Penguin Books, 1975.

An Historical and Moral View of the Origin and Progress of the French Revolution; and the Effect It Has Produced in Europe. London: Joseph Johnson, 1794. Facsimile by Scholars' Facsimiles & Reprints, 1975.

Letters Written during a Short Residence in Sweden, Norway, and Denmark. London: Joseph Johnson, 1796. Reprinted by University of Nebraska Press, 1976.

Posthumous Works of the Author of A Vindication of the Rights of Woman. London: Joseph Johnson, 1798. Facsimile by Garland Publishing Inc., 1974, and by Augustus M. Kelley, 1972.

The Wrongs of Woman: or, Maria (part of *Posthumous Works*). Reprinted by Oxford University Press, 1976, and as *Maria or the Wrongs of Woman* by W. W. Norton & Company, 1975.

II. *Major Collections of Letters*

The Love Letters of Mary Wollstonecraft to Gilbert Imlay, with a Prefatory Memoir. Ed. Roger Ingpen. London: Hutchinson & Company, 1908.

Supplement to *Memoirs of Mary Wollstonecraft.* Ed. W. Clark Durant. London: Constable & Co., Ltd., 1927.

Four New Letters of Mary Wollstonecraft and Helen Maria Williams. Ed. Benjamin P. Kurtz and Carrie C. Autrey. Berkeley: University of California Press, 1937.

Shelley and His Circle: 1773–1822. Ed. Kenneth Neill Cameron. Cambridge: Harvard University Press, 1961.

Godwin and Mary: Letters of William Godwin and Mary Wollstonecraft. Ed. Ralph M. Wardle. Lawrence: University of Kansas Press, 1966.

III. *Recent Biographies*

Flexner, Eleanor. *Mary Wollstonecraft: A Biography*. New York: Coward, McCann and Geoghegan, 1972.

George, Margaret. *One Woman's "Situation": A Study of Mary Wollstonecraft*. Urbana: University of Illinois Press, 1970.

Nixon, Edna. *Mary Wollstonecraft: Her Life and Times*. London: J. M. Dent and Sons, 1971.

Sunstein, Emily W. *A Different Face: The Life of Mary Wollstonecraft*. New York: Harper & Row, 1975.

Tomalin, Claire. *The Life and Death of Mary Wollstonecraft*. London: Weidenfeld and Nicolson, 1974.

Wardle, Ralph M. *Mary Wollstonecraft: A Critical Biography*. 1951; Lincoln: University of Nebraska Press, 1966.

IV. *Some Recent Comments on Wollstonecraft's Life and Works*

Boulton, James T. *The Language of Politics in the Age of Wilkes and Burke*. London: Routledge & Kegan Paul, 1963.

Detre, Jean. *A Most Extraordinary Pair: Mary Wollstonecraft and William Godwin*. New York: Doubleday & Co. Inc., 1975.

Janes, Regina. "Mary, Mary, Quite Contrary, Or, Mary Astell and Mary Wollstonecraft Compared," *Studies in Eighteenth-Century Culture*. Ed. Ronald C. Rosbottom. University of Wisconsin Press, 1976.

Lundberg, Ferdinand and Marynia F. Farnham. *Modern Woman: The Lost Sex*. New York: Harper & Brothers, 1947.

MacCarthy, B. G. *The Later Women Novelists 1744–1818*. Cork: Cork University Press, 1947.

Nicholes, Eleanor L. "Mary Wollstonecraft," *Romantic Rebels, Essays on Shelley and His Circle*. Ed. Kenneth Neill Cameron. Cambridge: Harvard University Press, 1973.

Pollin, Burton R. *Education and Enlightenment in the Works of William Godwin*. New York: Las Americas Publishing Company, 1962.

Rover, Constance. *Love, Morals and the Feminists*. London: Routledge & Kegan Paul, 1970.

Séjourné, Philippe. *Aspects Généraux du Roman Féminin en Angleterre de 1740 à 1800*. Gap: Louis-Jean, 1966.

Steeves, Harrison R. *Before Jane Austen: The Shaping of the English Novel in the Eighteenth Century*. London: George Allen & Unwin Ltd., 1966.

Todd, Janet M. *Mary Wollstonecraft: A Bibliography*. New York: Garland
    Publishing Inc., 1976.
Wardle, Ralph M. "Mary Wollstonecraft, Analytical Reviewer," *PMLA*,
    LXII, December 1947, 1000–1009.